VASSALS,
HEIRESSES,
CRUSADERS,
AND THUGS

University of Pennsylvania Press
MIDDLE AGES SERIES
Edited by
Edward Peters
Henry Charles Lea Professor
of Medieval History
University of Pennsylvania

A listing of the available books
in the series appears at the
back of this volume

VASSALS,

The Gentry of

HEIRESSES,

Angevin Yorkshire,

CRUSADERS,

1154–1216

AND THUGS

Hugh M. Thomas

upp

UNIVERSITY OF PENNSYLVANIA PRESS

Philadelphia

Library of Congress Cataloging-in-Publication Data
Thomas, Hugh M.
  Vassals, heiresses, crusaders, and thugs : the gentry of Angevin Yorkshire, 1154–1216 /
Hugh M. Thomas.
    p.   cm. — (Middle Ages series)
  Includes bibliographical references and index.
  ISBN 0-8122-3159-7
  1. Yorkshire (England)—History.   2. Gentry—England—Yorkshire—History.   3. Great
Britain—History—Angevin period, 1154–1216.   I. Title.   II. Series.
DA670.Y6T42   1993
942.8′1′008621—dc20

                                                                            92-42782
                                                                            CIP

To my Father and Mother

Contents

Tables and Figures

Acknowledgments

For westerners in the late twentieth century, one of the joys of pursuing medieval history is the chance to study a culture that is both radically different from, and yet the ancestor of, our own society. The medievalist has as subjects people whose physical environment and mental world were very different from our own, yet it is from their society that our own derives. This study is an attempt to explore, as much as is possible for a modern historian, the world of one small group of medieval people, the gentry of Angevin Yorkshire. It is also an attempt to explain how they changed that world, in some ways bringing it closer to our own. By carefully reconstructing insofar as possible the lives of this small but important group and by analyzing the changes in which they were involved, I hope to add to our knowledge and understanding of medieval society as a whole.

In carrying out this study, I have accumulated many debts of gratitude. I would like to thank the history department of Yale University for a grant which helped pay for one trip to the archives and the Mrs. Giles Whiting Foundation for a grant which gave me a year of uninterrupted time to work on this project when it was in the dissertation stage. I would equally like to thank the University of Miami for a Max Orovitz Summer fellowship and for travel money for a second trip to the archives.

In carrying out my research I received help from many librarians and archivists. Thanks are due to the staffs of Sterling Library at Yale, Richter Library at the University of Miami, the British Library, the Bodleian Library, the Public Record Office, the Yorkshire Archaeological Society, the Humberside Record Office, the John Rylands Library, the Shakespeare Birthplace Trust Record Office, and the York Minster Library. I would also like to thank Jean Thomas for making the map and Patricia Rosario for help with the index.

My intellectual debts are many. James Campbell first suggested the topic to me. Conrad Russell, despite the temporal distance of my subject from his own area of expertise, provided useful guidance in the early stages of the project. Paul Brand read an earlier version of the first two chapters and Robert Jackson, of the third chapter; both provided cogent and very useful criticisms. Their critiques and those of Harry Miskimin, who served as a reader of the dissertation, and of the anonymous readers to whom the manuscript was sent have helped me to revise and thereby improve this work greatly. Conversations with and advice from many other scholars have also aided me in formulating and refining my views on the subjects of this work. My greatest intellectual debts, however, are to my two advisors, John Boswell and Robert Stacey. John Boswell has played a fundamental role in shaping my view of the Middle Ages and has constantly provided a wider medieval perspective as well as useful advice and helpful criticism. Robert Stacey has done more to train me as a historian and to shape my view of English history than anyone else. Both have been wise and helpful mentors and dear friends. All of the scholars named above have helped me to make this a better book and to avoid errors. Any remaining errors are, of course, my own.

Finally, I owe thanks to the many friends and relatives who helped sustain me during the long and arduous process of writing a book. Within that category, as my dedication indicates, I owe special thanks to my parents, who have always stood behind me and who first inspired my love of learning and especially of history.

Public Record Office documents are Crown Copyright, reproduced by permission of the Controller of Her Majesty's Stationery Office. Permission to quote or reproduce other documents is acknowledged as follows: Documents from the York Minster Library (courtesy of the Dean and Chapter of York Minster; Rylands Latin MS 251 (courtesy of the Director and University Librarian, John Rylands University Library of Manchester); DDDC documents (permission of Humberside County Council); Gregory Hood Collection (permission of the Shakespeare Birthplace Trust on behalf of Colonel A.M.H. Gregory-Hood).

Abbreviations

Full publication information for sources given in the Bibliography, under editor or title.

BIHR	*Bulletin of the Institute of Historical Research.*
CRR	*Curia Regis Rolls.*
EHR	*English Historical Review.*
EYC	*Early Yorkshire Charters.*
Fountains Cartulary	*Abstracts of the Charters and Other Documents Contained in the Chartulary of the Cistercian Abbey of Fountains.* Ed. William T. Lancaster.
HMSO	Her Majesty's Stationery Office.
Meaux Chronicle	*Chronica Monasterii de Melsa.* Vol. 1. Ed. Edward A. Bond.
Pipe Roll 31 Henry I	*Pipe Roll 31 Henry I.* Ed. Joseph Hunter.
Pipe Roll 2-3-4 Henry II	*Pipe Roll 2-3-4 Henry II.* Ed. Joseph Hunter.
Pipe Roll 5 Henry II to *3 Henry III*	*Pipe Rolls 5 Henry II to 3 Henry III.* Pipe Roll Society.
Pleas	*Pleas Before the King or his Justices, 1198–1212.* Ed. Doris M. Stenton.
PRO	Public Record Office.
RCR	*Rotuli Curiae Regis.* Ed. Francis Palgrave.
Rot. Chart.	*Rotuli Chartarum.* Vol. 1, part 1. Ed. Thomas D. Hardy.
Rot. Litt. Claus.	*Rotuli Litterarum Clausarum in Turri Londinensi Asservati.* Vols. 1–2. Ed. Thomas D. Hardy.
Rot. Litt. Pat.	*Rotuli Litterarum Patentium in Turri Londinensi Asservati.* Vol. 1, part 1. Ed. Thomas D. Hardy.
Rot. Obl. & Fin.	*Rotuli de Oblatis et Finibus in Turri Londinensi Asservati, Tempore Regis Johannis.* Ed. Thomas D. Hardy.

Sallay Cartulary	*The Chartulary of the Cistercian Abbey of St. Mary of Sallay in Craven.* Ed. Joseph McNulty.
TRHS	*Transactions of the Royal Historical Society.*
YAJ	*Yorkshire Archaeological Journal*
YAS	Yorkshire Archaeological Society
Yorkshire Deeds	*Yorkshire Deeds.* 10 vols.
Yorkshire Eyre	*Rolls of the Justices in Eyre being the Rolls of Pleas and Assizes for Yorkshire in 3 Henry III.* Ed. Doris M. Stenton.
Yorkshire Inquisitions	*Yorkshire Inquisitions of the Reigns of Henry III and Edward I.* Ed. William Brown.

VASSALS,
HEIRESSES,
CRUSADERS,
AND THUGS

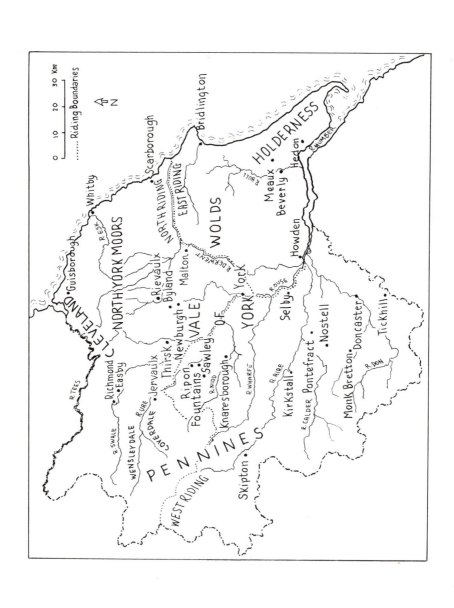

Riding Boundaries

0 10 20 30 Km

N

R.TEES

Guisborough

Whitby

R.ESK

CLEVELAND

NORTH YORK MOORS

Richmond
Easby

R.SWALE

WENSLEYDALE

R.URE

COVERDALE

Jervaulx

Thirsk

Newburgh

Ripon
Fountains

R.NIDD

Sawley

Knaresborough

Rievaulx
Byland

Malton

VALE

OF

R.WHARFE

Skipton

WEST RIDING

PENNINES

NORTH RIDING

EAST RIDING

WOLDS

Scarborough

Bridlington

HOLDERNESS

R.HUMBER

Meaux

Beverly

Hedon

R.HULL

R.DERWENT

York

YORK

R.OUSE

Selby

Howden

R.AIRE

Kirkstall

Pontefract

R.CALDER

Nostell

Monk Bretton

Doncaster

Tickhill

R.DON

Introduction

In recent decades, a large number of historians of early modern England have turned their attention to that segment of society loosely called the gentry. This attention is not misplaced, for the gentry, through their voices in parliament, their actions in war, their economic activities, and their religious proclivities, have played an important and sometimes crucial role in English history. Consequently, studies of local gentry communities have transformed our understanding of the social, political, and economic history of early modern England. More recently, historians of England in the Later Middle Ages have begun to carry out similar studies, which are bringing about a parallel transformation of our knowledge of England in that period.[1] This book takes the process back further still in history, to the earliest period in which sufficient information survives for a detailed regional study of the gentry and to a time when the gentry in some ways were first beginning to emerge as an independent force in English history. Despite the many changes in English society in the late twelfth century and thereafter, this study will reveal a remarkable number of similarities between the gentry of the Angevin period and those of later centuries. The most important of these is that the gentry in the Angevin period, like their later counterparts, played a key role in society and in social change.

The first purpose of this book is simply to describe the gentry of Yorkshire in the Angevin period and their role in society. Although several scholars have discussed the gentry in this period, often as tenants of a particular honor, no book-length study of this subject has been published and large gaps remain in our understanding of this group.[2] This book will

---

1. These studies include Nigel Saul, *Knights and Esquires: The Gloucestershire Gentry in the Fourteenth Century*; Nigel Saul, *Scenes from Provincial Life: Knightly Families in Sussex 1280–1400*; Susan M. Wright, *The Derbyshire Gentry in the Fifteenth Century*; A. J. Pollard, "The Richmondshire Community of Gentry During the Wars of the Roses"; Christine Carpenter, "The Fifteenth-Century English Gentry and Their Estates"; Simon Payling, *Political Society in Lancastrian England: The Greater Gentry of Nottinghamshire*.

2. For works which discuss gentry on specific honors, see F. R. H. Du Boulay, *The Lordship of Canterbury*; Edward King, *Peterborough Abbey 1086–1310: A Study in the Land Market*; "Large and Small Landowners in Thirteenth-Century England"; Eleanor Searle,

fill in many of these gaps and give a full picture of the gentry in at least one part of England during the reigns of Henry II and his sons.

The more important purpose of this book, however, is to use the gentry as a lens through which to view a group of simultaneous and often interconnected changes that transformed local society and particularly local power structures in the Angevin period. Between 1154 and 1216, patterns of power and landholding, relations between different levels of the elite, and relations with central government all shifted radically and a variety of institutions and social and political groupings, from honors, to judicial courts, to monasteries, underwent fundamental changes. In all of these changes the gentry were intimately involved.

The gentry, of course, were not the only actors in the changes to be described in the following chapters. Kings, magnates, clerics, and peasants were also involved. However, there are two reasons for studying these changes through the lens of the gentry. First, the gentry were heavily involved in the local transformations that occurred in the Angevin period and second, because the gentry were at the center of a network of connections with upward ties to magnates and the king, downward ties to peasants, and horizontal ties to monks, nuns, and clergy, a gentry study provides an excellent vantage point from which to view these transformations in English society.

Moreover, an advantage to studying historical processes from the vantage point of a particular group is that it allows one to see the interaction, within the history of that group, of a wide range of individual factors and changes, whether economic, social, political, or religious. History may consist of cause and effect, but generally there are a tremendous number of causes and effects occurring simultaneously. For this reason, the image of a tapestry is often used to describe history; at times, such is the complexity that it seems a tapestry designed by intoxicated Dadaists. To understand the history of a period, we must break it down into smaller parts. Many scholars prefer to do this by concentrating on particular questions within analytical fields such as legal, economic, or political history. This focus allows them to isolate certain specific chains of cause and effect, and thus help explain a part of the pattern. For all the advantages of isolating certain elements of change, this method can obscure the tremendous complexity of

Lordship and Community: Battle Abbey and Its Banlieu 1066–1538; Barbara Harvey, *Westminster Abbey and Its Estates in the Middle Ages*. Discussion of the gentry can be found in works on other subjects as well. Particularly important is J. C. Holt's chapter on knights in *The Northerners*, 35–60.

the inter-relations between different aspects of human life and history. People simply do not divide their lives into neat analytical categories. Unless complemented by studies using other approaches, scholarly works based on analytical fields can therefore inadvertently lead to a somewhat disjointed view of the past. By focusing on a group, one can investigate a number of topics from different fields of history and study the interaction of a wide variety of factors. One can explore how religious beliefs, family relations, politics, and economics can all interact, and how changes in one area will affect another, how even an area in which there is little change can, in conjunction with one in which change *is* occurring, bring radical changes in a third.

This book will, of course, make use of analytic categories, but will also try to show the connections between them. Each chapter has its analytic focus: the transformation and decline of the honor; gentry participation in lawlessness and in the legal system, including the growing system of royal courts; the gentry as improving landlords; gentry families and households; the religious life of the gentry; the economic crisis of the gentry; and gentry participation in the Magna Carta revolt. However, this last element cannot be fully understood without a clear picture of the rising impact of royal government on gentry or the economic troubles faced by the gentry. The rising impact of royal government cannot be fully understood in turn without an investigation of the decline of the honor. The economic difficulties of many gentry must be set in the context of great generosity by the gentry to cadet lines, followers, and the church. More interconnections could be described and ultimately all these topics are interconnected.

Before turning to these subjects and the main body of the book, I must discuss three issues. First, there are the problems posed by the fact that Yorkshire was in many ways unique. Second, there is the issue of the term gentry and the shortcomings of its use. Third, there are certain difficulties inherent in the sources.

I have chosen the county as the unit of study largely because that is the traditional unit of analysis for gentry studies. Yorkshire presented itself as the best county for this study partly for practical reasons. Because of circumstances that will be discussed below, the identification of individuals and families within the gentry or indeed in almost any class is extremely difficult for the Angevin period. The extensive and careful work done by William Farrer and even more so by Charles Clay has made this task much simpler for Yorkshire. A study of gentry in any other county would have required years of genealogical work before the main part of the project could even begin and therefore my debt to these earlier scholars cannot be overemphasized.[3] But Yorkshire was also an attractive locus because of its importance in the expansion of the new monastic orders in England, the Magna Carta revolt, and other trends and events in which the gentry, as shall be seen, played an important role.

However, the very trends and events that make Yorkshire interesting also point to its difference from the rest of England and, perhaps more important, to the north south split that then as now divided England. J. C. Holt has discussed the political aspects of this split in *The Northerners*.[4] It may be asked whether conclusions about the attitudes of gentry in the overwhelmingly rebellious county of Yorkshire are valid for areas with stronger royalist sentiments. Similar problems exist with the expansion of new monastic orders, for Yorkshire, lacking the large Anglo-Saxon Benedictine foundations of the south, was an unusually fertile field for monastic growth. Did Yorkshire gentry have a different attitude to monasticism from that of their fellows in areas replete with prosperous and well-fed black monks? Yorkshire had suffered extensive devastation after the Conquest, and even before this disaster its economy was relatively underdeveloped. Did this make a difference in the economic activities and decisions of Yorkshire gentry?

Such questions will not be fully answered until similar studies are done for other areas of England. However, in cases where comparisons can be made using information from the works of other scholars, patterns in Yorkshire seem to be similar to those found elsewhere. After all, many of the differences described above were differences of degree rather than of kind. The new monastic orders expanded most heavily in Yorkshire, but spread throughout England. More land was available for clearing in Yorkshire, but most parts of England saw assarting. Many of the problems faced by Yorkshire gentry were faced by others throughout the country. Moreover, large portions of the Yorkshire gentry, though by no means all, shared a Norman heritage common to much of the gentry throughout England, a heritage which in particular shaped the relations between the various layers of the local elites. Yorkshire, though in many ways unique, was certainly not an island unto itself. Future studies of other areas will certainly provide a more complete and nuanced picture of the English gentry in the Angevin

---

3. *Early Yorkshire Charters*, ed. William Farrer and Charles Clay. See also the many articles by Clay listed in the bibliography.

4. Holt, *The Northerners*, throughout.

period, but there is little danger that the Yorkshire gentry were so unique that conclusions drawn from this work will be uniformly invalid for England as a whole. Meanwhile, I will attempt to provide an indication in areas where Yorkshire particularities may have made a difference.

The second issue—terminology—is a particularly difficult one. By the end of the Middle Ages clear ranks had emerged within the elites. Landlords were divided into lords and gentry and the latter group were divided into knights, squires, and gentlemen. Mechanisms to distinguish between members of various ranks, such as personal summons to parliament, dubbing, or the possession of coats of arms, helped to delineate the different groups. Moreover, individuals advertised their status with titles. The system was not perfect, and at the borders between ranks there existed a wide overlap of wealth and power, but titles and rank clearly show how society perceived status and can help the historian in the same task.

Angevin elite society did not have these clear demarcations. Chroniclers often spoke of *maiores* and *optimates*, but these terms had rather vague meanings. Earls, of course, were set off as a group, but there were only a handful of them. No formal House of Lords existed to separate lords from gentry. The use of the term baron was extremely fluid, a fact that would cause both later royal administrators and modern historians severe headaches when they sat down to figure out just what a baron or barony was and whether individual cases fit.[5] In an earlier period, the term was used to designate important honorial vassals, including many of the sorts of people covered in this study. In later periods, it designated only nobles, except in the cases of the barons of London and of the Cinque Ports. The changing nature of this term limits its usefulness to help define which individuals should be included in this study.

A more promising term is *miles*, or knight, and some scholars have used the term knightly class to delineate a particular group within twelfth- or thirteenth-century English society.[6] Knighthood was clearly a distinct

5. For a discussion of the terms "baron" and "barony," see Frank Stenton, *The First Century of English Feudalism*, 83–113; Helena M. Chew, *The English Ecclesiastical Tenants-in-Chief and Knight Service*, 159–88; I. J. Sanders, *Feudal Military Service in England*, 1–28, and *English Baronies: A Study of their Origin and Descent 1086–1327*, v–vi.

6. Indeed, in an earlier version of this work, I also used the term knightly class. For discussions of knighthood and the status of knights in England from the late eleventh century through the early thirteenth, see Sally Harvey, "The Knight and the Knight's Fee in England"; R. Allen Brown, "The Status of the Norman Knight"; Donald Fleming, "Landholding and *Milites* in Domesday Book: A Revision"; "*Milites* as Attestors to Charters in England"; J. Quick, "The Number and Distribution of Knights in Thirteenth Century England: The

rank in Angevin England and knights were marked out by having received the "belt of knighthood," presumably as the result of a formal ceremony such as dubbing.[7] The belt of knighthood, and therefore the rank, could be lost; during the Third Crusade, when Richard prepared an attack on Tancred in Sicily, it was decreed that any knight who fled would lose his belt.[8] Those who had obtained the belt of knighthood received special privileges before the Exchequer, a further indication that knights were recognized as a distinct group and treated as such.[9] Moreover, certain judicial tasks, such as the grand assize, were reserved for knights and this suggests that knighthood was no longer perceived solely in military but also in social terms. A link between knighthood and social status can also be seen from the occasional comment in a narrative source. For instance, Roger of Howden described the Yorkshire knight Gilbert de Plumpton as "a youth of noble birth" and elsewhere as "a knight of noble birth."[10] Knighthood was seen not only as a distinct social category, but as one that could be associated with a high social status. Thus in using the term knightly class one is drawing upon the terminology used in the society in question.

Unfortunately, there are also problems associated with using this term. Contemporaries often described magnates as knights, as indeed they were, and it is not clear to what degree Angevin society differentiated between nobles and lesser local aristocrats in the absence of a clear boundary such as that later provided by summonses to parliament. Since this study does exclude magnates, the absence of a clear-cut boundary between magnates and knights, at least in Yorkshire sources, vitiates the usefulness of the latter term. This is only one aspect of a greater problem, which is that there is no way to know the exact make-up or scope of the knightly class as viewed by contemporaries. The practice of using knight as a title in documents and witness lists, which became standard later, is extremely rare in the Angevin

Evidence of the Grand Assize Lists"; P. R. Coss, *Lordship, Knighthood and Locality: A Study in English Society c. 1180–c. 1280*, 210–63.

7. Unfortunately, no evidence concerning dubbing survives from Angevin Yorkshire. For references to the belt of knighthood by monastic writers in Yorkshire during the Angevin period, see Hugh of Kirkstall, "Narratio de Fundatione Fontanis Monasterii in Comitatu Eboracensi," in *Memorials of the Abbey of St. Mary of Fountains*; "Selebeiensis Monasterii Historia," ed. J. T. Fowler, in *The Coucher Book of Selby*, 6.

8. *The Chronicle of Richard of Devizes of the Time of King Richard the First*, 22.

9. Richard fitz Nigel, *Dialogus de Scaccario*, III, 116–17.

10. In one version the Latin is "miles nobili prosapia ortus" and in the other version, found in the work later attributed to Benedict of Peterborough, the Latin is "juvenis quidam nobili exortus prosapia." Roger of Howden, *Chronica Magistri Rogeri de Hoveden* 2:286; Benedict of Peterborough, *Gesta Regis Henrici Secundi Benedicti Abbatis* 1:314.

period; thus it is very difficult to know whether specific individuals were considered knights.[11] Large lists of knights *can* be drawn up from the judicial records, which record those summoned as knights for particular duties restricted to that class. However, questions have been raised about whether all those summoned as knights actually were knights.[12] More important, the lists, though extensive, are clearly incomplete. Families which held one or more knights' fees in 1166, whose members used the title of knight later in the thirteenth century, and who had all the earmarks of rank and status, are not represented on the lists. These lists reflect not the entirety of Yorkshire knighthood in the period, but those knights called to serve in specific judicial cases, the records of which happen to survive. The usefulness of this contemporary social ranking is severely diminished because we do not know exactly who contemporaries placed in this rank, and no set of guidelines survives, if one ever existed.

The problem is exacerbated by the fact that the term miles, like the term baron, was fluid. The existence of knighthood as a sharply defined social rank rather than simply as a military profession may have been relatively new in England.[13] Indeed, the insistence by the Angevin government that only knights could perform certain judicial and administrative tasks may have played a role in the final stages of the transformation from military profession to social rank by sharpening the distinction between knights and non-knights and setting knights apart as a group with special rights and responsibilities.[14] If this is the case, knighthood may well have had different connotations at the beginning and at the end of the Angevin period.[15]

11. For the chronology of the designation of attestors as milites, see Fleming, "*Milites* as Attestors," 185–98.

12. See Quick, "Number and Distribution," 114, for some cases in which individuals who were not knights served in a knightly capacity. However, I do not think this was in fact a widespread occurrence. Certainly, some of those summoned were very obscure, but this may reflect more on the state of the records than on the status of those individuals. No clear examples of non-knights being summoned appears in the Yorkshire sources.

13. Myriad studies exist on the transformation of knighthood from profession to social rank. For England, the most important is Harvey's article, "The Knight and the Knight's Fee," 3–43.

14. An analogy could be drawn with the way in which the new Angevin legal remedies sharpened the distinction between free peasants and serfs. For this process see Paul Hyams, *King, Lords, and Peasants in Medieval England: The Common Law of Villeinage in the Twelfth and Thirteenth Centuries*. This analogy was first suggested to me by Robert Stacey.

15. The whole question of social categorization, the precise contemporary meaning of knighthood, and whether knights can be seen as a social class in this period is a knotty one and must be pursued more fully. However, to obtain sufficient information scholars will have to spread their nets more widely than Yorkshire, for the Yorkshire evidence alone is not a sufficient basis for broad conclusions. See above, n. 7, for existing work.

Another trend affecting the category of knighthood, at least in the thirteenth century, was the steady decline in the number of knights and the increasing tendency for only very wealthy landholders to take up the rank.[16] The records of royal courts show that knighthood was still spread widely among the landed classes late in the Angevin period and early in the reign of Henry III. These records, from the 1190s to the Yorkshire eyre of 1218–19, show nearly two hundred individuals fulfilling the tasks allotted by the royal government to knights and to this may be added over one hundred more named in records going up to 1230. Very few of these individuals came from the same family and these figures by no means represent all the families of Yorkshire knights.[17] Many individuals who in later periods would have been esquires or mere gentlemen apparently possessed knightly status in the Angevin period.[18] However, without earlier lists of knights it is impossible to know whether knightly status was even more widespread in an earlier period.[19] Moreover, if it is clear that knighthood was more widely spread in the Angevin period than later, the incompleteness of lists of knights makes it unclear how much more widely spread. Was the knightly class of the Angevin period synonymous with the entire gentry of later periods? How were household knights categorized?

Because the incompleteness of the records makes these questions impossible to answer, a less specific term such as gentry or lesser landlord seems better, for to use the term knightly class is to pretend to a precision which may have been possible for contemporaries but is not possible for modern historians. Of these terms, gentry has been chosen because of its historiographical connotations. This term is unfortunately not based on a contemporary term, at least not a common one.[20] Moreover, the advan-

---

16. Harvey, "The Knight and the Knight's Fee," 3–43; R. F. Treharne, "The Knights in the Period of Reform and Rebellion, 1258–1267: A Critical Phase in the Rise of a New Class," 6–7; Noel Denholm-Young, "Feudal Society in the Thirteenth Century: The Knights," 107–19.

17. This list is drawn from all the records of the royal courts relating to Yorkshire in that period, including the records of judicial eyres.

18. David Carpenter, using the same source for the knights of Oxfordshire, has also found that knightly rank was fairly widespread at the beginning of the thirteenth century; "Was There a Crisis of the Knightly Class in the Thirteenth Century? The Oxfordshire Evidence," 722–23, 724 n. 7. See also Coss, *Lordship, Knighthood and Locality*, 210–57.

19. If Sally Harvey is right about knights being fairly insignificant figures in the late eleventh and early twelfth century, this may well have been the case; Harvey, "The Knight and the Knight's Fee," 5–30. However, see Fleming, "Landholding and *Milites*," for a critique of Harvey's arguments.

20. Professor Holt has drawn my attention to the use of the term *gentiles*, which could quite readily be treated as gentry, but this is not a term found in the Yorkshire sources, at least to my knowledge.

tages of its historical connotations are accompanied by the dangers of distortion and anachronism. The disadvantages of this term, however, are outweighed by the fact that it describes the group of people I am studying in terms familiar to other historians, that it stresses continuities with later periods, and places the book in a wider historical context. No term is entirely satisfactory, and other scholars may reasonably disagree with my choice, but for the purposes of this study it seems the least unsatisfactory.[21]

The use of the term gentry still leaves the question of which families and individuals should be included in the study. In determining this, I have used a variety of measures of wealth and status. The chief of these is control of land, seen, however imperfectly, from the returns of the *cartae baronum* of 1166, from charter evidence, and from the evidence of land litigation. The appearance of family members as knights in the judicial lists has also been a factor, as have other, more miscellaneous indications of local prominence. Another factor is feudal tenure. Tenants-in-chief who held more than a handful of knights' fees of the king have been excluded. Subtenants, even when they held as many as fifteen knights' fees, have, conversely, been included.

The decision to include all subtenants, it must be noted, is somewhat problematic and illustrates the difficulties of trying to create a perfect system categorizing social rank. Certainly at the beginning of the Angevin period, when the honorial structure was still relatively strong, the situation of wealthy subtenants corresponded more closely to that of lesser subtenants than to that of magnates; they could not really be considered peers of their honorial lords. However, as the honorial system declined, a process that will be described in chapter one, wealth became more important and tenurial status less so. During the Magna Carta revolt, two wealthy tenants of the honor of Richmond were described as barons, in the later, more exalted sense of that term, indicating that they were already seen as more important than run of the mill knights.[22] The descendants of several of the greatest subtenant families were summoned personally to parliament, which would place them among the nobility of later periods, and in a few cases the families already possessed the estates in the Angevin period which

---

21. Peter Coss, for instance, would certainly disagree, for he develops a much narrower definition of gentry which would exclude the lesser elites of the Angevin period. In my opinion, however, his definition is far too narrow and includes such factors as parliamentary representation and participation in commissions of the peace which seem to me excessively specific. Coss, *Lordship, Knighthood and Locality*, 308–9.

22. Matthew Paris, *Chronica Majora* 2:585.

justified those later summons.[23] Thus, arguments could be made either for including or excluding this group. Because these families were at most on the fringes of the nobility in later periods, and always shared affinities with the gentry, and even more because the issue of the transformation of vassals into independent landowners is so important in this work, I have chosen to include these wealthy subtenants.

A secondary question in the area of terminology is which families qualify as *Yorkshire* gentry. Most held land only in that county, but some held land elsewhere as well and may even have had their chief residence elsewhere. Because it is often difficult to tell where a family's chief residence was, unless they took their name from it, and because it seems arbitrary to assign gentry active in two or more counties to only one of these, no distinction is made between gentry who were essentially based in Yorkshire and those who were based outside, as long as they had land in the county. The activities of gentry families within Yorkshire will be considered whether or not they were based there. Conversely, the activities of primarily Yorkshire families in other counties will largely be ignored. Thus, this study will include families which could be considered in the context of other counties as well as in a Yorkshire context.

Any system of social categorization, whether constructed by contemporaries or by modern historians, will have flaws. In this case, gaps in the evidence and the social shifts described in this book only increase the problems. These problems should not be exaggerated, however. There is certainly enough evidence to place large numbers of Yorkshire families in the Angevin period squarely within the category of gentry as that term is generally understood, and if the edges are slightly blurred that is nothing new in gentry studies. I have generally been cautious about placing families within the gentry, but even so this study is based on research concerning approximately 225 families. This may not have been the entire Yorkshire gentry in this period, but it is a sufficiently large portion to give a good picture of the gentry and their role in Angevin Yorkshire.[24]

The third issue is that of the sources. There are three major types of sources for this study: narrative sources, charters, and royal records. Each type of source is very rich in its own way, but none was written with the purpose of illuminating the lives of the gentry of Angevin Yorkshire. As so often in medieval history, the picture must be reconstructed from frag-

23. See chapter one.
24. Unfortunately, the records are too spotty and the difficulties of categorization too great to give a precise figure for the total number of gentry families in Yorkshire.

ments, like a jigsaw puzzle, to use a common analogy. And, as so often in medieval history, many pieces of the puzzle have been lost through the original lack or subsequent loss of written record. Landholding appears repeatedly in the sources, human emotion, rarely. Complex feuds were reduced to a few laconic entries in royal judicial records, and often not all of these entries survive. Most of the thousands of surviving charters were preserved by monasteries, and tell us about gentry property only at the point when it was transferred to a monastery. To take the jigsaw analogy a step further, much of the picture has to be reconstructed from pieces designed for other puzzles.

A second problem is the massive change in the quality and quantity of the sources during the twelfth and early thirteenth centuries. The number of charters expanded greatly and individual charters tended to become more detailed. New types of records appeared, such as the pipe rolls, curia regis rolls, and other records of the royal government.[25] The historian is confronted with a sharply rising information curve. This upward curve sometimes makes it very difficult to differentiate between what was actually new in the Angevin period and what simply appeared for the first time in the increasingly informative records. In many cases, the evidence does clearly show change, and in other cases common sense and historical analysis can make a strong case for real rather than apparent change. However, caution is called for, and I will endeavor to point out where there is uncertainty whether a change is real or only apparent.

The shortcomings of the evidence should not be exaggerated. Despite the difficulties of the sources, they provide a remarkably rich picture of the Yorkshire gentry in the Angevin period. More important still, they allow the historian to observe a series of transformations involving the gentry which would have profound effects on the patterns of English society and therefore the shape of subsequent English history. The most important of these was the transformation of the honor and it is to this transformation that we will now turn.

25. I might note here that I have relied heavily on the records of the eyre of 1218–19 throughout the book even though the eyre took place after John's death, because these records are particularly rich and many of the cases handled by the eyre would have started before John's death. Any case after John's death would have occurred extremely close to the Angevin period.

1. Vassals, Tenants-in-Chief, and the Transformation of the Honor

I

In the decades following the Norman Conquest, William the Conqueror and his followers killed, exiled, or dispossessed the vast majority of Anglo-Saxon aristocrats. This allowed them to completely reshape the aristocratic landholding structure of England and in so doing, to introduce a fundamentally important institution, the honor. William the Conqueror and his followers redistributed land and created honors through enfeoffments: grants that not only paid off followers but also created permanent ties and continuing expectations of service. Thus landholding became tied with personal bonds of lordship and loyalty. This link was common in the Middle Ages, but only in England and a few other "conquest" states, such as the Crusader states, was it made so ubiquitous.

This universality made the honor, with its powerful conjunction of landholding and aristocratic patronage, an extremely important institution in Norman England. Honors provided the units for the feudal host and thus played a key role in the military organization of the kingdom. The law courts attached to honors assumed an important share of the judicial business of the kingdom, particularly in the area of land law. Many elite social and religious activities became associated with honors. Thus honors formed the backbone for elite organization and control in the Norman period. Traditionally, the system that resulted from the creation of honors been described as "English feudalism," but I will use a more specific phrase, the honorial system, because the term feudalism has acquired so many definitions and meanings that it would have discouraged even the most ardent proponents of Universals in the Middle Ages, had they known of it.[1]

1. Elizabeth A. R. Brown, "The Tyranny of a Construct: Feudalism and Historians of Medieval Europe," 1063–88.

It is my contention that the conjunction of personal ties and landhold-ing, while strengthening the honorial system in the short term, made it inherently unstable in the long term, for the permanence of landholding, in a society in which inheritance was a norm and eventually a right, could not be accommodated to the fluidity of circumstances and of human relation-ships.[2] As a result, the honor gradually transformed from a vibrant system of patronage and governance to a collection of fixed and largely impersonal rights and obligations. Consequently, honors lost much of their impor-tance and new avenues of patronage had to be formed within the elite and new systems had to take over many of the functions of the honor. This process began practically from the creation of the system, but in many important respects culminated in the Angevin period, with important consequences for the gentry, which had in large measure emerged from the process of enfeoffment after the Conquest.

There is already widespread agreement among historians that the honor had gone into decline in the late twelfth century. Edmund King describes the honor of the abbey of Peterborough as patently decayed by 1200.[3] K. J. Stringer contrasts the importance and strength of Scottish honors with the relative weakness of English ones in the late twelfth century.[4] Poole suggests that by the end of the twelfth century social relations were based more on money than on tenure, which had been the basis of the honorial system.[5] Painter argues that from the beginning of the thirteenth century, the military resources of barons ceased to be feudal in nature.[6] Though lords continued to collect scutage and benefit from feudal incidents much longer, honors seem to have lost much of their political and social significance by the beginning of the thirteenth century.

In the past, explanations for the decline of feudalism have centered upon the royal government and in particular upon the legal innovations of the Angevin period, especially novel disseisin and mort d'ancestor. The most influential arguments in this respect are those of Maitland and Mil-som. These scholars' explanations of the purpose of Henry II's legal re-forms and their impact upon the honorial system are very different. Mait-land described the reforms as an intentional undermining of the system, and through it of noble power, by the king.[7] Milsom, drawing in part on

2. I will discuss the issue of whether inheritance existed before the Angevin legal reforms later in the chapter.

3. King, *Peterborough Abbey*, 36.

4. K. J. Stringer, *Earl David of Huntingdon 1152–1219*, 57.

5. Austin L. Poole, *Obligations of Society in the Twelfth and Thirteenth Centuries*, 3–4.

6. Sidney Painter, *Studies in the History of the English Feudal Barony*, 135–36.

7. See Frederick Pollock and Frederic W. Maitland, *The History of English Law* 1:144–51,

the work of Thorne, depicts the reforms as having unintended but disastrous consequences for the honor.[8] Both theories, however, describe legal change as the fundamental cause of the decline of the honor.

There can be no doubt that the Angevin legal reforms were closely intertwined with the fate of the honorial system, but it seems problematic to focus only on legal change; to do so places the weight of an extremely important political and social transformation *solely* on the shoulders of a handful of procedural changes in law. As legal historians, Maitland and Milsom naturally concentrated on legal change, but it is time to look for other factors in the decline of the honorial system.

Several very recent works provide new perspectives on lordship in medieval England and suggest new routes to an understanding of the decline of the honorial system. The first of these is J. M. W. Bean's book, *From Lord to Patron: Lordship in Late Medieval England*. Although Bean concentrates on what has traditionally been known as bastard feudalism rather than on the honorial system, he has one important conclusion that should be considered carefully by students of the latter system. Bean traces annuities, indentured retaining, and livery back to relationships within the households of lords in earlier periods. He then uses this information to argue for an essential continuity of lordship and service from the early Anglo-Saxon *gesithcundman* to the late medieval retainer. The types of reward may have shifted, and the growth of stability under a strong government may have altered the framework in which lordship operated, but the personal links between aristocratic lords and followers remained an important aspect of society throughout. This is a provocative view and one that suggests that the precise nature of bonds between honorial lords and vassals should be scrutinized more carefully and perhaps reevaluated.[9]

Another perspective comes from David Carpenter's contribution to the debate over Coss's recent argument about the rise of bastard feudalism.

202–3, 2:46–80 for Maitland's discussion of the changes. Maitland's views of Henry's motives, however, are stated much more directly in "The Beatitude of Seisin," in *The Collected Papers of Frederic William Maitland*, 412–13.

8. Samuel E. Thorne, "English Feudalism and Estates in Land," 193–209; S. F. C. Milsom, *The Legal Framework of English Feudalism*. Robert C. Palmer has strongly supported Milsom's view of the reforms, while at the same time offering several modifications; "The Feudal Framework of English Law," 1130–64; "The Origins of Property in England," 1–50.

9. J. M. W. Bean, *From Lord to Patron: Lordship in Late Medieval England*, 146–47, 232–37. Even earlier, G. A. Holmes argued that bastard feudalism was part "of a more permanent feature of English social organization: the grouping of servants and followers, household and retinue, noble and servile dependents, around the great estate, supported and attracted by its wealth and influence." *The Estates of the Higher Nobility in Fourteenth-Century England*, 83.

In his discussion of the decline of the honor, Carpenter emphasizes personal relationships and choices. He argues that to get good service from able followers, lords had to break out of the restrictions of the "honorial straitjacket." However, as land became scarce and tenure more firmly established in the late twelfth century, enfeoffments became increasingly problematic for lords. They switched to other forms of patronage and began to establish followings that were increasingly independent of their honors. Carpenter is not certain whether this was happening at such an early time in the North where honors were more compact but is certain that it was happening on many southern honors. At the same time, tenants were often willing to seek out new patrons. Carpenter sees the willingness of both lords and tenants to seek new patronage ties outside their honors as an important factor in the shift from "real" to "bastard" feudalism envisioned by Coss. Carpenter does not deny the importance of the Angevin legal reforms, but slightly shifts the focus away from them.[10]

David Crouch, in his contribution to the same debate, and in his recent book on William Marshall, makes a stronger break with traditional historiography.[11] He too focuses on the declining flow of land, starting in Stephen's reign, and argues that this decline weakened the ties between lords and their traditional followers. Knights became more mobile in their allegiance from the 1180s on and many magnates began to create affinities similar to those of the late Middle Ages. Crouch goes further than Carpenter and suggests that the decline of lands, rather than the rise of the royal courts, caused the decay of the old system, for magnates were making certain adjustments even before the Angevin legal reforms. Crouch, like Bean, argues for continuity. Citing the existence of forms of patronage outside the honorial system from the Norman period and the early existence of strong public authority in England, Crouch asserts that the changes between 1100 and 1300 were "matters of degree and cosmetic."[12]

Even before the publication of these recent works, I had independently come to the conclusion that an investigation of personal ties between lords and tenants and of the membership of the retinues of lords was key to the understanding of the decline of the honor as an important political and social institution. Bean's work highlights the need to consider the ties

10. David Crouch, D. A. Carpenter, and Peter R. Coss, "Debate: Bastard Feudalism Revised," 177–89.

11. Crouch et al., "Debate: Bastard Feudalism Revised," 165–77; Crouch, *William Marshal: Court, Career and Chivalry in the Angevin Empire*, 133–70.

12. Crouch et al., "Debate: Bastard Feudalism Revised," 168.

between lords and followers independently of the institutional framework of those ties. In studying such ties, the contrast between "bastard" feudalism and "real" feudalism is, as Bean suggests, somewhat misleading. Studies of patronage and lordship in the later Middle Ages show that patronage networks could be extremely fluid, with retainers serving more than one lord and moving from one noble retinue or affinity to another, depending upon their own needs and political circumstances.[13] By implicit contrast, "real" feudalism is seen as stable or even static, and the neat uncluttered diagrams of feudal pyramids sometimes found in textbooks reinforce the picture of a rigid, unchanging feudal structure. One imagines a world in which generation after generation of tenants loyally served generation after generation of lords without interruption from clashes of personality or alterations of loyalty due to political circumstances.

When described in such explicit terms, of course, this perfect feudal or honorial world is difficult to believe, and few if any scholars would, I think, advance such an oversimplified picture. Until recently, however, scholars of "real" feudalism have largely concentrated on abstract or institutional matters such as quotas of knights' service, and this has obscured the human element. Partly this is a matter of historiographical trends, but it is also partly due to the sources. Many of our perceptions of feudalism depend on thirteenth century records, which provide survey after survey of knights' fees and ample information about knights' quotas and feudal incidents. These do show the durability of honors and of honorial ties, but only in terms of standardized rights and obligations such as scutage and wardship rather than personal links between vassals and lords.

By concentrating on the personal rather than impersonal aspects of the honorial system, I hope to place honorial lordship in the broader context of medieval English patronage. Equally important, I hope to shed light on the transformation and ossification of the English honorial system, processes I regard as far more than matters of cosmetic change. As this chapter will show, in some respects lordship in the Angevin period shows startling continuity with lordship in later periods. In other respects, however, lordship underwent radical change under Henry II and his sons.

---

13. See particularly Wright, *The Derbyshire Gentry*, 60–82, and Michael J. Bennett, in *Community, Class and Careerism: Cheshire and Lancashire Gentry in the Age of Sir Gawain and the Green Knight*, 215–23. Christine Carpenter, in "The Beauchamp Affinity: A Study of Bastard Feudalism at Work," 514–32, describes a comparatively stable retinue, but even here, struggles for local dominance caused shifts in the patronage structure.

II

Lords throughout the Middle Ages depended on active service and loyal support to help maintain their power. Ties that were merely institutional or strictly legal were of limited use to them. To succeed, and in dangerous times to survive, they needed loyal followers closely bound to them through personal ties. Indeed, personal ties lay at the very origin of the English honorial system. William the Conqueror did not conquer England because he had a large feudal levy, for his rights as lord did not extend to overseas invasions. He conquered England because his ties with his followers were close enough that he could persuade them to accompany him on his perilous invasion. Eleanor Searle argues that earlier Norman political history also needs to be seen in the light of personal links rather than institutions.[14] Personal ties, active service, and interaction between lord and followers continued to be important long after the Conquest, and indeed to some degree long after the Middle Ages.

The Jervaulx chronicle provides some rare and vivid glimpses of the personal relations and interaction between a lord and his followers in the twelfth century, shortly before the Angevin period. This chronicle shows Count Alan, lord of the honor of Richmond from 1136 to 1146, hunting with his barons and knights in Richmondshire, rebuking honorial officials for their neglect of his forest, cajoling his knights to make gifts to Jervaulx abbey, and taking counsel with his followers upon further requests from the monastery.[15] This chronicle was written years after the events described had taken place and contains some errors; to some degree it may represent the way a monk imagined the interaction.[16] In any case, what is so striking about these passages is that they record or envision a high level of interaction and cooperation between the lord and his followers. Here the personal element of lordship is very strong.

Personal lordship, however, must by its nature be somewhat fluid, especially over the course of generations. A lord might find a loyal follower's son to be equally loyal but less competent than his father. The heir to a lordship might have new favorites or find less favor in the eyes of many

14. Eleanor Searle, *Predatory Kinship and the Creation of Norman Power: 840–1066*.

15. William Dugdale, ed., *Monasticon Anglicanum* 5:569, 572.

16. At the earliest, the chronicle was written after Alan's son, Duke Conan, had died and been succeeded by his daughter in 1171; Dugdale, *Monasticon* 5:573. The most important error is that some of the actions ascribed to Count Alan must chronologically have occurred during the period his son Conan held the honor; *EYC* 4:25.

vassals. In times of unrest, a follower might find it prudent to gain a new patron, especially in England, where a vassal might hold land far from any of his lord's strongholds. Given the dual loyalty to king and to immediate lord expected of vassals, disputes between kings and magnates could severely strain and even break personal ties. So too could the existence of rival lords to an honor.[17] Both lords and tenants could have reasons to sever or simply ignore traditional bonds of personal lordship. None of these reasons would necessarily break the tenurial bonds of the honorial lordship, but they would certainly alter the composition of a lord's retinue.

The story in the Jervaulx chronicle provides little information about the precise identity of Count Alan's followers, though it is likely that most were local Richmondshire vassals. Fortunately, other sources do allow one to reconstruct the retinues of great magnates. References to estate officials and attorneys and miscellaneous descriptions of links or cooperation between tenants-in-chief and specific followers provide some of this information. Witness lists, however, are the most important source for the constitution of retinues and have been used as such by other scholars.[18] Witness lists cannot always provide precise and complete information about a given lord's retinue at a given time, and should always be used with caution, but when they survive in sufficient numbers they can provide solid evidence about shifts in the patterns of retinue formation.[19] The membership of retinues can then be compared to the lord's tenantry, whose identity can be garnered from the *cartae baronum* of 1166 and other lists of vassals and fees, and this can be used to explore the role of honorial tenantry within retinues.[20]

Particularly plentiful evidence survives for the retinues of two magnate

17. In one local war during King Stephen's reign, a member of the Foliot family, who were tenants of the honor of Pontefract, was fighting against the Lacys, who were traditional lords of the honor; Fowler, "Selebeiensis Monasterii Historia," 35; W. E. Wightman, *The Lacy Family in England and Normandy*, 77.

18. Most notably, C. Warren Hollister has used witness lists to determine which nobles were close followers of the Norman kings; see his articles on the relations between kings and nobles in his collection *Monarchy, Magnates and Institutions in the Anglo-Norman World*. For the use of witness lists to reconstruct a magnate's retinue and the problems with this method, see Stringer, *Earl David*, 150, 155–58. See also Charlotte A. Newman, *The Anglo-Norman Nobility in the Reign of Henry I*, 91ff.; Wightman, *The Lacy Family*, 106; and Crouch, *William Marshal*, 134.

19. Only when one gathers sufficient charters do patterns begin to emerge. Out of the scores of individuals attesting the charters, a few names appear again and again. Not surprisingly, these tend to be honorial officials, men who served as attorneys or in some other role, and followers who received land or other rewards from the lord in question.

20. For the *cartae baronum*, see Hubert Hall, ed., *The Red Book of the Exchequer*, 186–445.

families, the Mowbrays and Percys.[21] The Mowbrays, descended from one of Henry I's new men, Nigel d'Aubigny, held approximately one hundred fees in 1166, and played an important role in national events, including the 1173–74 rebellion and the Magna Carta revolt. The Percys, who received much of their land before 1086 but only had about one third the number of fees in 1166, played a smaller role than the Mowbrays in national affairs of the Angevin period, in part because the honor was split for much of the period by two coheiresses, Matilda and Agnes, and then, in an unusual arrangement owing to the *casus regis*, between the grandson and younger son of Agnes.[22] Nevertheless Richard de Percy, the younger son, did play a role in the Magna Carta revolt. Locally, both families were extremely important. An analysis of the witness lists of the many charters produced by these families reveals much about the nature of retinues in the Angevin period and the shifting role of tenants in those retinues.[23] The charters of the heads of these families, their heirs presumptive, and of the husbands of Matilda and Agnes de Percy, where they pertain to the Percy honor, will be considered.[24]

The primary point to be made about the Mowbray and Percy retinues is that they were fluid; as decades passed, membership changed slowly but constantly. This fluidity reflected not only generational change within the families of tenants, which one would expect, but also declining participation by some established families and the replacement of their participation by that of new families. The figures in Table 1 cannot be seen as absolutely

21. It should be noted that these discussions will include gentry from outside Yorkshire. It simply does not make sense to speak of only a portion of the tenants of an honor or of the members of a retinue.

22. The term *casus regis* refers to the problem of whether the son or the brother of an heir should succeed as heir if the original heir died before his father, and is so called because of the debate whether John or Arthur should take the throne after Richard's death. In the Percy case, a compromise was made.

23. The information is drawn from the 11th volume of *Early Yorkshire Charters*, and from D. E. Greenway, *Charters of the Honour of Mowbray, 1107–1191*. In order to extend discussion of the Mowbray retinue to the end of the Angevin period, I have collected a number of William de Mowbray's charters; *Fountains Cartulary* 1:18, 141, 142, 211–12, 2:662, 746–47, 749; *Yorkshire Deeds* 7:128–29; John Brownbill, ed., *The Coucher Book of Furness Abbey*, vol. 2, part 2, 340–42; Dugdale, *Monasticon Anglicanum* 6:318–19; *Calendar of Charter Rolls* 2:442; BL, Egerton MSS 2827:71, 77, 78, 87; Cotton MS Nero C XII, 3v, 44r; Harley Charter 83 G 53; Cotton Charter V 13; Bodleian Library, Dugdale MSS 13:356; Dodsworth MSS 8:298; Shakespeare Birthplace Trust Record Office, DR10 42; DR10 59.

24. The charters of heirs presumptive are being included largely for a practical reason; it is not always possible to tell whether a charter was issued before or after an heir inherited. The only heir presumptive who issued large numbers of charters was Nigel de Mowbray, and there is such a large overlap between the witnesses to his charters and those of his father that factoring out the charters he issued as an heir does not alter the picture in any significant way.

Table 1   Average Number of Attestations by Category of Vassal

Decade	Number of charters	Pre-1135	1135–1166	Post-1166[a]
			Tenants	
Mowbray retinue				
30s, 40s	51	2.35	.63	.22
50s	46	3.24	1.93	.41
60s	38	2.00	1.68	.89
70s	104	1.88	1.25	1.04
80s	42	1.62	.79	.86
1194–1224[b]	26	1.46	1.15	0.00
Percy retinue				
50s	6	3.83	.83	
60s	15	2.53	1.13	
70s	15	1.47	1.27	
80s	11	1.37	1.64	
90s	17	.35	.41	

a. This includes a family introduced to the honor through marriage to an heiress, a marriage in which Roger de Mowbray probably had a hand.
b. The dates 1194–1224 represent the dates in which William de Mowbray controlled the honor. His charters are too few to warrant breaking down by decade.

precise indicators of change within retinues; most charters can only be placed in approximate decades.[25] Nevertheless, the table provides a good, if rough, illustration of the way in which participation in the retinues passed from families long established on the honors to new families over the course of the Angevin period.

In addition to the new tenants included in Table 1, all of whom held at least a substantial fraction of a knight's fee, several more new men joined retinues who either received no land or very small grants. In Roger de Mowbray's later years, for instance, Robert de Beauchamp and John and Robert Crevequer attested so many charters that Diana Greenway suggested they were probably household knights.[26] Roger's grandson, Wil-

25. Charters were rarely dated in this period. I have therefore placed charters within decades by taking a date in the middle of the span suggested by Greenway or Clay in their editions. Because these spans are often long, and because charter dating is of necessity an inexact science, even for such excellent editors, the tables will only be imprecise indicators of change over time. However, dating techniques are good enough to give a good, if rough, sense of change over a period of time, especially with such large samples.
26. Greenway, *Mowbray Charters*, lxi, n. 9.

Table 2   Declining Attestations by Established Vassals

Decade	Number of charters	Average number of attestations	Percentage
Mowbray			
30s, 40s	51	3.20	48.41
50s	46	5.59	54.59
60s	38	4.58	53.76
70s	104	4.16	41.31
80s	42	3.26	32.21
1194–1224	26	2.54	29.73
Percy			
50s	6	4.67	41.79
60s	15	3.67	37.16
70s	15	2.73	22.53
80s	11	3.00	38.82
90s	17	.76	9.77

liam, recruited at least one important new follower, Philip son of John, described as William's associate in one royal record, and probably recruited others as well.[27] Similarly, Matilda de Percy recruited two new men, Robert de Beaugrant and Robert her chamberlain and one new woman, a second chamberlain named Juliana.[28] If these and others were factored in, the shift seen in Table 1 would be even greater, though one would be moving beyond the core of the honorial tenantry to figures with at best a minor landed interest in the honor.

The fluidity of retinues was accompanied by a slow but steady decline in the participation of established tenants. As time went on, many vassal families, though they continued to thrive, attested fewer and fewer charters of their lord or even none at all. The overall decline of participation in the Mowbray and Percy retinues by established tenants with at least a substantial fraction of a knight's fee, from the 1150s on, is illustrated in Table 2. This table shows the decline of attestations by such vassals not only in absolute

27. Thomas D. Hardy, ed., *Rotuli de Liberate ac de Misis et Praestitis Regnante Johanne*, 45. Philip attested eleven of William's charters. Another likely new retainer was Roger de Fontibus, who witnessed eight charters.

28. Both Roberts attested more than twenty percent of the charters of Matilda and her husband relating to her honor. Women almost never appear in witness lists and Juliana was no exception, but Matilda identified her as her chamberlain in several charters; *EYC* 11:52, 61, 63.

terms, as an average number of attestations per witness list, but also in relative terms, as a percentage of total attestations in each period, since the average size of witness lists seems to fluctuate over time.

This decline in attestations by established vassals had clearly begun early. Eleven of the thirty-six families of vassals established before 1135 on the Mowbray honor attested none of the charters of Roger de Mowbray, who was lord of the honor from 1129 to 1187 (the rise in attestations on the Mowbray honor in the 1150s was in large measure due to the participation of the many new vassals enfeoffed in this period by Roger de Mowbray). More striking still, over half of the tenants on the Percy fee in 1166 attested none of the charters of William de Percy, who held that honor in the middle of the twelfth century. As the decline continued over the course of the Angevin period, it began to include new families as well as old; some of the new families active in Roger de Mowbray's retinue are conspicuously absent from the witness lists of his grandson's charters.

Not all vassal families ceased to participate actively in retinues and the overall decline did not completely eliminate established tenants from the retinues by the end of the Angevin period. For instance, members of the Daiville and Malebisse families were in the retinues of four generations of Mowbrays, from Nigel d'Aubigny to William de Mowbray.[29] William de Mowbray still relied on vassals for an important part of his retinue at the end of the Angevin period. Nevertheless, the general trend was for established tenants to participate less and less in retinues. As a result, there developed a growing gap between the membership of retinues and the core of honorial vassals. By 1216 vassals were less likely to be members of their lord's retinue than in 1154, and even then the shift had already begun.

Investigation of a third retinue indicates that the declining participation in retinues by lords might extend to political and military affairs. The retinue in question is that of Conan, earl of Richmond from 1146 to 1171 and duke of Britanny from 1156 to 1166. The earls of Richmond were among the greatest magnates in England and held close to two hundred knight's fees in England.[30] Conan, son of earl Alan, thus had a vast number of tenants from which to form his retinue. In a pattern that is similar to that found for the Mowbray and Percy retinues, some of these families provided officers,

29. Hugh Malebisse, tenant of an old fee and steward to Roger, may even have accompanied Roger on his final, fatal crusade; The antiquary, Dodsworth, stated that Hugh Malebisse died on Crusade in 1187–88; *EYC* 3:457; Bodleian Library, Dodsworth MSS 63:64.
30. For a series of lists enumerating fees on the honor of Richmond in the twelfth century, see *EYC* 5:2–3, 11–12.

some frequently attested his charters, and a large number were conspicuous by their absence. Conan himself had new men.[31]

But Conan's retinue is especially interesting because he had a claim to the Duchy of Britanny through his mother and was able to make good on this claim in 1156 after he invaded Britanny and captured his stepfather. However, Conan's tenure of the Duchy was so precarious that in 1166 he surrendered custody of it to Henry II when he betrothed his daughter and heiress, Constance, to Henry's son, Geoffrey. Over half of Conan's charters were issued in Britanny, most of them during the period he was trying to rule the Duchy, when he needed all the support he could get. Given the fact that William the Conqueror's success depended so heavily on persuading followers to follow him to England, it is interesting to note that Conan was able to draw only very limited support for his Breton ambitions from his vast English honor.[32] Even individuals who did attest English charters, such as Ralph son of Ribald, Conan's kinsman and tenant of one of the largest fees on the honor, Hervey son of Acaris, another kinsman and important tenant, or Warner son of Wimar, Conan's steward, were conspicuously absent from the Breton assemblies in which he issued charters.[33] The only one of Conan's most important tenants to serve actively in Britanny was his constable, Alan.[34] Conan's other English supporters who frequently followed him to Britanny were all the sons or brothers of English tenants or Conan's own new men.[35]

31. These statements are based on a study of the witness lists and lists of tenants in *Early Yorkshire Charters*, vol. 4.

32. Conan occasionally locked horns with Henry II over issues relating to Britanny and Paul Brand has suggested to me that Henry's displeasure may have been a factor in limiting the support Conan received in Britanny. Unfortunately, there is little evidence for the relations between Conan and Henry II aside from the occasions when they were in dispute and it is difficult to know if this would have been a factor throughout Conan's involvement in Britanny; indeed, W. L. Warren argues that Henry supported Conan's bid for the duchy; W. L. Warren, *Henry II*, 76. In any case, disputes between kings and lords, as suggested earlier, must be considered as part of the picture in studying personal relations between lords and vassals.

33. Ralph attested four of Conan's fifty authentic charters and three spurious ones containing plausible witness lists. None of Ralph's attestations were in Britanny. Only one each of Warner's and Hervey's eight attestations was of a Breton charter.

34. Alan attested nineteen charters, seven of them Breton. In some cases tenants may have been too old to fight or otherwise unsuitable, but this alone cannot explain the presence of one established tenant out of dozens.

35. The relatives of tenants included Henry, son and heir of Hervey son of Acaris; Hervey's younger brother, Walter; Conan's chamberlain, Ralph, the younger son of a native English tenant who held of Conan by drengage service; and the twins, Alan and Richard de Moulton, younger sons of Lambert de Moulton. Henry attested one English and six Breton charters; Walter, four of each; Richard thirteen Breton charters and three English ones; his twin; all of these and a fourteenth Breton charter; Ralph, eight Breton charters and four English ones. The new men included John son of Mengi and perhaps Henry Bertram.

Thus Conan's English support came largely from that youthful element in society that Georges Duby has shown played such an important
role in twelfth-century society: heirs who were not yet established and
younger sons in search of land to call their own.[36] Even the sons of tenants,
however, played only a limited role in Britanny. The vassals of the honor of
Richmond were probably willing to hunt with Count Alan in Richmondshire, but most were not willing to help Alan's son, Conan, uphold his
claim to the Duchy of Britanny.[37] Had William the Conqueror received the
same level of support from his Norman vassals, the Norman Conquest
would never have succeeded.

Each honor had its own history and its own circumstances, and these
undoubtedly affected relations between lords and tenants. Henry I's placing of Nigel d'Aubigny, founder of the Mowbray family, over tenants-in-
chief and over vassals enfeoffed by earlier lords may have given the Mowbray honor a weak base.[38] Many different factors could affect the history of
individual honors: geographical shape, the personality of lords, national
politics, and so forth. The Lacy and Brus families, for instance, seem to have
had better success than most at keeping older families in their retinues.[39]
On the honor of Skipton, in contrast, most of the older families disappeared from witness lists early on, but the holders of the honor greatly and
effectively expanded their retinues through many new enfeoffments.[40]
Over the long haul, however, all honors showed the same patterns of

36. Georges Duby, "Au XII^c siècle: les 'jeunes' dans la société aristocratique dans France
du nord-ouest," 835–46; trans. by Cynthia Postan as "Youth in Aristocratic Society," in *The
Chivalrous Society*, 112–22.

37. An interesting parallel, though from the end of the Angevin period rather than the
beginning and involving rebellion rather than the upholding of a more or less legitimate claim,
is Janet Meisel's analysis of Fulk Fitz Warin's following when he revolted against King John in
the first decade of the thirteenth century. Only twenty percent of the men who went into
rebellion with Fulk were tenants, and only two of Fulk's five tenants by knight's service joined
him. Many of the rebels came from the region where Fulk had powerful local influence; *Barons
of the Welsh Frontier: The Corbet, Pantulf and Fitz Warin Families, 1066–1272*, 113–15.

38. However, the split between those who remained in Roger's retinue and those who
did not does not correspond exactly to the split between fees created by Nigel and those
created before him. The Arches, who had once held of the crown, and the Wyvilles, who had
probably received their lands from the Stutevilles, produced two of Roger's most faithful
followers (Greenway, *Mowbray Charters*, xxxiv). At the same time, it is likely that some of the
tenants who had drifted out of the Mowbray retinue had been enfeoffed of their lands by
Nigel.

39. This statement is based largely on a study of the witness lists to charters of the two
families. It is notable that their honors were fairly compact, though the same could be said for
the Yorkshire portion of the honor of Richmond.

40. For the large number of new enfeoffments on the honor of Skipton, see *EYC* 7:94–
95. A study of the witness lists of charters issued by the holders of the honor reveals their
reliance on these new tenants for their retinues.

shifting retinues and declining participation in retinues by established vassals.

So far, the discussion has focused on the point of view of the honor and the honorial lords. What of the vassals? More particularly, what was becoming of the vassals who disappeared from retinues but not from the body of the tenantry? Undoubtedly some simply concentrated on their own interests and provided whatever minimal service was necessary to retain their lands. Others, however, sought new patrons; it was not just lords who sought to break out of the honorial straitjacket. Many examples can be found of individuals with roots in one honor serving the lord of another; for instance, Peter de Billinghay, originally a tenant of the Archbishop of York, who attested some of Roger de Mowbray's charters and received land from him; Ralph de Tilly, constable of the Archbishop of York, whose family held of the Warennes and Lacys; and Henry son of Conan, one of Peter de Brus's stewards, who held of the honor of Richmond.[41] One Stuteville vassal, Thomas de Etton, even entered the service of Thomas Becket, presumably when the latter was, among other things, provost of Beverley.[42] Just as lords could seek out new followers, vassals could seek out new lords. Since several families held tenancies of different honors even in 1166, this was probably not a new practice in the Angevin period.[43] Thus, fluidity of lordship and the growing gap between retinue and honor derived not only from the actions and decisions of lords but also from those of vassals.

In some respects, at least, the fluidity described so far had its advantages for both lords and vassals, for both were enabled to search out the most advantageous link possible. Vassals could seek the best patron. Lords could pick and choose whom they pleased for their retinue and could recruit the ablest followers regardless of honorial affiliation.

However, there was another factor in the equation, one that created difficulties for lords and ultimately forced a radical reconstruction of the relations between patrons and followers, namely the close connection be-

41. Greenway, *Mowbray Charters*, 224–25; *EYC* 8:143–47; Roger of Howden, *Chronica* 2:60; *EYC* 5:54, 57–58; J. S. Purvis, ed., *The Chartulary of the Augustinian Priory of St. John the Evangelist of the Park of Healaugh*, 152.

42. J. C. Robertson and J. B. Sheppard, *Materials for the History of Thomas Becket, Archbishop of Canterbury*, 1:153, 2:92. The Mowbray tenant, Thomas de Coleville, was in the retinue of another national figure, William Marshal; Crouch, *William Marshal*, 138, 202.

43. For the frequency with which important families might hold of several honors, see Barbara English, *The Lords of Holderness, 1086–1260*, 153–54, 156; David Crouch, *The Beaumont Twins: The Roots and Branches of Power in the Twelfth Century*, 127–30; Stringer, *Earl David*, 127.

tween recent or impending reward and active personal service revealed by a study of retinues. The connection is obvious in the case of newer tenants; however, it is also true for established families. Roger de Mowbray can be shown to have given new fees or increments to existing fees to members of seven of the thirty-six families established on his honor before 1135. These seven families provided more attestations to Roger's charters than the remaining twenty-nine established families. On most honors, certain families and individuals provided far more attestations than others. Table 3 indicates the correlation between the families who received rewards from Roger and those who were most active in his retinue; the correlation would perhaps be even higher if all of Roger's secular charters had survived. Table 3 also indicates that the families who received rewards were far more likely to provide honorial officials and to participate in the 1173–74 revolt, presumably in support of Roger.[44] Similarly, of the eleven individuals who appear most frequently in the charters of William de Percy, three certainly and two more probably came from established families who had received new rewards; one was a new vassal; and four held at most only minor interests which their families received at an unknown date. Only one came from an important established family and received no known grant of land.[45]

The Mowbrays and the Percys were not the only lords to reward the established tenants most active in their service. Duke Conan gave lands and offices in England and Britanny to members of several honorial families, especially those who supported him in Britanny. Indeed, it was probably the only way he got them to serve him in Britanny.[46] Similar examples of rewards to established tenants could be drawn from other honors as well.[47] Clearly tenants were not willing to provide the sort of active service lords needed simply because of an enfeoffment made in a previous generation.[48]

44. The officials were drawn from the Cundy, Daiville, Malebisse, Wyville, Belvoir and Bellun families. The rebels included members of the Arden, Moreville, Malebisse, Wyville, Buscy, and Beler families and Warin, son of Simon. For the placement of these families in the respective categories, see Appendix one. For the Mowbray officials, see Greenway, *Mowbray Charters*, lx–lxiii. See *Pipe Roll 20 Henry II*, 143; *Pipe Roll 21 Henry II*, 33, 92, 95, for the vassals who can be shown to have participated in the 1173–74 revolt.

45. These eleven appeared in at least five of the twenty-six witness lists in William's charters. For more detail, see Appendix 1.

46. *EYC* 4:35, 58–59, 82; *Rot. Chart.*, 88b.

47. For some instances, see *EYC* 1:413, 416, 431; *EYC* 3:305; Dodsworth MSS 117:122v; Humberside Record Office, DDCC/135/2:1, 3, 5; Richard Holmes, ed., *The Chartulary of St. John of Pontefract*, 2:lxii.

48. Stringer argues that knights of old tenant families often served without new rewards; *Earl David*, 168, 173–74. I suspect, however, that these tenants did receive rewards of some sort,

Table 3   Service and Reward on the Honor of Mowbray

Number of attestations	Pre-1135 (no reward)	Pre-1135 (reward)	1135–66	Post-1166	Total
Frequency of attestation by family					
0	11	0	3	0	14
1–5	5	2	2	0	9
6–15	9	0	0	1	10
16–35	4	2	4	0	10
36+	1	3	2	3	9
Other types of support by family					
officials	1	3		2	
rebels	2	2	3		

Instead, tenants who served in the retinues of their lords probably expected to obtain new rewards and grants as a matter of course. Conan's constable, Alan, though he held one of the larger fees on the honor of Richmond, expressed such an expectation in a charter in which he granted fifteen librates of land to Jollan de Neville in marriage with his daughter, and promised another five librates from the first increment his lord might give him.[49] Alan, in other words, did not simply hope that he might receive a grant of land but counted on getting at least five librates as a reward at some point.

That such expectations existed and were frequently met must have encouraged the fluidity of retinues and the declining participation of established vassals in the retinues of their lords. Vassals whose expectations were not met might well seek a better patron. Moreover, if lords were expected to reward established vassals and non-vassals alike, they gained no particular advantage by recruiting their own tenants.

More important, the apparent need for lords to reward most if not all

---

but that the evidence has not survived. See Crouch, *The Beaumont Twins*, 102–14, for a discussion of how rewards effected loyalties on the honor of Breteuil. For the problems kings had in maintaining loyalty over several generations, see Holt, *Magna Carta*, 39–40, and Newman, *Anglo-Norman Nobility*, 18, 46, 98, 100, 105–6. The need to reward established followers was probably not new, for Searle has argued that in Normandy before 1066, "a clientele could not be 'purchased' once for all." *Predatory Kinship*, 200.

49. *EYC* 5:153. Alan was the only major English tenant to appear frequently in Conan's Breton witness lists. However, Clay dates this to c. 1175, and since Conan died in 1171, it is not certain that Alan was referring specifically to Conan.

active followers, even if these followers were already wealthy vassals, placed a strain on the resources of magnates. Historians have remarked on the financial strain caused by the need to reward new men, but in fact the situation was far worse since magnates also had to reward "old" men.

For a time, lords continued to reward their followers within the framework of the honorial system. In King Stephen's reign and the early Angevin period tenants-in-chief still frequently rewarded followers, both old and new, with grants of land. Many of the "new fees" in the *cartae baronum*, the fees created between 1135 and 1166, were for this purpose. Some magnates, such as Roger de Mowbray, continued to give land after 1166.[50]

As Carpenter and Crouch pointed out, however, lords were running out of land and their traditional generosity with grants of land could not continue. One temporary expedient was simply to make smaller grants. The Daivilles gained four knights' fees on the Mowbray honor before 1135. Between 1135 and 1166, Robert Daiville, the most frequent attester to Roger de Mowbray's charters and sometime constable of Axholme, received one knight's fee. After 1166, Robert's brother William, a member of Nigel de Mowbray's retinue, received one quarter fee. The grants by the earliest members of the Percy family to their followers were measured in knights' fees and carucates. Matilda de Percy's gifts to her chamberlains, Robert and Juliana, and another faithful follower, Robert de Beaugrant, were measured in acres.[51] However, even smaller gifts could cumulatively create a serious drain on resources. Therefore, grants of land became progressively rarer.[52] In the Angevin period, there was still a little give in the honorial straitjacket, for lords had enough land to recruit some new men within the honorial system, but that give rapidly vanished as the Angevin period proceeded.

As their supplies of land dwindled, lords increasingly turned to forms of patronage that did not require further depletion of their demesne lands. One form of patronage, the use of feudal incidents to reward followers, remained within the honorial framework. Lords could expect to gain

50. Greenway, *Mowbray Charters*, 220–22, 224–25, 242–43. For gifts of land after 1166 on the honor of Pontefract, see Dodsworth MSS 155:151r; *EYC* 3:204; M. L. Faull and S. A. Moorhouse, eds., *West Yorkshire: an Archaeological Survey to A.D. 1500*, 2:409, 509.

51. Greenway, *Mowbray Charters*, 231, 256–57, 264; *EYC* 11:52, 63–64; M. T. Martin, ed., *The Percy Cartulary*, 68.

52. Of the fees that existed in 1166, 87.7 percent had been created between 1066 and 1135, and only 7.5 percent between 1135 and 1166 (the remainder were held in demesne). The increase in fees after 1166 was minimal; Thomas Keefe, *Feudal Assessments and the Political Community Under Henry II and His Sons*, 43.

control of the occasional marriage, wardship, or escheat and these could be used for the purposes of patronage. This form of patronage is best reflected in the surviving evidence by the occasional marriage of a retainer to the heiress of one of his lord's vassals.[53]

However, there were other forms of patronage that lay entirely outside the honorial system. First, despite having given away a great part of their lands, the tenants-in-chief still tended to be the richest landowners and the growing economy of the Angevin period gave them access to money with which they could reward followers. It was probably no accident that in the late Angevin period, baronial officials were among the most active buyers in the land market.[54] Second, lords could obtain offices, favors, and even land for their followers if they themselves had good contacts in the royal government. For instance, when William de Stuteville and Roger de Lacy became sheriffs of Yorkshire, their undersheriffs were gentry followers and Richard de Percy gained a pardon for one gentry follower, Robert de Baldersby.[55] In 1204, lands confiscated from Normans were granted to Sampson de Pomerai, a follower of the magnate Robert de Turnham, and in similar grants to William de Buscy and Philip son of John these men were explicitly described as associates of William de Mowbray.[56]

A third factor that undoubtedly helped great magnates to support retinues as land grants dried up is the sort of intangible favors and support a powerful figure could provide his followers. It is striking that many of the knights who are recorded as having heard pleas in the York county court in 1212 had close connections with magnates, a pattern that can be matched elsewhere.[57] There is better evidence for gentry attempting to manipulate the judicial system than for magnates, but that may be because this evidence

53. Greenway, *Mowbray Charters*, xxxix; *EYC* 3:253; *EYC* 6:215; *EYC* 9:141–42; *EYC* 11:227; *Yorkshire Eyre*, 124.

54. Baronial officials who were members of the gentry and purchased land include Roald, constable of Richmond; Thomas de Horbury, steward of the Earl Warenne; Alan de Wilton, steward of Robert de Turnham; William de Tameton, steward of Peter de Brus; and Robert de Linton, steward of Matilda de Percy. See chapter 6 for their purchases. A practice earlier in the Angevin period was for lords to buy land which they then gave to followers; *EYC* 1:110; *EYC* 8:158–59.

55. For gentry undersheriffs, see *EYC* 10:71; *Pipe Roll 3 John*, 158, *Pipe Roll 7 John*, 40. For the pardon, see *Rot. Litt. Pat.*, 67b; *EYC* 11:345. For other examples of intercession by Yorkshire lords, see *Rot. Litt. Claus.*, 191b; *Rot. Obl. et Fin.*, 232–33; *Pipe Roll 31 Henry II*, 72.

56. *Rot. Litt. Claus.*, 12b; Hardy, *Rotuli de Liberate*, 45, 76. Sampson was a new man, at least in terms of Yorkshire, who was introduced into Yorkshire society by Robert through marriage to a local heiress; *EYC* 2:320. His relationship with the more powerful Devonshire family of the same name is unclear, but see Edward B. Powley, *The House of de la Pomerai*, 22.

57. Hugh M. Thomas, "The Knights of the York County Court in 1212," 142, 150; Robert Palmer, *The County Courts of Medieval England, 1150–1350*, 72–73, 113–38.

appears in royal court records only when the gentry were caught at it. Magnates may have been better able to cover their tracks.[58] Thus there is at least the possibility that magnates were practicing what later would have been called maintenance. Even if they were not, powerful lords were always in a position to help out loyal followers in one way or another.

Thus, when lords became increasingly chary of granting out demesne lands, and the honorial system therefore became less viable as a vehicle for patronage, they turned to other avenues of patronage that did not diminish their own resources.[59] Though the development of indentured retaining and of bastard feudalism lay in the future, the seeds were already being sown in the Angevin period.[60] Lords and their followers could and did adjust to new circumstances, and the strong ties between magnates and lesser members of the landholding classes remained a fundamentally important aspect of medieval English society.

The ability of lords and followers to adjust allowed the broad continuity in lordship described by Bean and Crouch.[61] Moreover, the retinues of Angevin magnates, like the affinities of late medieval lords, were built upon personal ties, continuing rewards, and active service, and were therefore very fluid. Honorial lordship was less distinct from other forms of lordship than might first appear.

In another respect, however, there was severe discontinuity. Patronage may have survived unscathed as an important aspect of English society, but the honorial system did not. The fluidity found in the retinues of honorial lords meant that there was an ever growing gap between retinues and tenantry, especially after lords ceased to incorporate new men into their honorial tenantry through enfeoffments. As a result of this growing gap, the honor slowly ceased to be a focus of personal lordship. This change could not but have consequences for the honor and was perhaps the most important factor which in the long term doomed the honor as an important political and social institution.

58. The ability of lords to harass enemies and support followers remained crucial in constructing patronage networks throughout the Middle Ages. See especially Carpenter, "The Beauchamp Affinity," 524–31. See chapter two for gentry manipulation of the judicial system.

59. As J. E. Lally has shown, Henry II was able to make a similar sort of adjustment; "Secular Patronage at the Court of King Henry II," 159–84. In contrast, Earl David of Huntingdon still seems to have relied largely on grants of land; Stringer, *Earl David*, 165–76.

60. For the growth of contractual arrangements as the basis of patronage, see Scott L. Waugh, "Tenure to Contract: Lordship and Clientage in Thirteenth-Century England," 811–39.

61. See above.

III

In discussing the history and fate of the honorial system, it is of primary importance to stress the sheer volume of land transfered from tenants-in-chief to vassals. In 1086, Count Alan the Red held 199 manors in the castlery of Richmond, as well as other lands in Yorkshire. One hundred thirty-three of the Richmondshire manors were already in the hands of tenants at the time of *Domesday Book*[62] and when the honor of Richmond was taken into the king's hand early in King John's reign, only Richmond and six other Yorkshire manors were held in demesne.[63] The detailed survey of Richmondshire carried out in *Kirkby's Inquest* in the late thirteenth century reveals that despite the recovery of some manors by the lords of Richmond in the thirteenth century, their demesne contained less than four percent of the carucates belonging to the honor in that region, despite the fact that Richmondshire was the heart of the honor. Because carucates were taxation units rather than precise measures of land and because the lords of Richmond had developed new sources of income including huge ranches in what had previously been forest, this figure does not provide an accurate picture of their relative economic position in the late thirteenth century. However, the picture it gives of the extent of subinfeudation is exaggerated only slightly if at all.[64]

Similarly, by 1129 there were only thirteen demesne manors on the Mowbray estates and by the end of the Angevin period the Mowbrays had only six demesne manors in all of England.[65] William de Percy held about one hundred manors in Yorkshire at the time of *Domesday Book*, and approximately sixty more were subsequently added to the family estates, so that the Percys eventually held more than 575 carucates in that county from the king. They also held another 150 or 160 carucates as tenants of other lords.

62. Margaret L. Faull and Marie Stimson, eds., *Domesday Book*, Yorkshire, 381. These figures are drawn from the summary of Count Alan's estates. See R. Welldon Finn, *The Making and Limitations of the Yorkshire Domesday*, 27–28, for a discussion of the problems concerning these figures. Despite the problems, they give a good idea of the scale of subinfeudation at that point.

63. *Pipe Roll 2 John*, 87–88.

64. One of the important demesne manors, Catterick, had had its assessment revised from ten carucates to none, but this was an isolated case and may be partially balanced by the subinfeudated lands recovered by the lords of Richmond. Since there was demesne in only eight of 175 villages within the honor recorded in the survey, the figure of less than four percent cannot be far off the mark, at least as far as arable farmland is concerned. Robert H. Skaife, ed., *The Survey of the County of York, taken by John de Kirkeby, Commonly Called Kirkby's Inquest*, 148–86.

65. Greenway, *Mowbray Charters*, xliv.

An inquisition post mortem of the middle of the thirteenth century, however, shows that Richard and William de Percy, who held the honor split between them, held only six demesne manors, and a few small holdings associated with them, with a total Domesday Book assessment of approximately sixty carucates.[66] Other thirteenth-century inquisitions post mortem show the same pattern. Yorkshire lords whose predecessors had held scores, even hundreds of manors and berewicks, possessed only a handful (between four and twenty-five) of manors themselves.[67]

These figures raise the question of why tenants-in-chief granted away such a large percentage of their lands, much of it within a generation or two of the Conquest. Motives were varied.[68] Some grants were meant to provide for relatives; others to pay off allies of equal or greater rank. Most grants were made to followers; many early grants were undoubtedly rewards for support during the Conquest and the difficult times thereafter and reward, as we have seen, continued to be an important reason for giving land. However, grants were made not simply to pay off vassals for past service but were also investments in future support. Enfeoffment of land to vassals was designed to allow the lord and vassal to share the fruits of the land, the vassal getting the direct benefits and the lord indirect benefits through the active service of the vassal. The idea was clearly that enfeoffment created a lasting personal bond.

The whole honorial system was designed around this principle. The ceremonies surrounding the granting of land and the passage of land from one generation to the next were originally rituals constructed to symbolize and perpetuate the bond between lord and tenant. The feudal host was built around the assumption that honorial lords could draw loyal and effective war bands from their bodies of vassals. The feudal custom of marriage presumed that the lord would have a continuing interest in the

---

66. *EYC* 11:19, 364; *Yorkshire Inquisitions* 1:66–72; *Calendar of Inquisitions Post Mortem* 1:124–25.

67. Besides the Percy inquisition, there are inquisitions for Edmund de Lacy, William de Fortibus III, who held the honors of Aumale and Skipton, Peter de Brus III, Peter de Maulay II, who held the Fossard lands, Peter of Savoy, who held the honor of Britanny, and Baldwin Wake, who held the Stuteville lands; *Yorkshire Inquisitions* 1:47–65, 73–84, 139–50, 191–200, 222–53; *Inquisitions Post Mortem* 1:115–16, 132–33, 258–62, 265–68; *Calendar of Inquisitions Post Mortem* 2:169–73, 213–15, 222–23. See also Stringer, *Earl David*, 104–25, for a discussion of the massive subinfeudation on the honor of Huntingdon.

68. For discussions of the motives of lords in giving out land, see Chew, *Ecclesiastical Tenants-in-Chief*, 116–18; Painter, *English Feudal Barony*, 29–30; J. M. W. Bean, *The Decline of English Feudalism, 1215–1540*, 3–4; Harvey, "The Knight and the Knight's Fee," 5–9; Stringer, *Earl David*, 80–81; Richard Mortimer, "The Beginnings of the Honour of Clare," 119–41; "Land and Service: the Tenants of the Honour of Clare," 177–97.

identity and personal loyalty of the tenant. The custom of wardship was not only designed to compensate the lord for any loss of personal service while the tenant was a minor, but also gave the lord a chance to develop close personal ties with the new tenant by raising him or her in the lord's household. Even the existence of honorial courts may be related to personal lordship, specifically to the idea that honorial affairs should be settled internally between a lord and his men. Honorial lordship was in its origins a very personal matter, and this is what gave it its strength. A lord and his tenants could work closely together to aid the king, fight their own enemies, and govern and profit from the land that the king had granted to the tenant-in-chief and he had shared out among his followers. The honor was one of the key institutions of the Norman period precisely because of the strength of personal ties.

Moreover, the scattered nature of most English honors, including many Yorkshire ones, made personal ties even more crucial to lordship in England than in other countries; honorial lordship could only rarely be combined with regional lordship. Personal ties of lordship rather than geographical proximity necessarily provided the glue for most English honors.[69]

However, over the course of generations the honor was transformed by a decline of the personal element in honorial ties. Milsom, in noting that the term felony had once been used not only in its criminal sense but also to describe a denial of a lord's proprietary rights by a tenant, argues that the disappearance of this broader meaning indicates that "the personal element in homage was waning rapidly."[70] Though I would disagree with Milsom on the timing of this change, and in large measure on its cause, the change was certainly occurring.

To a certain degree impersonal ties were built into the honorial system from the beginning, and throughout the history of the honorial system, enfeoffments were made which were never intended to create a personal bond of lordship. The honorial system was so all encompassing that almost all transactions between members of the upper classes had to be made within its scope. *Domesday Book* shows that even before 1086 magnates sometimes gave land to other magnates who were equally or more powerful and this practice continued long after 1086. In some cases magnates were

69. See Crouch, *The Beaumont Twins*, 134–38, for a comparison of feudal geography in England and France. See also Holt, *Magna Carta*, 23, and Christopher John Wales, "The Knight in Twelfth Century Lincolnshire," xxxiii–xxxv.

70. Milsom, *Legal Framework*, 28.

even forced to make enfeoffments to rivals and enemies; a number of
Mowbray enfeoffments were of this nature.[71] This created awkward anom-
alies within honors. Similarly, straightforward sales were also treated as
grants in return for service. Early in the Angevin period, when Reginald de
Warenne bought a manor for £100 from the Warenne tenant, Elias de
Bosville, the two went through all the formalities associated with the grant
of land by a lord to a tenant, although it is extremely unlikely that Warenne,
a younger son of Elias's lord, sometime caretaker of the Warenne estates,
and a powerful man in his own right, was ever Elias's vassal in any true
sense.[72] The granting of land and the taking of homage sometimes created
lordship in only the most abstract and legalistic manner.[73] In a sense, a
fictional personal relationship was created.[74] This maintained the integrity
of the honor in a legal or theoretical respect, but eroded the element of
personal lordship that had helped make the honor so important.

Far more important than the creation of fictional personal lordship
was the decline of the personal element where it had once existed. We
cannot know how far the honorial system ever lived up to the ideal of
intense personal lordship suggested by the rituals and conditions of enfeoffment described earlier, but certainly in the first generation after the Conquest lords and men must have been quite close. By 1154, however, the
personal bonds between lords and vassals had ruptured in a large number of
cases, and the process would continue through the Angevin period. One
important demonstration of this is the evidence for retinues presented in
the previous section. Each decade saw a growing rift between the body of
retainers and the honorial tenants as established tenants disappeared from
retinues. At first this rift could be papered over by new subinfeudation, but
as lords ceased to make new enfeoffments this became impossible. Established tenants who did not serve in retinues may well have maintained
casual contacts with honorial lords, but nevertheless their absence from
retinues clearly indicates a widespread erosion of personal ties.

There is other evidence for the decline in personal relationships between tenants-in-chief and their vassals as well. Vassals often held land in

71. For instance, the enfeoffments of the Stutevilles and Eustace fitz John. Roger of
Howden, *Chronica* 4:118; Greenway, *Mowbray Charters*, xxvi–xxviii.
72. *EYC* 8:158.
73. See Wales, "The Knight," 27.
74. J. Ambrose Raftis makes a similar point about grants of fee farms, which were often
strictly economic grants but were placed in the same legal structure as grants for knight service
through what was in many ways a legal fiction; *The Estates of Ramsey Abbey*, 39. It should be
noted, however, that fee farms were sometimes granted as rewards and in these cases, the
relations between donor and recipient genuinely were those between lord and follower.

the boroughs founded by their lords. For instance, the Featherstones, Stapletons, Reinevilles, and Dais, all tenants of the honor of Pontefract, held four dwellings right in a row along Southgate in Pontefract, and the Foliots, another family that held of the honor, also held property in the borough.[75] It is possible that when lords founded boroughs, they gave tenements to their vassals to help encourage development, but more likely the tenements were originally intended as dwelling places for followers and their households when they came to attend the courts of their lords or even for the periods when they performed castle guard. Yet such gentry holdings in honorial towns appear only when they were sold or given away, and this would have been likely to happen only when honorial ties decayed.

Two grants support this suggestion. In one, William son of Walding and his wife granted two tofts in Pontefract to the priory of that town, but reserved the right of hospitality there in case there was a call for castle guard duty (necessitas fuerit pro custodia castelli).[76] William was willing to fulfill his obligation of castle guard, but apparently saw no other need for a house at his lord's caput. In the other, dated between 1175 and 1189, Richard de Huddleston granted his chief dwelling in Clementhorpe in York to Avenal for a rent of two shillings, but inserted a clause stating that if war broke out Avenal was to turn over the actual house to Richard and move to one of the other buildings on the tenement.[77] Richard was a tenant of the archbishopric, and York, besides being a safe place to be during a war, was probably also the place where the archbishop rallied his tenants. Richard's ties with the Archbishop had apparently declined to the point where Richard no longer felt he needed a permanent home in York, but he still saw the possibility of being summoned for military service. In both cases, ties had attenuated though not broken. In all other similar grants, however, the gentry made no arrangements whatsoever to maintain any lodging rights in dwellings near the caputs of their lords.

Moreover, there is strong evidence not just for the passive decay of individual ties but also for many conflicts. Court records show the great

75. *EYC* 3:249–50, 293–94, 217–18. Similarly, the Constables of Richmond and the Burghs, both important tenants of the honor of Richmond, held land in Richmond, and Odo Fribois, a tenant of the Counts of Aumale, held land in the borough of the Count of Aumale's castle at Skipsea; *CRR* 6:328; Egerton MSS, 2827:252; *EYC* 3:72. Parallels can be found in England and on the Continent; Coss, *Lordship, Knighthood and Locality*, 61–66; Georges Duby, *La société aux xie et xiie siècles dans la région mâconnaise*, 190; G. T. Beech, *A Rural Society in Medieval France: the Gâtine of Poitou in the Eleventh and Twelfth Centuries*, 76, 90–91; M. Parisse, *Noblesse et chevalerie en Lorraine Médiévale: les familles nobles du XIe au XIIIe siècle*, 51–53.

76. Holmes, *Chartulary of Pontefract* 1:147.

77. *EYC* 1:180.

frequency of disputes between tenants-in-chief and their vassals. Of course, one would expect disputes between lords and even their closest followers, since the relationship involved personalities, mutual obligations, and transfers of property. Such disputes did not necessarily destroy otherwise close ties. The Jervaulx chronicle describes how Count Alan grew angry at his constable and steward for their lax keeping of the forest in Wensleydale, but this was no more than one would expect between a lord and his officials.[78] On another occasion Nicholas Bellun, a member of Nigel de Mowbray's retinue, placed himself in Nigel's mercy and allowed him to decide the issue when a dispute over woodland arose between them, thus preventing the dispute from destroying the close relations between them.[79]

However, tenants frequently sought outside support in disputes, thus undermining the strength of honorial ties. A number of cases exist in which Yorkshire tenants or would-be tenants went to the royal courts to seek land, dower, or other rights from their lords.[80] Sometimes, even the close relatives of people who had been members of their lord's retinue were involved in disputes. For instance, Sampson de Beler sought an assize of mort d'ancestor against William and Robert de Mowbray after the death of his uncle Hamo, a faithful Mowbray follower.[81] Tenants were quite willing to turn against their lords to protect their interests, something that was both a result and a cause of the decline of personal ties.[82]

Lords, faced with diminishing amounts of land, a continuing need to reward retainers, and a large body of vassals who were not contributing to their retinues, were equally willing to enter into disputes with tenants in hopes of recovering land or offices, or at least getting some cash. In one particularly remarkable case, Gerard de Furnival, a royal favorite who gained wardship of the heiress to the Luvetot honor and married her to his son, successfully seized land from a Luvetot tenant despite initial judgments for the tenant by a royal court and by a group of arbitrators. Gerald had agreed to arbitration in return for a proffer of one hundred marks from the tenant; to add insult to injury, he also persuaded the royal government

78. Dugdale, *Monasticon* 5:572.

79. Greenway, *Mowbray Charters*, 221–22.

80. *Pipe Roll 16 Henry II*, 41; *Pipe Roll 25 Henry II*, 21; *Pipe Roll 27 Henry II*, 45; *Pipe Roll 31 Henry II*, 75; *Pipe Roll 33 Henry II*, 90; *Pipe Roll 2 Richard I*, 66; *Pipe Roll 5 John*, 212; *Pipe Roll 6 John*, 188; *Pipe Roll 13 John*, 29; *RCR* 1:127; *CRR* 1:405; *CRR* 7:76–77; William Brown, ed., "Pedes Finium Ebor., Tempore Ricardi Primi," 183; *Yorkshire Eyre*, 79; *EYC* 3:254; *EYC* 11:43–44; *Fountains Cartulary* 2:48–49.

81. *Pipe Roll 7 Richard I*, 91.

82. See Crouch, *William Marshal*, 92–107, for the support many Leinster vassals gave to King John's representative in his struggle against their honorial lord, William Marshal.

to force the tenant to pay the one hundred marks despite the fact that he ignored the decision of the arbitrators.[83]

This was not an isolated case. Lords, and especially lords with close connections to the king, could use royal courts and the royal administration to hound lesser people, and honorial tenants were particularly vulnerable to this sort of treatment. Angevin land law generally protected tenants, but because it was originally based on feudal relationships there were plenty of loopholes that unscrupulous lords could exploit, aided sometimes by corruption and influence peddling. Some lords, in fact, systematically used the royal courts to bring pressure on tenants. The royal favorite, Robert de Turnham, made a large sum of money challenging grants made by the Fossards, his predecessors, and then withdrawing his claims in return for compensation. Most of his victims were religious houses, but one knightly tenant was forced to pay forty marks to end a case.[84] Maurice de Gant, who inherited part of the Paynel lands, brought cases against nearly twenty tenants, including several Yorkshire vassals, on one occasion alone.[85] During the Magna Carta revolt, King John was able to lure magnates to his side partly with the promise that they could seize and keep the land of any of their tenants who were in revolt.[86] This was a lure that at least some tenants-in-chief took seriously. Indeed, William de Fortibus, Count of Aumale and lord of Holderness, went into revolt in 1220 partly because the minority government under Henry III attempted to make him relinquish the land of his Lincolnshire tenant, William de Coleville, which he had seized during the war.[87] A surprising number of lords and vassals were in sharp conflict with each other.

Perhaps the most striking sign of the decline of the personal element in lordship was the practice of giving away or even selling lordship. In certain circumstances, one could imagine a gift of lordship that would fit into a situation in which personal ties were still strong, for instance, a father

83. *Pleas* 1:304; *CRR* 1:396; *Rot. Obl. et Fin.*, 118, 342; *Rot. Litt. Claus.*, 56; *Pipe Roll 3 John*, 158–59; *Pipe Roll 4 John*, 64; *Pipe Roll 8 John*, 208. Gerard was able to carry out this legal swindle in part through clever manipulation of his position as guardian rather than lord of the honor; agreements binding on him were not binding on his son, the new lord.

84. *CRR* 1:265; *CRR* 2:226; William Brown, ed., *Pedes Finium Ebor. Regnante Johanne*, 89, 99–100, 112–13; *Meaux Chronicle*, 232, 289–91.

85. *CRR* 5:189. Maurice claimed four manors from John de Birkin alone, *CRR* 5:282.

86. John made this offer to many lords, including to two Yorkshire magnates, John de Lacy and the Count of Aumale; *Rot. Litt. Claus.*, 255b, 266b.

87. For this revolt, see Ralph V. Turner, "William de Forz, Count of Aumale: An Early Thirteenth-Century English Baron," 238–42; English, *Lords of Holderness*, 42–46, 166–67; Robert Stacey, *Politics, Policy, and Finance under Henry III, 1216–1245*, 22–24; D. A. Carpenter, *The Minority of Henry III*, 229–34. Not surprisingly, few tenants went into revolt with him.

transferring the service of a loyal and active tenant to a beloved younger son. However, it is harder to explain the grant of knight's service from William Fossard to another tenant-in-chief, William de Stuteville, in this light.[88] It is even harder to explain sales. William Paynel sold the seven knights' fees held of him by Robert de Meinil to Hubert Walter, Archbishop of Canterbury.[89] Nicholas de Stuteville sold the lordship over half a knight's fee held by Thomas de Etton to Meaux Abbey, which was busily acquiring the land itself from Thomas.[90] In some cases at least, honorial lordship had become a commodity rather than a relationship.

The decline and frequent rupturing of personal ties was accompanied by a major shift in the nature of honors and therefore of the honorial system. As retinues shifted and as honorial ties lost their personal element, the honor lost much of its ability to function as a network of patronage and a focus of cooperation among the upper classes. No longer did honors have a central role in the relations between magnates and gentry. David Crouch, it is true, has warned us against seeing the honor as the only focus of such relations even in the Norman period, and Stenton's picture of an elite overwhelmingly organized and governed through the honorial system may be modified by future research.[91] Nevertheless, honors were clearly very important in the Norman period and the evidence shows that they subsequently had a declining role in certain aspects of aristocratic organization, and not only in terms of the contribution of honors to retinues.

An example can be seen in the area of religious patronage. In the middle of the twelfth century, gentry often gave land to the monasteries favored by their lords and as seen earlier, the Jervaulx chronicle describes Count Alan of Richmond actively persuading some of his knights to do so.[92] Guy Barnes and Toby Burrows have shown how important a role honorial ties played in the early donations to two other Yorkshire houses, Kirkstall and Bridlington. However, they have also showed how quickly the importance of honorial ties in monastic benefaction declined.[93] Vassals occasionally requested prayers for the souls of their lords, and though these were never common, proportionally they were more common in earlier

88. *Rot. Chart.*, 54b; *EYC* 9:186.

89. *EYC* 6:188.

90. *Meaux Chronicle*, 376.

91. Crouch, Carpenter, and Coss, "Debate: Bastard Feudalism Revised," 168–70.

92. Dugdale, *Monasticon* 5:569.

93. Guy D. Barnes, *Kirkstall Abbey, 1147–1539: An Historical Study*, 10, 12, 15–18; Toby Burrows, "The Geography of Monastic Property in Medieval England: A Case Study of Nostell and Bridlington Priories," 85.

gifts.[94] Tenants-in-chief and vassals, at least in the religious sphere, were no longer working together as a unit.

Honors were losing other important functions as well. Although honorial courts survived as institutions long past the Angevin period, there is a widespread perception that their importance was declining and passing to the royal courts. There were many reasons for this, many of them to be found in the changes in royal law. However, it is also likely that this shift in jurisdiction should also be seen at least partly in the context of the decline of personal ties between lords and vassals. When personal ties were close, disputes could be settled internally. A problem would come when ties loosened. If a court consisted of an increasingly atomized collection of tenants, it could not have been very effective in reaching and enforcing decisions, in mediating between individuals, and in mediating between a lord and his followers. If the honorial court was dominated by the lord's retinue, as the surviving evidence suggests, a tenant at loggerheads with a lord, as many tenants clearly were, would not readily accept the judgment of a court when an alternative was available.[95] The royal courts may have provided the alternative but the breakdown in personal ties clearly provided the incentive for litigants to transfer jurisdictions.

The breakdown of personal ties may also have affected the viability of the feudal host. On a number of occasions, the Angevin kings demanded fractions of the traditional quotas from their tenants-in-chief. On other occasions, tenants-in-chief brought smaller contingents of varying size.[96] Smaller contingents became the norm, and by the end of the thirteenth century, new quotas had come into being which were tiny in comparison to the old ones. Magnates were required to bring handfuls of knights where their ancestors had brought dozens or scores.[97]

94. Problems of dating and the lack of numerous examples make statistical analysis impossible. Roughly, however, there were three or four in every decade from the 1130s on. What is important is that the numbers of charters including such requests remained more or less constant while the number of charters issued by vassals soared.

95. In documents in which an honorial court is explicitly described, the members of the court tend to be active retainers. For instance, Roger de Mowbray's curia in one case included seven knights, all of whom were among the most frequent attestors to Roger's charters; *EYC* 9:239.

96. Sanders sees the earliest evidence for reduced as opposed to fractional service coming from 1213–1214; Sanders, *Feudal Military Service*, 59. See, however, my suggestion about the Irish campaign of 1210 in chapter seven. For the arrangements to distribute the burden from the reduced quota summoned for the 1214 campaign from the Yorkshire honor of Holderness, see English, *Lords of Holderness*, 162–64.

97. See particularly, Sanders, *Feudal Military Service*, 50–90; Michael R. Powicke, *Military Obligation in Medieval England: A Study in Liberty and Duty*, 65–67. There is a

Unfortunately, the reasons for this are never made very clear in the records. Scholars have suggested a number of factors, including the rising cost of military equipment, the fact that English knights were increasingly called to fight in distant places, and subinfeudation.[98] However, another factor may be that as personal ties declined, lords had problems raising satisfactory contingents from their honors. If vassals were no longer active as retainers, and if they were selling or giving away the houses they held near their lords' strongholds, when and how did they gather in order to train as a unit? If a vassal served in the retinue of a lord other than his honorial lord, with which lord would he fight? What if he held fees of more than one lord? Would a lord want to undergo the dangers of war backed up by a group of supporters with lukewarm feelings of loyalty or, worse yet, feelings of discontent over some dispute? Because the surviving records are extremely reticent about the causes of the decline of the feudal host, explanations for this decline must remain largely hypothetical; nevertheless, the probability is strong that it was related to the decline of personal ties on the honor.

Whatever the truth of this last hypothesis, the decline of ties and the frequent occurrence of animosity was certainly affecting the honor, frequently in corrosive ways. However, too much was invested in the honor and the honor was too important for it to disappear altogether. Even in the Norman period, when strong personal bonds were presumably still prevalent, temporary circumstances, such as sickness or inheritance by a minor, forced the creation of certain practices designed to offset the resulting loss of personal service. Since these by their nature did not depend on ties of personal loyalty, they survived and could provide the basis for restructuring the relations between lords and vassals once those personal ties were gone.

Thus wardship, marriage, reliefs, suit of court, scutage, and castle guard dues continued to be part of the scene long after personal lordship had declined within the honorial framework. While a lord might not relish having a tenant whose loyalty and enthusiasm were lukewarm follow him to battle or guard his castle, he would certainly be happy to receive payment

---

possibility that English kings never expected more than a fraction of the feudal host to fight in foreign wars, but this cannot be proved; Sanders, *Feudal Military Service*, 32–44; Michael R. Powicke, "Distraint of Knighthood and Military Obligation under Henry III," 458–59.

98. Painter, *English Feudal Barony*, 40–42; Harvey, "The Knight and Knight's Fee," 31, 40–41. R. Allen Brown has disputed the first two of these, pointing out that military equipment did not change drastically in the Angevin period, and thus would not have increased in price at a much greater rate than other goods, and that overseas service did not deter knights in the Norman period. Brown, "Status of the Norman Knight," 31.

for scutage or castle guard. Feudal incidents could be exercised whether or not the lord had a close relationship with a vassal family. Honorial courts could still function, with attendance required by suit of court, even if much of their work had passed to the royal courts. A demand for loyal and enthusiastic support could not be enforced against the will of a vassal, but payments and certain limited obligations could. Thus lordship and therefore the honor became transformed. Tenurial lordship was no longer a matter of service, patronage, and cooperation, but of escheats, reliefs, and narrowly defined services.[99] A charter from late in John's reign or early in Henry III's demonstrates this, for it shows that tenure could already be seen largely in terms of feudal incidents. In this charter, Ralph de Scotton granted to Fountains Abbey the homages, services, reliefs, escheats, and lordship of the whole vill of Wigglesworth, the gift comprising four carucates held by three tenants.[100] In this case there was no longer even the pretense of a personal bond.

I do not wish to advance a single, oversimplified explanation for the transformation of the honor; in the next section I will return to the role of the Angevin legal reforms. Excessive subinfeudation, as is well known, also forced change in the honorial system by causing many practical problems in the functioning of the honor. Tenants who gave away too much of their land might not be able to afford the arms and equipment necessary to fulfill their military service. The multiplication of mesne lords between the tenant-in-chief and the lesser tenants holding much of the land also created practical difficulties.[101] However, if the decline of the personal element of honorial lordship was not the only cause of the transformation of the honor, it was certainly a fundamentally important one; indeed, perhaps the single most important factor.

A chronology of this transformation of the honor and of the decline of personal lordship within the honorial system, unfortunately, is very difficult to obtain because the strength of personal ties are intangible and thus difficult to measure, because the process was gradual, and because the

99. See Edward Miller, "The State and Landed Interests in Thirteenth Century France and England," 111, for a similar point.
100. *EYC* 11:179. Clay dated this charter as c. 1215–1230. Ralph was only a mesne tenant, but the principles still apply.
101. For instance, the multiplication of mesne tenants weakened honorial justice by creating lords who could not possibly hold effective courts and by making multiple layers of lordship which increased the chance of dues and services going astray and caused distraint to be a trickier process than it would be if the holder of the land was also the direct tenant of the tenant-in-chief. See *CRR* 4:220 for a case in which mesne lordship caused problems in the collection of dues and in distraint for those dues.

chronology varied from honor to honor and indeed from family to family of vassals within honors. However, it is possible to describe the approximate situation at the beginning and end of the Angevin period.

Clearly the transformation began, in certain respects, even before the Angevin period. The fluidity of the Mowbray retinue is apparent even in the 1140s and 1150s. The absence of many families from witness lists already found in the middle of the twelfth century for the Mowbrays, Percys, and the lords of Richmond indicates that the attenuation of personal ties was already under way. The multiple tenancies that already existed in 1166 suggest that vassals too had already begun to break out of the honorial straitjacket and this too probably began before Henry II's accession. The early history of honors remains obscure because of the lack of evidence, but because of the inherent instability of the honorial system, its gradual transformation must have begun very early. In a way, the decay and transformation of the English honor began not in 1166, with the earliest Angevin legal reforms, but in 1066.

However, the honor was an important focus of personal lordship and patronage in the early Angevin period and was still an extremely important social and political institution, even if it was already suffering damage. To what degree was this still true at the end of the Angevin period? How far had it been transformed into nothing more than a collection of rights and obligations by 1216?

There are a few indications that strong personal ties still occasionally mattered within the honorial framework and that honors therefore had some viability as political and social institutions early in the thirteenth century. As late as 1207, a gentry heir named Hugh de Bolton had to turn his land over to Richard Malebisse because he absolutely refused to accept Malebisse as his lord, though Hugh's heirs were assured the reversion of his land. Hugh's reasons for his refusal are not stated, but he apparently felt that the identity or character of his lord were important. Moreover, at least a few vassals served in the retinues of most lords late in the Angevin period; indeed, instances of vassals serving their honorial lords can be found long after the Angevin period. Most important, Holt argues that honorial ties affected political loyalties in the Magna Carta revolt, an indication that the honor still had political meaning.[102]

However, all these indications of strong personal lordship within honors and of the continuing political importance of honors need to be

102. See Holt, *The Northerners*, 35–53, for this.

strongly qualified. The Bolton/Malebisse case was unique among Yorkshire cases in the surviving royal records and moreover it illustrates the rupturing of personal ties as well as their strength. Equally important, the circumstances were unusual; Hugh de Bolton's predecessors had been tenants of the Percys and the lordship of his fee had only recently been transferred to Malebisse by his aunt Matilda de Percy. Moreover, Malebisse, the leader of the York pogrom, was extraordinarily unscrupulous and aggressive even by the standards of Yorkshire gentry in this period; Hugh de Bolton had unusual cause for concern.[103] The number of vassals in the retinues of their honorial lords was very limited after 1200 and it must not always be assumed that they served because they were tenants. Tenants may have entered the retinues of their own honorial lords simply because they were the most generous or most accessible patrons.[104]

Holt's argument for the political vitality of honorial ties is the strongest reason to suppose that honors may still have been important institutions at the end of the Angevin period. This argument comes from the correlation Holt found between the political loyalties of tenants-in-chief and the political loyalties of their vassals; rebel lords tended to have rebel vassals and royalist lords, royalist vassals. This correlation surely indicates that lords had influence on at least some vassals. I am not sure, however, that the evidence shows a strong enough correlation to argue that honorial ties had more than a moderate influence on loyalties in the rebellion. Unfortunately, as Holt himself makes clear, the evidence for the loyalties of vassals is problematic and difficult to find; in most cases insufficient evidence survives to trace the loyalties of more than a handful of vassals on any given honor. However, the shortcomings of the evidence might best be illustrated by examining Holt's strongest case for honorial loyalty to a rebel, namely that of the honor of Mowbray.

William de Mowbray was one of the leading rebels and Holt shows that thirty of his vassals can be shown definitively (and one probably) to have been rebels, while only two were definitely loyalists. At first glance, this seems very strong evidence. However, Holt draws this out of a figure of seventy-eight tenants from a survey of the Mowbray fees made in the 1220s.[105] Thus fewer than forty percent of William's vassals can be shown to

103. *CRR* 5:77–79; *Rot. Obl. & Fin.*, 379; *EYC* 11:62, 77–78.
104. See Crouch, *William Marshal*, 138–39, for a vassal who sought out the patronage of his honorial lord.
105. Because this survey includes tenants holding tenancies as small as three bovates, there are more tenants in this list than are factored into Tables 1 through 3. For the survey, see *Book of Fees* 2:1460–62.

have been rebels. Perhaps others were rebels whose participation simply was not recorded in the surviving records, but it must be stressed that because of the formal procedure for receiving rebels back into the king's peace after the rebellion, the names of rebels were far more likely to be recorded than those of royalists, while the names of those who were neutral would not appear at all. On balance, then, those who were not recorded as rebels were likely not to have been rebels, while the royalist sympathies of many may simply be absent from the record. Moreover, there is no reason to assume that all the rebels of the Mowbray honor rebelled because of the honorial links or as supporters of William; as I will show in chapter seven, the gentry had plenty of reasons of their own to rebel.[106] Many Mowbray vassals lived in rebel areas and may have been influenced more by neighborhood ties than honorial ones.

In contrast to the evidence for tenurial influence, there is also evidence for independence by vassals. Holt, who by no means sees tenurial ties as the only determinants of knightly or gentry loyalties, displays much of this evidence. Many vassals did oppose their lords, particularly on some honors; for instance, on the honor of Richmond, the majority did so.[107] Moreover, the admittedly limited evidence for the actions of specific members of the gentry during the military campaigns of the rebellion indicates that they were acting independently. The records show knights fighting, negotiating, and surrendering without any reference to their honorial lords.[108] To all appearances, the disjointed fighting went on in Yorkshire without being affected by feudal ties at all. More striking still, the Close Rolls, which name so many rebels, do not give any indication of tenants accompanying magnates to their surrender; tenants-in-chief and their vassals are scattered far apart in the lists of rebels returning to allegiance. Moreover, John's practice

106. Similarly, the relative lack of rebels on the honors of some royalist tenants-in-chief does not necessarily mean that most vassals were actively supporting their lords; many may have been neutral.

107. However, they were less unified in their opposition than Holt argues. Holt suggests that the tenants of Richmondshire worked as a unit under the Constable of Richmond castle. In fact, however, only some of the tenants were captured in Richmond. Two of the most important tenants, Ranulf son of Robert and Brian son of Alan were not recorded in the castle, but seem to have been operating with Adam de Staveley, a prominent knight who had no connections with Richmond at all, for the three received letters of safe conduct from the king jointly. Holt, *The Northerners*, 46; *Rot. Litt. Pat.*, 165.

108. For fighting, see *Yorkshire Eyre*, 370, 373, 386, 418. For letters issued to knights who wished to negotiate, see *Rot. Litt. Pat.*, 163–65. For the results of such negotiations, or rather surrenders, see *Rot. Obl. & Fin.*, 569, 573–74, 588. It should be noted that Holt does not find such surrenders to be particularly strong indication of knightly independence; *The Northerners*, 51–53. For independent action by the Kyme family in Lincolnshire, see Wales, "The Knight," 30–31, 109–10.

of promising the lands of rebel vassals to their lords as a means of enticing rebel lords back to his side indicates that these rebel vassals were not acting in conjunction with their lords. Though Holt's evidence certainly cannot be ignored, I would argue that the evidence from the Magna Carta revolt is insufficient to warrant seeing the honor as a particularly important political institution late in the Angevin period.

In sum, the honor still retained some of its old character even in 1216. Nevertheless, the cumulative evidence for the declining participation of vassals in retinues, disputes between lords and tenants, the giving and selling of lordship, and the difficulties faced by honorial courts and the feudal host indicates that in 1216 the honor was in an advanced state of senescence as an institution governing the loyalty and actions of both lords and vassals. The large number of feodaries of later periods record the continuing survival of the honor, but only as a collection of impersonal rights and obligations.

IV

The transformation of the honor, as Crouch has said, involved ossification, and in many ways feudal incidents and dues represent the fossils of the honorial system.[109] They were important fossils, not least because they continued to provide money and sources of patronage to tenants-in-chief, and the ossified honor would have a long history of its own as lords sought to maintain these rights. The importance of these fossils, however, should not hide the fact that the honorial system as a whole lost many of its important functions in the late twelfth and early thirteenth centuries as links of personal lordship ceased being formed within the honorial framework.

The importance of feudal incidents and dues should also not be allowed to disguise the cumulative loss of land and power faced by lords as a result of subinfeudation and the subsequent decline of personal ties and active service. Such feudal incidents as wardship and marriage had originally been only peripheral aspects of lordship. They had been created to ensure that a lord was not deprived of the service that an adult male heir could have provided, and it was only because lords could no longer expect active service from adult male tenants that these peripheral and incidental

---

109. Crouch, Carpenter, and Coss, "Debate: Bastard Feudalism Revised," 167.

aspects of the honorial system assumed central importance. It was only because tenants could no longer be expected to serve in the retinues of their honorial lords that the strictly financial renders such as scutage and relief assumed center stage. However, the rare or even frequent windfalls brought by feudal incidents were no substitute for steadfast loyalty and active service by wealthy and powerful tenants.[110] This is why magnates continually made new investments of land to attract or retain active service.

Equally, the value of feudal dues and incidents was no substitute for the income that lords would have received had lands remained in demesne. To the extent that grants to vassals were investments for future service, they were investments which quickly lost most of their value, often within a generation of the grant. The chief losers in all this were the great tenants-in-chief, who had the most invested in lordship. As Barbara Harvey points out in the case of Westminster Abbey, the monks would never have wanted for money if so much land had not passed into the hands of feudal tenants and hereditary farmers.[111] The earlier discussion of the extent of subinfeudation provides some idea of the cumulative loss to tenants-in-chief in the generations after the Norman Conquest. This, of course, raises the question of why the powerful tenants-in-chief allowed this to happen. Why did they permit a system that drained their resources from generation to generation? The traditional answer is that after the Angevin legal reforms the royal courts forced them to do so, but this assumption needs to be questioned.

In this context the question of security of tenure and inheritance before Henry II's legal reforms is very important. The great flaw of the honorial system was that it combined the fluidity of personal lordship with the relative permanence of landholding. If, however, lords had great latitude in matters of inheritance, this problem would not be severe, for lords could periodically transfer fees from lukewarm supporters to their most loyal and active followers. Indeed, under those circumstances, vassals would be unlikely to provide lukewarm support or seek new patronage for fear that their families would lose their inheritance.

Thorne and Milsom have argued that inheritance, at least as a legal right, did not exist until late in the twelfth century, after the Angevin legal reforms had time to take effect. Milsom likewise argues that in the earlier period security of tenure depended on a lord's acceptance of a tenant, and

110. Milsom makes this point well in *Legal Framework*, 112, 154–55. In contrast, Bean argues that feudal incidents were of central importance from the beginning; *Decline of English Feudalism*, 5–6.

111. Harvey, *Westminster Abbey*, 70. See also Raftis, *Ramsey Abbey*, 60.

outside that acceptance the tenant had no right or recourse. These arguments are not in fact as radical as they first appear. Both Thorne and Milsom allow for inheritance as a customary or normal practice (Thorne, from the second quarter of the twelfth century) and in Milsom's view the relationship between a lord and his tenant would normally give the latter security as long as he fulfilled his obligations. However, both give lords the final say.[112] If this is right, then the fatal flaw of combining static landholding with fluid patronage within the honor did not become fixed until after the Angevin legal reforms.

There is at least some evidence from Yorkshire charters to support the idea that lords had great latitude in the control of their fees. The lords of Richmond occasionally deprived heirs of their tenants of subtenancies by making the subtenants direct vassals, thus at least diminishing their tenants' fees.[113] In a famous charter, Nigel d'Aubigny, fearing he was about to die, repented of disinheriting or disseising a number of men, restored land to some, and asked his brother to make reparations to others.[114]

It is notable, however, that Nigel saw his actions as wrong. Holt and others have argued that notions of heritability already existed among the Normans at the time of the Conquest and that inheritance became increasingly entrenched in the early Norman period.[115] Despite the examples mentioned above, it was certainly very common, and probably the norm, for fees to pass to heirs in Norman Yorkshire as elsewhere. Paul Hyams has suggested a way of partially reconciling the two views by shifting from Thorne and Milsom's focus on the rights and powers of lords to a focus on lords' obligations and the rights of tenants. Lords had strong obligations to tenants, which extended to their heirs and thus created customary rights of security and inheritance and limited the latitude of lords more than Thorne and Milsom would perhaps allow.[116] Most recently, John Hudson has argued for the strength of inheritance before the Angevin legal reforms. He also argues that kings may have been deeply involved before the reforms in supporting inheritance.[117] The evidence described earlier in this chapter for the lack of service provided by many vassals even before 1166 and for the

112. Milsom, *Legal Framework*, 154–86; Thorne, "English Feudalism," 193–209.

113. *EYC* 4:28; *EYC* 5:5, 17, 77.

114. Greenway, *Mowbray Charters*, 7–9.

115. J. C. Holt; "Politics and Property in Early Medieval England," 3–52; "Feudal Society and the Family in Early Medieval England: II. Notions of Patrimony," 193–220. See also Wales, "The Knight," 17, 16 n. 45.

116. Paul Hyams, "Warranty and Good Lordship in Twelfth-Century England," 437–503, especially 473–74.

117. John Hudson, "Life-Grants of Land and the Development of Inheritance in Anglo-Norman England," 67–80.

continuing need of lords to expend new resources indirectly supports the finding that inheritance was strongly in place before the Angevin legal reforms; if lords could have transferred lands from the heirs of lukewarm followers to their leading retainers, why did they continually give away demesne lands to recruit active retainers? What Thorne and Milsom have described is more a legal than a social revolution, since for the most part inheritance proceeded as before, and even in the legal sphere the change may have been less radical than they suggest. The Angevin legal reforms may have provided heirs with a new recourse against arbitrary lords, but earlier customary rights had limited lords from willy-nilly replacing heirs. Tenants who stopped providing active service or adopted new loyalties seem by and large to have been safe even before the Angevin legal reforms.

However, this raises a new set of questions. Inheritance was always conditional; even after the ossification of honors tenants were expected to pay feudal dues. Why did lords settle for so little? More specifically, why did lords permit heirs to avoid active service and remain outside the retinue? Why did lords have to buy loyal service from the same family repeatedly? Why were lords eventually forced to be content with only the feudal incidents, rather than the loyal service owed their ancestors? Again, one important answer is the royal judicial system, which protected tenure against all but the most blatant violations of a vassal's obligations. Once again, however, the legal reforms are not the only answer and indeed they cannot account for the drift of tenantry away from the retinues of their lords even before the Angevin legal reforms. Moreover, they only take the question a step back to why lords did nothing to counteract the effects of the legal reforms.[118] Hyams's views about customary rights only sharpen the issue, for he views these rights as being based on ideals of good lordship. Surely good lordship deserved good service in return. After all, vassals and their heirs held and inherited obligations as well as lands. Why did lords have to put up with so little loyalty and service from their tenants?

Several factors limited the ability of lords to dispossess less than active followers or to demand more service from vassals. The first was the fact that enfeoffment often had multiple purposes and that one of these was to reward followers for past services. The emphasis on reward must have been particularly heavy in the years immediately following the Conquest, when

118. Both Maitland's and Milsom's theories provide explanations for an initial lack of response, in Maitland's theory because lords were tricked by the king, in Milsom's, because the effects were accidental, but neither explain the lack of much obvious reaction when the consequences of the reforms became clear.

the greatest amount of subinfeudation occurred. Just as William the Conqueror had to reward his followers, so they had to reward theirs. Later retainers also saw grants of land as the proper form of reciprocation for their service. Grants of land were not simply another way of paying a salary for future service; to a degree, recipients had already earned their lands by past service, and this gave them and their descendants a certain claim to the land that was independent of their continuing relationship with lords.

An analogy may be drawn with a famous story from Edward I's reign in which the Earl Warenne defied the king, whose *quo warranto* proceedings were seriously challenging baronial privileges, by waving a rusty sword and tracing his privileges back to the role of his predecessors in conquering England.[119] So theoretically could an honorial tenant react when questioned about his or her rights. No such incidents are recorded from Angevin Yorkshire, but there is some indication that when some gentry families thought about the source of their tenure they looked back not to a grant by a lord to an ancestor, but to the participation of an ancestor in the Norman Conquest. On two occasions, at least, knights referred to tenure from the time of the Conquest.[120] Tenants may have felt that the service of their ancestors entitled them to keep lands without performing more active service than the minimum required by the terms of tenure by knight's service. Such a view would have shaped social expectations, including those of lords. This would have been especially important when the decline of a personal bond came from the lord's side—a lord who excluded the son of a loyal follower from his retinue for reasons of personality or incompetence rather than active disloyalty might have felt very hesitant about disinheriting the son on such grounds, given the past service of the son's family.

Another factor restraining lords was that they had the same relationship to the king that their followers had to them. As Paul Hyams points out, there could be no lords' lobby when all lords were someone else's men.[121] Lords could not deprive their tenants of rights without in the long run undermining their own rights. If the English kings had been weak, as were the earlier French kings or the later German emperors, powerful lords could have ignored the implications of their own vassalage to the king. Except for King Stephen's reign, however, the crown remained strong throughout the Norman and Angevin periods. It was thus in the lords' own

119. H. Rothwell, ed., *The Chronicle of Walter of Guisborough*, 216. For a recent discussion of this story, see Michael Clanchy, *From Memory to Written Record*, 21–28.

120. *EYC* 12:79; *CRR* 7:258.

121. Hyams, "Warranty and Good Lordship," 481.

interests to maintain the rights of tenants. Their families might lose some power, but would not risk complete disinheritance at the hands of a king freed of social expectations about inheritance and tenurial stability.

Yet another factor restricting the ability of lords to maintain complete dominance over their tenants was the collective power of tenants and their importance within the honorial structure.[122] The men who made judgments in honorial courts and upon whom the lord relied for much of his power, and particularly his coercive power, were either themselves tenants or hoped to be. Naturally, they would have had the interests of tenants in mind. Moreover, tenants were seen and saw themselves as a body with a set of well defined, if customary, rights against the lord. Thus, when William de Arches gave land to Elias de Hou, he defined both Elias's obligations and his rights by reference to those of another tenant, Robert son of Fulk. Similarly, when Alan son of Torfin made an exchange with his lord, Archbishop Roger, it was stipulated that his new land was to be held for one twentieth of a knight's fee "as Simon Ward and his other knights of Riponshire hold in knights' fees."[123] In others words, lords were expected to treat the tenants on their honors in a fair and uniform way and indeed some charters used the term peer to describe honorial tenants, reflecting language that would later be used in Magna Carta to define group rights.[124] Moreover, the tenants of an honor could act as a unit in opposing the demands of their lords. Outside of Yorkshire, Jocelin of Brakelond, for instance, recorded the struggle between abbot Sampson of Bury St. Edmunds and the tenants of his East Anglian monastery over their obligations for scutage.[125] Abbot Sampson won that dispute, but tenants, many of them well-armed warriors, were dangerous men to push too far, as illustrated by what happened to William Maltravers, a favorite of Henry I, who was granted the honor of Pontefract for a time. Shortly after Henry I's death, a knight named Pain, described as William's man, murdered William.[126]

122. Hudson points in this direction in his article, "Life-Grants of Land," 79–80. See also Paul R. Hyams and Paul A. Brand, "Debate: Seigneurial Control of Women's Marriage," 125, for the problems that might occur because of the power or connections of individual tenants.

123. *EYC* 1:113–14, 413; Riponshire was presumably the area attached to the Archbishop's holding of Ripon.

124. *EYC* 8:158; Greenway, *Mowbray Charters*, 114.

125. Jocelin of Brakelond, *The Chronicle of Jocelin of Brakelond*, 27–28, 65–67.

126. The reasons for Pain's actions are unknown. Perhaps Pain had a grudge, or perhaps he was simply a tenant who killed William out of loyalty to the exiled Lacys. The Campeauxs, an important tenant family, were also involved, as apparently were other tenants. Richard of Hexham, *The Chronicle of Richard, Prior of Hexham*, 140; *EYC* 3:143, 154, 183.

Because of social expectations about tenurial security, the reliance of lords on tenants and would-be tenants, and the potential for a violent backlash, lords tended to be extremely careful in their dealings with their vassals. When lords took land away from tenants, they took care to make an exchange that was fair or more than fair. William, Count of Aumale, about the middle of the twelfth century, took the manor of Meaux away from John de Meaux, first to make a park and then to found the abbey of Meaux. In compensation, he gave John the manor of Bewick, which was assessed at twice the number of carucates, to be held for the same service.[127] Other similar examples of equal or favorable exchanges exist.[128]

When lords were involved in disputes with their tenants, moreover, they often treated them with kid gloves. In one instance, Roger de Mowbray brought a case in his own court on behalf of the monks of Rievaulx against Alan de Ridale, a tenant on Roger's honor who plowed up the monks' way into a moor that Roger claimed was common to three villages and Alan claimed belonged to his own demesne. Roger made sure that not only were his own followers present, but that knights from the area and representatives of the king were also there, presumably to prevent any accusations of unfairness. The dispute was put to a trial of battle, and Roger's champion began to best Alan, whereupon Alan's friends persuaded him to compromise. Alan quitclaimed whatever Roger had given to the monks. Roger then allowed the dispute over whether or not the moor should be common to go to the arbitration of twelve neighboring knights, who decided that it should, but that any works of Alan's (perhaps assarts or sheepfolds) should remain. Nevertheless, the dispute continued, and was eventually settled by Roger lowering a rent owed by Alan from ten shillings to one pound of pepper in return for Alan's quitclaim of rights to Rievaulx. Roger, acting on behalf of an abbey, won in a properly constituted trial by battle, got a favorable settlement in arbitration by neighbors and still ended up making a compromise at his own expense.[129]

Other cases also show the anxiousness of lords to treat their tenants fairly. When the Mowbray follower Nicholas de Bellun put himself in Nigel de Mowbray's mercy in a dispute over a wood, Nigel conceded half the proceeds (exitibus) from the wood.[130] In a case similar to the one between

127. *EYC* 3:89–90; *Meaux Chronicle*, 77.

128. For example, *Meaux Chronicle*, 83; *EYC* 1:42–43; *EYC* 2:119, 361, 397; *EYC* 3:91.

129. *EYC* 9:238–42. It might be noted that much of the information comes from Roger's point of view. Alan might have had a different story.

130. Greenway, *Mowbray Charters*, 221–22.

Roger de Mowbray and Alan de Ridale, Gilbert de Gant stated that Ralph son of Richard claimed a wood from Rufford unjustly, because the wood had been part of Gilbert's demesne and he had given it to the monks. Gilbert prohibited Ralph from interfering with the gift, but he also prohibited the monks from bringing a case against Ralph, and he further stated that if Ralph or any other had a complaint about the situation, that person should come before him, whereupon he would do him right.[131] Undoubtedly, a lord could deprive a follower or disinherit his heirs for a gross act of treachery or an egregious failure of service. Undoubtedly if a lord disliked a tenant enough he could run roughshod over his rights. But lords could not do this easily, or as a matter of course. To do so would have been to incur great opprobrium and to risk losing one of the most important elements of baronial power, the loyalty of one's followers.

Because individual lords had so much more power than individual vassals, it is easy to forget the collective power of vassals and the extent to which lords depended on their tenants, or at least some of their tenants, when the honor was still strong. Moreover, it is all too easy to see honorial lords as absolute owners and tenants as therefore very insecure. In fact, the power and importance of tenants, along with the various ideas and ideals discussed earlier, strengthened the tenurial position of vassals vis-à-vis their lords. This is why vassals could reduce or transfer their service without losing their lands even before 1166. Thus the unstable combination of personal lordship and permanent landholding was weakening the honor long before the Angevin legal reforms.

The Angevin legal reforms did of course make a difference by adding another strong layer of protection to tenure and inheritance. Although the laws did not create security and inheritance out of nothing, they certainly provided an additional source of protection for tenants as they gradually transformed customary rights into legal ones. In Henry I's reign, Nigel d'Aubigny had been constrained by his conscience to make restitution to the tenants he had disinherited and disseised.[132] His descendants were constrained by law. By reinforcing the security of tenants, the royal courts

---

131. J. C. Atkinson, *Cartularium abbathiae de Rievalle*, 252. Though the charter is in the cartulary of Rievaulx Abbey, apparently the dispute refers to Rufford; Mary Abbott, "The Gant Family in England, 1066–1191," 329–30. For two other cases showing the conciliatory attitudes of lords towards the tenants with whom they were in dispute, see *EYC* 1:42–43; E. K. Clark, ed., "Fundacio Abbathie de Kyrkestall," 178.

132. Greenway, *Mowbray Charters*, 7–9.

ensured that the strain between the permanence of landholding and the impermanence of human ties would only become stronger. By helping to turn tenure into property, they ensured that lords would continue to get a diminishing amount of active service and loyal support.

The legal reforms helped weaken and transform the honor in other ways. Although Milsom's theory that the reforms caused a shift in the way in which landholding was conceived will need to be modified in light of the work by Hyams and Hudson, it would be unwise to discard the theory altogether. Moreover, as Maitland long ago pointed out, the legal reforms undermined the importance of honorial courts.[133] In doing so it weakened the power of lords, for the administration of justice was always an important source of power and prestige. Thus, the Angevin legal reform hastened the transformation that was already occurring because of the internal contradictions of the honorial system.

This conclusion may place Henry II and his legal reforms in a new light. Henry did not craftily undermine the honorial system in order to weaken his barons; indeed, the decline of the honor probably affected him as well by weakening the feudal host. Nor did he inadvertently destroy a going concern through the unexpected results of legal reform. Instead, Henry tried to deal with a mess created not only by the specific circumstance of the anarchy, but by the long term instability of the honor.

It is clear that feudal or honorial concepts played an extremely significant role in the development of law under the Angevins. This is hardly surprising, for the massive amount of subinfeudation after the Conquest created a situation in which fiefs became the standard manner of landholding for the elites and enfeoffment the standard manner of transfer. As seen earlier, even sales and transfers made under duress could be made under the guise of enfeoffments, and this testifies to the close identification between the honorial system and landholding for the upper classes. Yet the decline of personal lordship within the honor made it less easy for disputes to be kept within the confines of that honor. Henry's reforms and his new mechanisms could provide a certain amount of oversight to honorial justice and keep the system functioning, even if they undermined the system at the same time.

Moreover, the traditional view that the reforms served only the inter-

133. Milsom, *Legal Framework*, 36–39. Pollock and Maitland, *History of English Law* 2:202–3.

ests of vassals and harmed those of lords needs to be modified. Royal justice, for all the benefits it brought gentry, in some ways allowed lords to attack their tenants more freely; in royal courts, lords no longer had to rely on tenants and would-be tenants to deliver judgment and enforce it. With the decline of the personal element of honorial lordship, lords were less constrained by personal ties from challenging the rights of vassals and at least some lords made free use of the royal courts to profit at the expense of their tenants. Moreover, the royal courts did help preserve the fossilized skeleton of the honorial system, and did work against the most egregious flouting of feudal law, as in the case of Hugh de Bolton. Even weak lords could turn to the royal government and courts in order to seek the enforcement of feudal incidents and dues.[134] Finally, the honor was already being transformed because of its own internal contradictions; because the oversight of the royal courts could standardize the impersonal rights and obligations of lords and vassals, it could thus smooth the transition. A smooth transition was in the interests of all members of the elite. Lords gained as well as lost from the intervention of the royal court and this helps explain why the great magnates accepted the Angevin legal reforms so readily.

Ultimately, it was the internal contradictions of the honorial system combined with the collective power of vassals that forced the transformation of the honor. The royal courts, however, accelerated that transformation and more importantly, they helped shape it by providing oversight and standardization. Together, these factors slowly destroyed the honor as an important political and social institution and by 1216 this process was nearly complete. Thereafter, magnates and gentry would have to create new vehicles for personal lordship and this led, eventually, to what has traditionally been described as bastard feudalism.

V

The transformation of the honor had very important implications for the gentry. The vast majority of the gentry in the Angevin period were honorial vassals and the changes described in this chapter left them in a very strong position. The great generosity of tenants-in-chief left them with vast amounts of land. Some vassal families received a sufficiently large landed

134. For instance, *Rot. Litt. Claus.*, 11; *Yorkshire Deeds* 7:51.

base to eventually work their way into the parliamentary nobility when that emerged in the late thirteenth and early fourteenth centuries, though often they did so with the help of profitable marriages or subsequent acquisitions.[135] Most remained within the gentry, and the massive subinfeudation after the Norman Conquest created the financial basis of the medieval gentry. Although much of this land subsequently passed to monasteries and cadet lines, or in later periods to new and old noble families, the initial "endowment" of the gentry was so large that gentry landholders continued to hold a large percentage of land in England.

The long term implications of the transfer can be seen from studies of lands held by the gentry of later periods, most of whom were descended at least tenurially, if not always biologically, from the vassals of the Norman period. For instance, R. B. Smith calculated that the West Riding gentry in the reign of Henry VIII received about half the landed income of that area.[136] Tenants-in-chief may have had to grant out a larger percentage of lands in Yorkshire than elsewhere in order to attract or satisfy followers, for much of that county was relatively poor and had suffered severe depredations during the Conquest. Nevertheless, it is clear that everywhere tenants-in-chief granted out massive amounts of land, and the results on landholding patterns elsewhere was similar. Nigel Saul has estimated that the gentry held over half the manors in Gloucestershire in the fourteenth century and Michael Bennett, that they held over three quarters of the manors in Cheshire and Lancashire around the year 1400.[137] Of course, the flow of land to the gentry dried up in the Angevin period, and as later chapters will show, this had unfortunate consequences for some gentry families. Nevertheless, by that time the gentry as a group had already secured an extraordinarily strong financial basis as a result of subinfeudation.

Of equal importance to the amount of land received by the gentry was the fact that by 1216 they held it firmly and largely independently of their earlier honorial ties. Their descendants would continue to do so.[138] Vas-

135. These included the FitzHughs of Ravensworth, the Fauconbergs, Vavasours, Foliots, Everinghams, and Meinils. See Painter, *English Feudal Barony*, 48–56, for the shift from the feudal to the parliamentary baronage.

136. R. B. Smith, *Land and Politics in the England of Henry VIII: The West Riding of Yorkshire, 1530–1546*, 69–79.

137. Saul, *Knights and Esquires*, 5; Bennett, *Community, Class and Careerism*, 68–70.

138. The essential independence of the gentry in the later Middle Ages, despite the importance of noble retinues, can be seen in Wright, *The Derbyshire Gentry*, 60–82; Bennett, *Community, Class and Careerism*, 33; A. J. Pollard, "The Richmondshire Gentry," 527; Ian Rowney, "The Hastings Affinity in Staffordshire and the Honour of Tutbury," 44–45.

salage had brought their ancestors the land which was the source of their wealth and power, but also brought them duties, restrictions and close bonds to specific lords. Obviously vassals always had some leeway; this is one reason the honor declined. Nevertheless, as personal ties declined, tenure became ever more secure, and the honorial system decayed, the gentry gained ever more freedom of action. The decay of the honor did not bring unalloyed good to the gentry; those who did not gain protectors through the new avenues of patronage might be vulnerable to competition from powerful magnates for land and wealth. Nevertheless, by 1216, the gentry had great freedom to dispose of their lands, to pursue their own paths, to make their own connections outside the honor and eventually to begin creating their own political voice.

2. Violence, Lawlessness, and Law in Gentry Society

The Yorkshire gentry were in origin an aristocracy of service and much of that service was martial in character; the founders of most gentry families were warriors. Martial abilities continued to have importance for gentry families even as the old bonds of service decayed, for the gentry could use violence effectively in their own interest as well as for their lords and kings. Coercion and violence, whether legal or extralegal, are fundamental sources of power in any society. Heavily armed and supported by family and retainers, members of the gentry committed violent crimes ranging from brawling with enemies to leading the great pogrom against the Jewish community of York in 1190. Yet they also drew power from the important roles they had in the the the administration of justice. As justices, suitors, court officials, and jurors, they kept local courts functioning and often had a large say in the outcome of legal cases. This chapter will explore the role of gentry both as the breakers and as the upholders of law and the ways in which these roles came into conflict, often to the detriment of justice. It will do so, however, in the context of the rise of royal justice under the Angevin kings.

The course of the Angevin legal revolution is well known, and need not be discussed in detail here.[1] However, two facets that need to be stressed are the growth of standardized law and procedures and the growth of oversight from the central government. Van Caenegem has written of the local courts in the early twelfth century that "What was usually expected of a law court was not a clear-cut decision, of right or wrong, on an issue on which the parties had failed to agree, but much more something in the nature of an effort to bring about a settlement of the litigation by an acceptable, honorable compromise," and "The feeling seems to have been that a real court decision of right or wrong, excluding anything that looked

---

1. See the works cited in chapter one, notes 7 and 8. See also Doris M. Stenton, *English Justice Between the Norman Conquest and the Great Charter*, 22–114; R. C. van Caenegem, *The Birth of the English Common Law*.

like compromise, was a harsh and extreme measure."[2] These local English courts must have resembled those French ones described by Stephen White in which cases were settled not by strict and rigid laws, but by a fluid and varying set of customs and norms, the flexibility of custom being more conducive to reaching a compromise.[3] The use of more fluid customs and the emphasis on compromise had advantages, for ideally they could not only end disputes but bring the parties back into harmony. However, there was also a danger that powerful people could use their power to ensure that courts accepted those norms and customs that supported their position, or to win compromises that heavily and unjustly favored them.

The royal government had many aims in expanding royal justice, but one of the theoretical goals was to prevent powerful people from unjustly oppressing the weak. Drawing from and elaborating upon a passage from the prologue to Justinian's *Institutes*, the writer of the treatise attributed to Glanvill stated

> Not only must royal power be furnished with arms . . . but it is also fitting that it should be adorned with laws for the governance of subject and peaceful peoples; so that in time of both peace and war our glorious king may so successfully perform his office that, crushing the pride of the unbridled and ungovernable with the right hand of strength and tempering justice for the humble and meek with the rod of equity, he may both be victorious in wars with his enemies and also show himself continually impartial in dealing with his subjects.[4]

By providing strict procedures and oversight by royal justices, and by punishing wrongdoers impartially, the royal government could in theory hope to curb the injustice and violence of the powerful. The final section of this chapter will discuss the degree to which the Angevin reforms succeeded in achieving that goal. Legal systems generally function somewhat differently in theory than in practice and focusing on the identities and positions of people involved in crimes and legal cases will shed light on what happened when the theories of royal justice met the realities of local power structures.

2. R. C. van Caenegem, "Studies in the Early History of the Common Law," in *Royal Writs in England from the Conquest to Glanvill*, 42.

3. Stephen D. White, *Custom, Kinship, and Gifts to Saints: The Laudatio Parentum in Western Europe, 1050–1150*, 69–74; "*Pactum . . . Legem Vincit et Amor Judicium*. The Settlement of Disputes by Compromise in Eleventh-Century Western France," 281–308.

4. G. D. G. Hall, *The Treatise on the Laws and Customs of the Realm of England commonly called Glanvill*, 1; Hall's translation. For the passage on which this draws, see Peter Birks and Grant McLean, eds., *Justinian's Institutes*, 30.

The modern myth of the knight in shining armor is drawn partly from medieval literary sources, but in the Middle Ages there were much more sinister images that could also be used, images of the robber knight, of the marauding plunderer, of the oppressor of the poor and defenseless. Medieval chroniclers were often loud in their condemnations of the lawless rich. Modern historians have also recorded their depredations. Almost every study on the gentry or their equivalents such as the German ministerials during the Middle Ages reveals this violence and lawlessness.[5] Rodney Hilton, in his study of the Western Midlands at the end of the thirteenth century, wrote of the gentry that "disorder appears almost to be a by-occupation of the class."[6]

Here, as with many other aspects of gentry life, there was continuity. The gentry of Angevin Yorkshire, as their fellows in other times and periods, were capable of extreme brutality. In 1198, John Gramary testified that Ralph Mauleverer, a member of a prosperous gentry family, and five others broke into the house of John's lord, Ralph Follifoot, killing him and wounding John in the head.[7] A knight named William Mauleverer nearly lost three fingers when an enemy, Gilbert de Levinton, unexpectedly attacked him in the road with a sword and he threw his hand up to ward off the blow.[8] These are but two of the multitudinous examples of gentry violence that survive from the Angevin period in Yorkshire.[9]

Why were the gentry so violent? In discussing this question, it must be remembered that many members of the gentry were knights and formed part of a warrior elite. Yorkshire gentry fought on both sides in the 1173–74 revolt and one knight, Ralph de Tilly, played an important role as leader of the Archbishop of York's contingent in the force that captured King William of Scotland.[10] Incidental references in the copious royal records of

5. For instance, Bennett, *Community, Class and Careerism*, 184; Wright, *The Derbyshire Gentry*, 119–42; Saul, *Knights and Esquires*, 168–204; Payling, *Political Society*, 188–90; Benjamin Arnold, *German Knighthood, 1050–1300*, 22, 225–47. For a good study of violence, lawlessness and the law focusing on one individual, see Bernard McLane, "A Case Study of Violence and Litigation in the early Fourteenth Century: The Disputes of Robert Godsfield of Sutton-Le-Marsh," 22–44.

6. Rodney Hilton, *A Medieval Society: The West Midlands at the End of the Thirteenth Century*, 254.

7. *CRR* 7:340.

8. *Yorkshire Eyre*, 266–67.

9. For examples of gentry violence or alleged gentry violence not mentioned elsewhere in the chapter, see *CRR* 1:49; *CRR* 2:100; *CRR* 4:267; *CRR* 5:267; *Pleas* 4:96, 99, 102–4, 109, 110; *Yorkshire Eyre*, 95, 224–25, 263–64, 340–41, 365, 367, 385, 386; *Pipe Roll 5 Richard I*, 72.

10. See chapter one for the participation of Roger de Mowbray's men; see *Pipe Roll 21 Henry II*, 174; Roger of Howden, *Chronica* 2:60, for the participation of others. Two Yorkshire knights, Alan, Constable of Richmond, and Torfin son of Robert, also provided men for the

John's reign, whether to delay in legal cases granted for service overseas, to letters of protection accorded to those serving overseas, or to loans to gentry on campaign, show the widespread participation of Yorkshire gentry in royal campaigns.[11] One prominent knight, Robert Meinil, died in John's service in Poitou.[12] As later chapters will show, many Yorkshire gentry participated in the Crusades and the Magna Carta revolt. War was a fact of life for many gentry.

A good illustration of the role of warfare and martial skills even in everyday life comes from the records of the 1218–19 eyre. These include a note that William Aguillun killed Adam de Monceaux with a sword as they played (*ludebant*) in Robert de Percy of Bolton Percy's house.[13] All three were from knightly families and this may well have resulted from some sort of training. The use of such a term as play shown how casual the use of weapons was.

It seems likely that knights and other gentry, as members of a warrior class, would accept and even glorify the use of violence. Unfortunately, this assertion is difficult to prove, for in the absence of diaries, letters, and similar sources it is not always easy to discover what the attitudes of the gentry were. However, one important clue is provided by the surnames of some gentry families. Richard Malebisse, the leader of the York pogrom in 1190, had a surname that meant "evil beast." In Latin documents this was sometimes translated as Mala Bestia and in one Jewish document it was translated into Hebrew.[14] William of Newburgh, mentioning Richard's role as a leader of the attack on the Jews, described him as "Richard, appropriately surnamed Evil Beast" (vero agnomine Mala Bestia).[15] The modern person hearing or reading the surname "Smith" does not automatically envision a person standing over a forge, nor does a person with that surname routinely translate it into Schmidt in a German or Forgeron in a French context. "Smith" is simply a family name and its origins as an

garrisons of castles in the war or its aftermath; *Pipe Roll 21 Henry II*, 165. Alan later had custody of one of these, Edinburgh castle, for a time; *Pipe Roll 26 Henry II*, 141.

11. *CRR* 1:409; *CRR* 2:92; *CRR* 4:202; *CRR* 5:162; *Pleas* 1:411–12; *Pleas* 3:21; *Pleas* 4:300; *Rot. Obl. & Fin.*, 105; *Rot. Litt. Claus.*, 33b, 116b, 141b, 200–201; J. C. Holt, ed., "Praestita Roll 14–18 John," in *Pipe Roll 17 John*, 91, 92, 94, 97; Hardy, *Rotuli de Liberate*, 23, 180, 182–84, 187, 189, 198, 201, 203, 205, 207, 212, 214–15, 219, 221–23; *Pipe Roll 3 John*, 160–61; *Pipe Roll 13 John*, 31–32; *Pipe Roll 16 John*, 95; *Pipe Roll 3 Henry III*, 204.

12. Egerton MSS 2823:109; Dodsworth MSS 94:43.

13. *Yorkshire Eyre*, 297.

14. For two examples of the translation of the name into Latin, see *EYC* 3:441, 462. For translation into Hebrew, see Israel Abrahams, H. P. Stokes and Herbert Loewe, eds., *Starrs and Jewish Charters Preserved in the British Museum* 1:118–19.

15. William of Newburgh, *Historia Rerum Anglicanum*, in *Chronicles of the Reigns of Stephen, Henry II, and Richard I* 1:321.

occupational name are forgotten in day to day use. In the Angevin period, however, family surnames were relatively new and people thought about what they meant. William of Newburgh and the writer of the Hebrew document containing Richard's name were not punning, as has sometimes been suggested. The latter was simply translating and the former commenting on the appropriateness of the name.[16] The name Malebisse did not simply identify a family but also conjured up an image of a wild, evil beast. This was not unique. Another family of Yorkshire gentry, the Mauleverers, had a name that meant evil hound and one member of the family, at least, had a greyhound on his seal.[17] These names were examples of a group of Anglo-Norman surnames that, as Holt points out, described evil physical or moral characteristics.[18] That families should choose or at least accept names with such violent and asocial connotations is striking, and is suggestive of a mentality that not only accepted but even glorified violence. If such a mentality was widespread, which seems likely, it is not surprising that gentry violence was such a problem in Angevin Yorkshire.

Gentry violence, however, was common not simply because many glorified it, but also because coercion could be an important source of power. A study of the judicial records shows that many if not most acts of violence were carried out either to reinforce subordination of less powerful people or to pursue some tangible economic gain.

Violence against peasants and tenants could help keep them under continued domination. In the 1218–19 eyre, Nicholas son of Bernulf accused the gentry landowner, Thomas de Lascelles, of putting him in stocks, keeping him in prison for four days, sending servants to seize chattels worth the surprisingly large sum of eighty marks, expelling his wife and children from the family home, and killing his son. Thomas replied that Nicholas was his serf and reeve, had not rendered his account, and was much in arrears. Nicholas in turn said that he was not a serf and put himself on the judgment of the "poor free men" of the county. The jurors found that Thomas had not killed Nicholas's son and substantiated Thomas's claims; therefore Thomas's other actions had been legal and permissible.[19] Such

---

16. It is true, however, that people made jokes about the meanings of names. Gerald of Wales tells a story of a Jewish traveller who made an elaborate joke on the names of his Christian companions and of the places through which they were passing; Gerald of Wales, *Itinerarium Kambriae*, 146. This, however, only underscores the degree to which people were aware of the meanings, or possible meanings, of names.

17. *EYC* 7:147.

18. J. C. Holt, *What's in a Name? Family Nomenclature and the Norman Conquest*, 10.

19. *Yorkshire Eyre*, 371–72. For a discussion of this incident in relation to villeinage and the common law, see Hyams, *King, Lords, and Peasants*, 116, 136–37.

coercion and such verdicts helped landowners maintain their dominance over serfs. Cases of violence that were clearly directed towards subordinate peasants can rarely be found in the court rolls, but the jury reply may show why. Within certain bounds, violence was permissible against serfs, and therefore would not have been recorded. Only because there were doubts about the status of Nicholas, who was clearly well-to-do, and because he claimed his son had been killed, did the case appear in the royal courts. It is likely that minor acts of violence against serfs were relatively common.

In surviving records, one more frequently finds acts of violence involved in disputes over land. Of course, the use of force in defending one's right to land was permitted in certain very circumscribed circumstances.[20] However, what might appear to one party in a dispute as a licit use of force might appear to the other as illicit. Moreover, disputants often ignored the legal limitations on self-help. In any case, arguments over land often resulted in violence and bloodshed. For example, the skirmish in which William Mauleverer nearly lost three fingers resulted from a novel disseisin suit.[21] Sometimes a single individual could be involved in a string of violent disputes over land. Herbert de St. Quintin suffered a raid on his lands in one such dispute and saw some of his men imprisoned in another. In the latter dispute, he retaliated by raiding the land of his enemy, William de Rocheford, while William was in a royal prison for striking a third knight in the eye in what was apparently an unrelated incident.[22]

In disputes over land, the gentry did not restrict their violence to other gentry but sometimes even attacked unarmed monks or conversi. Incidents of both assault and murder are recorded.[23] In a slightly less serious but more colorful incident, a disagreement over his father's gifts to Meaux abbey sent one East Riding knight, Saer de Sutton, on a rampage against that monastery. Backed by an armed band, he took one hundred shillings, twenty-two quarters of grain, and other goods from Meaux's property, and destroyed two sheepfolds. He also helped the Nuns of Swine steal a corpse, presumably so that they would get the land or goods promised with the

---

20. Pollock and Maitland, *History of English Law* 2:50, 52–53, 574–78.

21. *Yorkshire Eyre*, 266.

22. Brown, *Pedes Finium Ebor.*, 76–77; RCR 1:38; RCR 2:298; CRR 1:162, 219, 457; CRR 2:26, 71, 194; CRR 3:37, 176, 234–35, 262, 313; *Pleas* 4:97.

23. *Yorkshire Deeds* 6:54; Clark, "Fundacio Abbathie de Kyrkestall," 184–85. In the latter case, in which three conversi of Kirkstall were murdered, the perpetrators were unnamed, but given the size of the property in dispute they were almost certainly gentry. For a less serious but more typical instance of harassment, see the problems faced by Rievaulx abbey in its early days; Atkinson, *Cartularium de Rievalle*, 194–95; EYC 9:218–19.

burial.[24] Religious scruples seem to have had only limited effect in protecting those devoted to religion, though the fact that the religious themselves were not always very scrupulous when it came to property disputes may be a factor.

Sometimes the pursuit of power and wealth through force took on more indirect forms. Late in the reign of Henry II, Gilbert de Plumpton, brother of the powerful knight Nigel de Plumpton, abducted the daughter and heiress of the recently deceased Roger de Gulewast and married her. Since Gilbert's bride had been in the wardship of Henry II's justiciar, Ranulf de Glanvill, who had intended her for one of his own followers, Gilbert's actions had disastrous consequences for the short term. In the long term, however, he successfully gained a rich bride and eventually was treated as a knight in the royal judicial system.[25]

At other times, gentry violence was nothing more than robbery. On one occasion the inhabitants of dozens of villages plundered a Norwegian ship and members of the gentry clearly participated.[26] On another occasion, William Malesoures accused William Fairfax of forcibly imprisoning him in order to extort a charter for land in York during the confusion of the Magna Carta revolt.[27] Members of the gentry, inured to violence, did not hesitate to make blatant use of it to protect or advance their holdings and thus their power and wealth.

These individual acts of violence, as calculating and extreme as they may seem, pale before the most infamous incident of gentry violence in the Angevin period, the York pogrom of 1190, an incident which has been carefully studied and admirably discussed by R. B. Dobson in his work *The Jews of Medieval York and the Massacre of March 1190*.[28] The attack at York was the last of a series of assaults on English Jewish communities that began when the attempt of several Jews to enter Westminster Palace during King Richard's coronation, on September 3rd, 1189, sparked a riot in London. In York, a series of attacks forced the Jews to take refuge in a royal castle where, fearing treachery, they subsequently shut out the royal constable. The constable went to the sheriff who then ordered a siege. A mob gathered around the castle and the sheriff lost control of events. Eventually, the Jews,

24. *Meaux Chronicle*, 356–58; BL, Lansdowne MSS 424:112.
25. Roger of Howden, *Chronica* 2:286; Benedict of Peterborough, *Gesta Regis* 1:314–16; *Pipe Roll 30 Henry II*, 29, 38; CRR 6:344.
26. Other gentry aided the unsuccessful attempt to conceal the crime. *Pipe Roll 26 Henry II*, 67–69.
27. *Yorkshire Eyre*, 419–23.
28. R. B. Dobson, *The Jews of Medieval York and the Massacre of March 1190*.

realizing the hopelessness of their position, decided upon mass suicide, which they carried out on the evening of Friday, March 16. Only a few Jews remained alive the next morning, and though they left the castle offering to convert they were nonetheless slaughtered by the mob at the instigation of its leaders. The leaders of the mob then went to York Minster, seized the Jewish bonds that recorded debts, and burned them in the cathedral.[29]

Mob activity was evident throughout the assaults on the York Jews. However, the mob was led by a group of indebted gentry and contemporaries recognized that these men had engineered the attacks in York. It is not clear how many gentry were involved. Both William of Newburgh and the *Meaux Chronicle* identified Richard Malebisse as a leader and the *Meaux Chronicle* also listed Philip de Fauconberg, William de Percy of Bolton Percy, and Marmaduke Darel, all prominent knights, as leaders.[30] Entries in the pipe rolls show that Alan Malecake and Richard de Tong, also members of the gentry, were involved as well.[31] It is likely that this is a very incomplete list.[32] More important than numbers, however, was the leadership provided by the gentry. Elsewhere in England, the rioting was disjointed and the majority of the Jews were able to take refuge in royal castles and escape bodily harm. In York, the existence of an organized conspiracy of gentry caused the persecution to be pursued to its brutal end.

The York pogrom must be seen in light of the violent religious particularism of the Crusades and the growing anti-Semitic hysteria affecting Latin Christendom, partly as a result of the blood libel accusations originating in England. Only in this context is the destruction of an entire community of people explicable, for lawless violence against Christians was never carried out on such a scale. The pogrom must also be seen, however, in the context of the willingness of many members of the gentry to use lawlessness and violence to protect or gain power and wealth. The chronicler, William of Newburgh, stated that many of the instigators of the attack were deeply

29. Dobson, *Jews of Medieval York*, 24–28.

30. William of Newburgh, *Historia Rerum Anglicanum* 1:321; *Meaux Chronicle*, 251.

31. *Pipe Roll 4 Richard I*, 221; *Pipe Roll 6 Richard I*, 161. Some other men mentioned in the pipe rolls may also have been from gentry families.

32. The chroniclers were concerned only with naming the leaders. The royal government sought all the perpetrators of the attack, but many of the attackers immediately left on the Third Crusade, making it hard to track them down. The difficulties faced by the royal government in the absence of King Richard also increased the likelihood that gentry attackers would escape detection. Philip de Fauconberg and Marmaduke Darel, for instance, were never amerced despite their involvement in the pogrom. Thus, many more than those named above may have participated.

indebted to the Jews,[33] and indeed a document recording a repayment of £4 by Richard Malebisse reveals that he owed a "great debt" to Aaron of Lincoln.[34] Moreover, the eagerness of the gentry leaders of the pogrom to burn the Jewish bonds in York cathedral after the massacre is indicative of their motives. Clearly many of the attackers hoped to get out from under heavy indebtedness to Jews first by destroying the Jewish community in York and then by destroying the records of their own debts. Members of the gentry were accustomed to solving their problems through violence and their actions in the York pogrom fit neatly into this pattern.

Though the leaders of the York pogrom failed to achieve their economic goals, coercion and violence could be effective, and the Yorkshire gentry used them as a means of securing or advancing their position in society.[35] This is not to say that all illegal violence resulted from calculated motives of power and wealth. William son of Gilbert de Ayton, member of a prominent family, killed his brother-in-law, Ignald de Furneaux, for mistreating his sister and here it was clearly family tensions that produced violence.[36] Hot anger may have been as great or greater a factor in gentry violence as cold calculation. In a society honoring violence, considerations of prestige and proper behavior may also have promoted thuggishness. Nevertheless, for the gentry, violence was chiefly a tool for maintaining power.

S. F. C. Milsom, discussing the origins of novel disseisin, has argued that a world in which "Malefactors hurry about attacking people, ejecting them from their lands, hoping to get away with obvious wrongs" is not one in which we can consciously believe.[37] In light of the accounts of gentry and non-gentry violence in the legal records of the reigns of Richard and

33. William of Newburgh, *Historia Rerum Anglicanum* 1:313. The *Meaux Chronicle* also discusses the indebtedness of the nobility, 244.

34. Abrahams, Stokes, and Loewe, *Starrs and Jewish Charters* 1:118–19. Aaron was dead by the time of the attack and his bonds had passed to the royal government, but Richard may have owed money to other Jews as well.

35. See Scott L. Waugh, "The Profits of Violence: The Minor Gentry in the Rebellion of 1321–1322 in Gloucestershire and Herefordshire," 843–69, for the use of violence by gentry in a later period in the specific circumstances of civil war.

36. BL, Cotton MSS Claudius D.XI, 142r. Unfortunately, I am unable to date this incident accurately, as I have been unable to identify Ignald and there were at least two members of the Ayton family who were named William and whose fathers were named Gilbert. One lived in the middle of the twelfth century, but the second survived beyond the Angevin period. If the incident took place outside of the Angevin period, however, it was not far outside.

37. Milsom, *Legal Framework*, 5.

John, after decades of strong royal government, this world does not seem so unbelievable after all.[38]

Despite their proclivities toward violent lawlessness, gentry played a key role in the administration of justice. The judicial role of the gentry in later periods, as justices of the peace or in other offices, is well known. Once again, continuity can be traced from at least the Angevin period, though the specific roles and offices changed. In the Angevin period the gentry had a large role in all the secular courts above the manorial level (and in their own manorial courts as well, of course, though little is known of these).[39] The decline of the honorial court and the rapid rise of royal justice did not substantially alter this, but altered the venue and to a degree the nature and context of gentry participation in the administration of justice.

The gentry, and particularly knights, were ubiquitous in what evidence remains for regional courts. A case from 1212 reveals the names of men hearing pleas in the York county court and almost all of these were members of prominent knightly families.[40] That this was not unique can be seen from two county court final concords, modeled on those of the royal courts, in which prominent members of the gentry appear in the portion of the document allotted to royal justices in fines of the royal court.[41] A charter issued by Peter de Brus governing the conduct of justice in the court of Langbargh wapentake was addressed to the knights and free tenants of Cleveland, which shows that prosperous local landholders were expected to have a role in wapentake courts as well.[42] Another document shows twelve knights perambulating certain boundaries on behalf of a wapentake court.[43] Members of the gentry often served as bailiffs for collections of wapentakes or ridings,[44] and occasionally served as undersheriff or even, on

38. This in turn would suggest that novel disseisin may well have had a possessory aspect.

39. For instances where the private courts of gentry are mentioned, see Egerton MSS 2823:67; *EYC* 5:143; *EYC* 2:150; *Pleas* 3:139. See also an agreement between Adam de Staveley and William de Mowbray in which Adam gave up a claim to have an ordeal pit and gallows in one of his manors; *Pleas* 3:136.

40. *CRR* 6:214–15. This is discussed in detail in Thomas, "Knights of the County Court," 137–50.

41. *EYC* 7:287–88; Bodleian Library, Fairfax MSS 9:34r.

42. W. Brown, *Cartularium Prioratus de Gyseburne* 1:92–94. This remarkable document, and its political implications, are discussed at greater length in Appendix four.

43. *Fountains Cartulary* 1:734.

44. Late in the reign of Henry II, Conan de Aske, a Richmondshire knight, had care of the various wapentakes that make up Richmondshire; Roger Gale, *Registrum Honoris de Richmond*, 21. Gentry riding bailiffs included Hugh de Leathley, Ralph de Normanville, Robert de Mohaut, William de Stapleton, and William de Marton; *Yorkshire Deeds* 6:23, 25; *EYC* 7:136, 234–35; *Fountains Cartulary* 2:671. It may have been as bailiff of the West Riding that William de Marton was amerced 40 marks for having a badly kept roll; *Pipe Rolls 5 John*, 219. If so this would be an interesting illustration of the use of writing in local administration.

one occasion, as sheriff, though the last two offices were generally held by royal favorites and their followers.[45] The gentry clearly had a large role in running regional courts.[46]

As one might expect, gentry tenants and especially gentry retainers played a role in honorial justice as well. The best evidence comes from the honorial court of Roger de Mowbray. In two documents, Roger's tenants state that they have quitclaimed land "before Roger de Mowbray and his knights in his court of Thirsk," showing that it was knights who came to mind when one thought of an honorial court.[47] A third document, in which the members of Roger's curia were distinguished as such in the witness list, shows that after Roger's two sons and his chaplain, the other members of the court were seven of Roger's chief retainers, all of whom were or became important gentry landholders.[48]

The gentry even played a large role in the arbitration and unofficial judgments that often settled disputes in Angevin Yorkshire as throughout medieval England.[49] Geoffrey Fossard, member of a gentry branch of that important family, helped settle one dispute; when the magnate Robert de Turnham, acting as guardian of Stephen Meinil, sought to settle a boundary dispute between the Meinils and Byland abbey, he sent for local gentry to perambulate the boundaries.[50]

45. Most of Ranulf de Glanvill's associates, for instance, were relatives or neighbors from East Anglia; Richard Mortimer, "The Family of Rannulf de Glanvill," 11. However, when Roger de Lacy became sheriff he appointed Robert Walensis, who was his own seneschal, as undersheriff and likewise the Yorkshire magnate William de Stuteville appointed two members of the local gentry, Walter de Bovington and William de Percy, to the same office; *EYC* 10:71; *Pipe Roll 7 John*, 40; *Pipe Roll 3 John*, 158, 293. Robert de Percy, who, like William, was a member of one of the gentry branches of that family, became sheriff late in John's reign; *Pipe Roll 16 John*, 84.

46. Robert Palmer sees the county courts as being dominated by professionals, even at this early date; *County Courts*, 129–38. However, see Thomas, "Knights of the County Court," 137–50, and Peter R. Coss, "Knighthood and the Early Thirteenth-Century County Court," 45–57.

47. *EYC* 9:246–47.

48. *EYC* 9:239. In a witness list to a quitclaim made in Roger's court, Roger himself heads the witness list, followed by his son, Nigel, two clerics, several knights from his retinue and some outsiders; *EYC* 9:242–43.

49. It is difficult to tell how prevalent arbitration was in this period, but it seems to have been fairly common. It was extremely common in the later Middle Ages. In his article, "Arbitration in Gentry Disputes of the Later Middle Ages," Ian Rowney discusses the advantages of this means of dispute settlement; 367–76. See also, Wright, *The Derbyshire Gentry*, 122–27; Bennett, *Community, Class and Careerism*, 30–33; and Pollard, "The Richmondshire Gentry," 50.

50. *Yorkshire Deeds* 2:12–13; *EYC* 2:143–44; Egerton MSS 2823:109; Dodsworth MSS 94:43–48. The fact that Robert de Turnham addressed the knights not as his men or in any official capacity but as his beloved friends (*dilectis amicis*) shows the informal nature of this settlement.

Given the examples cited above, it will be no surprise that knights and other gentry appear in almost every witness list of charters drawn up at honorial and regional courts and often dominate these lists.[51] Clearly, almost any court above the level of the manor would have included a gathering of gentry. Moreover, individual gentry could participate in and move between various courts. For instance, Adam de Reineville appeared as a member of the county court in one document, witnessed an agreement made in Staincross wapentake court, and appeared three times in the court of Roger de Lacy, lord of Pontefract.[52] Thus, individuals and the gentry as a whole had a very large role in the conduct of justice in local courts even before they became involved with royal courts. The evidence for this role, it is true, largely comes from late in the Angevin period, well after the royal courts had begun to expand, but everything we know about local courts in earlier periods suggests that the participation of gentry would have been nothing new. When Henry II began his legal reforms, there was almost certainly a strong tradition of gentry involvement in justice.

The new royal courts did little to alter this tradition. Indeed, the royal government welcomed and even mandated the participation of gentry and in particular knights, and soon royal justice came to depend heavily on their service. Knights performed an enormous number of routine tasks necessary for the functioning of royal courts, including bringing the records of local courts when cases were transferred to royal courts, checking up on people who essoined for bed sickness, perambulating boundaries, and guarding other knights who were suspected of serious crimes. In 1179 Henry II created the grand assize as an alternative to the duel as a means of trial, and it was knights who elected and served as jurors for this new procedure. Jurors for the petty assizes such as novel disseisin were drawn from a broader social range, but knights and other members of the gentry often participated in juries for such assizes. Knights could also be consulted on specific points of local information such as an individual's reputation and legal standing.[53] The records of the royal courts, from the earliest ones that survive up to and including those of the 1218–19 eyre, show nearly two hundred Yorkshire knights electing jurors, serving on a grand assize, check-

---

51. Unfortunately, the small number of witness lists explicitly associated with various courts (about a dozen each from honorial, wapentake, county, and royal courts) makes any statistical study of these lists futile.

52. *EYC* 8:174; *EYC* 3:403, 213, 333, 340.

53. See Hall, *Glanvill*, 11–12, 16, 30–31, 33, 35–37, 98–99, 102, 139 and Poole, *Obligations of Society*, 53–56, for the general duties of knights.

ing essoins, or performing other tasks.[54] Quite simply, the royal courts could not have functioned without the routine service of knights.

Some members of the gentry had more important individual responsibilities. From 1194, knights were chosen as keepers of the crown pleas, or coroners.[55] In 1206, Bernard de Ripley proffered twenty marks and a palfrey to have an assize of mort d'ancestor heard before the sheriff of Yorkshire, Brian de Lisle, and four knights. The proffer was accepted and the sheriff was ordered to choose four knights who "best knew the law and customs of England."[56] More important, six or seven Yorkshire knights served on an occasional basis as royal justices under the Angevin kings and several more who were alive during the Angevin period served in that capacity under Henry III.[57] Thus, from the performance of routine tasks to the more exalted duties of a royal justice, members of the gentry kept the machinery of royal justice operating.

In using the gentry, the royal government was not innovating but building on a traditional pattern and using the same sort of people that were already involved in the exercise of justice. Indeed, it often used not just the same sort of people, but the same individuals. John de Birkin appeared in the court of Roger de Lacy and a final concord was made before him and other knights and the undersheriff in the county court. John is also recorded as a juror on a grand assize in King John's reign, and served the royal judicial system in several capacities early in Henry III's reign, when he frequently served as a justice in specific novel disseisin cases.[58] Thus, in one respect there was much continuity between traditional local courts and the new royal courts. A litigant was likely to see many of the same people in

54. If one investigates the court rolls from up to 1230, more than one hundred other knights can be added to the list; see the introduction.

55. See *CRR* 6:115, for a list of Yorkshire coroners in 1210.

56. *Rot. Obl. & Fin.*, 363. This seems to have been a precursor to a practice during the reign of Henry III whereby four local knights would be appointed to judge specific petty assizes, for which practice see Donald Sutherland, *The Assize of Novel Disseisin*, 62.

57. William Vavasour, Geoffrey Haget, Richard Malebisse, Henry son of Hervey, Walter de Bovington, and Robert de Percy of Bolton Percy served under the Angevin Kings. A William de Percy who served on one occasion was probably also of Bolton Percy. John Daiville, Brian son of Alan (who also served as sheriff of Yorkshire and Northumberland during Henry III's reign), Ranulf son of Henry, Ranulf son of Robert, Jordan de Hairun, Adam de Novo Mercato, and William de Tameton all served under Henry III. In addition, Roger Arundel and Eustace de Fauconberg, clerical members of gentry families, served as justices under the Angevin kings. David Crook, *Records of the General Eyre*, 59–93; Edward Foss, *The Judges of England* 1:422, 384–85; 2:31–32, 42–43, 58–59, 93–94, 102–5, 307–8, 324–27, 332–33, 366, 430–31, 482–83.

58. *EYC* 3:213–14, 333; *EYC* 7:287; *CRR* 3:2. For John's appointments as a justice for novel disseisin cases in Henry III's reign, see *Patent Rolls of the Reign of Henry III, A.D. 1216–1225*, 174–75, 310, 343, 391, 392, 396, 479, 487, 488.

different courts, in some cases performing similar activities and in other cases performing very different functions.

The benefits this continuity provided both to the royal government and the local gentry are clear. The royal government got free labor in the running of royal courts from people who were experienced and powerful and had the leisure to devote to carrying out judicial tasks. As for the gentry, the power and prestige that judicial activity gave them was enormous. Their actions and decisions within the judicial system determined the fates of many individuals and the dispositions of many properties. For members of the gentry in later periods, service on commissions of the peace provided power, prestige, and status.[59] The same was undoubtedly true of the various judicial activities of Angevin gentry and Gaillard Lapsley, in his article on the Gloucestershire *buzones* of 1212, draws some very apt parallels. He saw these men as local squires, dedicated to the business of government, and analogous to similar groups of gentry who ran local governments in later periods.[60] Significant participation in any form of judicial activity would have emphasized an individual's status and allowed him to influence the course of events in the neighborhood. As the decline of the honor made elite society less structured and more competitive, the royal courts offered gentry a new source of prestige and standing. As honorial courts declined in importance, gentry could turn to service in the royal courts. By participating in royal justice, the gentry adapted to new circumstances and retained an important source of power and prestige in a new venue. It is not clear whether gentry participation in royal justice came from royal or local initiative, but even if the former was the case, it is hard to believe that the crown could have shoved new duties down the throats of the gentry. The crown was able to use the gentry because service in the royal courts had its attractions.[61]

However, the differences between local and royal courts meant that the gentry were not simply stepping from one identical situation to another. Honorial courts would have been headed, either in person or by

59. See for instance Wright, *The Derbyshire Gentry*, 93–109. Much work has been done on this for the Early Modern period.

60. G. Lapsley, "Buzones," 177–93, 545–67.

61. Such service could also be a burden, of course, but because knighthood, the criterion upon which much judicial activity was based, was still a relatively broad social category, the burden of carrying out these tasks was not as onerous as it later became. Only two Yorkshire knights, Roald son of Alan and Alan de Wilton, sought to purchase exemptions from such duties in John's reign; *Rot. Chart.*, 127; *Pipe Roll 6 John*, 189.

proxy, by a lord who would have had an important, perhaps dominant say in the outcome and who could rarely be disinterested even if he desired.[62] No such figure loomed directly over the gentry in regional courts, but there, powerful local pressures could be brought to bear. The return of royal power, however, brought some oversight and regulation to these local courts.[63] In the royal courts, moreover, the gentry were working within a framework with increasingly standardized rules and increasingly experienced justices, often from outside the county, who oversaw the conduct of cases. Theoretically, this should both have limited local pressures and also prevented members of the gentry from using, or perhaps misusing, their judicial responsibilities to further their own ends. Although the growth of royal justice did not change the fact of gentry participation in dispute settlement, it should at least have carefully regulated it.

This raises a group of related questions. What was the effect of the paradox that so lawless a group as the gentry continued to play so important a role in the conduct of justice? To what extent were gentry content with the prestige that came from their judicial services, and to what extent did they seek to misuse their positions for their own ends? To what extent were gentry willing to accept the new rule of law under the Angevins? To what extent was the Angevin government willing and able to impose order upon this group? These questions may be gathered under one broader question. To what degree did royal justice live up to the standards set in the statement from *Glanvill* quoted earlier, particularly when it came to the gentry? In other words, to what degree was lawless coercion by the powerful prevented and to what degree was an impartial system of justice that gave no advantage to the elite created? Stated in such terms, the question is relatively straightforward. The answer, alas, is not.

There are several difficulties in answering this question. First, there are the shortcomings of the sources. Because of the spotty survival of judicial records, even from John's reign, some of the most interesting cases survive only partially, thus leaving crucial questions unanswered and sometimes the outcome unknown. Even when the case is relatively complete, the entries can be very laconic, thus leaving out factors that would show why a case was decided one way or the other. Moreover, plaintiffs or defendants sometimes resorted to outright fabrication, leaving the historian with two wildly

62. Milsom would say never; *Feudal Framework*, 45, 58–59, 73–74.
63. See Palmer, *County Courts*, 297–306, for the increasing oversight of regional courts by the central government.

differing stories and no way to differentiate between them.[64] As shall be seen, it is not always possible to tell whether truth or perjury triumphs in a given case.

Second, this straightforward question contains many facets. There are many levels on which the system could fail to meet the ideal. The favoritism of the king, corruption on various levels, lack of enforcement, inability to enforce; all these and more could deflect the course of justice. It must be asked to what degree those who ran the royal courts, from the king to the gentry, actually desired to live up to the standards found in *Glanvill*, and given such desire, to what degree they were able. Third, different answers will be found to the question in different cases. In one, justice may appear to triumph; in another, the most blatant perversion of justice can be seen. Thus, there will be no single, simple answer. Nevertheless, the investigation of a number of individual cases yields very interesting results when one considers the identities, status, and power of those involved and though a discussion of royal justice on the ground, as it were, is not easy and will not present simple conclusions, it will nevertheless greatly illuminate the impact of the growth of the royal courts.

Not surprisingly, such a study reveals a host of failures and shortcomings. In cases involving royal favorites, blatant favoritism could be practiced. The use of royal courts by favored tenants-in-chief to extract land or money from their tenants has been discussed elsewhere.[65] After Gilbert de Plumpton kidnapped the heiress in Ranulf de Glanvill's custody, Ranulf persuaded the royal court to condemn him to death. Roger of Howden, who recorded this incident, felt Ranulf used his power and position in an unjust manner to obtain this unusually harsh sentence against Gilbert and so, apparently, did a large crowd of people who gathered to protest the planned execution. Public sentiment and the intervention of Bishop Baldwin of Worcester was strong enough to save Gilbert, but clearly he had had a close shave. As it was, Gilbert's brother Nigel was only able to purchase his freedom from prison after Glanvill's death.[66]

Favoritism toward royal favorites and officials was more likely to harm than to help the gentry, who generally had little access to royal favor. Another factor undermining justice, one more likely to favor the gentry, was corruption and influence peddling by royal justices, many of whom

---

64. For instance, *CRR* 1:296, 397; *CRR* 5:267; *CRR* 6:355; *Yorkshire Eyre*, 341–42.

65. See chapter one, section three.

66. Roger of Howden, *Chronica* 2:286; Benedict of Peterborough, *Gesta Regis* 1:314–16; *Pipe Roll 30 Henry II*, 29, 38; *Pipe Roll 2 Richard I*, 66.

were gentry in origin and a few of whom came from a local Yorkshire background. During the Angevin period, much criticism was directed against the royal justices for their corruption. Ralph Turner, who has discussed this criticism, is probably right that it is exaggerated.[67] Nevertheless, corruption existed and justices drawn from the area may have been especially susceptible. A later account of the history of the ownership of Bolton in Bolland reveals that William Vavasour, a royal justice and wealthy knight, received half the village from William de Leathley after he presided over a case in which William de Leathley recovered the village from his brother-in-law. Given the size of the reward, it is unlikely that William Vavasour simply provided sound legal advice.[68] At least upon occasion, members of the gentry were willing to use their authority or the authority of friends in the judicial system for their own ends.

More important than corruption were the difficulties of enforcement, possibly exacerbated by the distance of Yorkshire from Westminster. Powerful landholders could use their influence, and power to avoid the consequences of their own lawlessness. The trial of Malger Vavasour, a son of the royal justice, and of his retainers for attacking the followers of William son of Everard, illustrates well the strategies a prosperous local landholder might employ to escape punishment for misdeeds. William's man, Henry de Irton, before the justices in eyre, accused several men of the attack, stating that Stephen Carter had wounded and robbed him, that Thomas Lymer had wounded him, and that John Hardy participated in the attack.[69] In a separate statement, Henry accused Malger of masterminding the attack, accompanying his followers, and attacking and wounding Henry's boy (*garcio*) when the latter tried to raise the alarm by sounding a horn. Malger essoined for sickness and thus was absent.[70] His men, however, were present and answered Henry's accusation. Stephen Carter, the first of the accused, began by denying the whole charge word for word. Second, he accused Henry of making up the accusation because of the enmity between William son of Everard and Malger Vavasour arising from a lawsuit over

67. See Ralph V. Turner, *The English Judiciary in the Age of Glanvill and Bracton, c. 1176–1239*, 3–9, 54–56, 123–24, 181–82, 280–98.

68. The account containing this story is much later in date and some odd details within it have led Clay to describe it as a "strange story." However, the Vavasours certainly acquired half of the village and it seems an odd story to make up out of whole cloth; *Sallay Cartulary* 1:67–68; *EYC* 11:126.

69. He also accused two others of participating in the attack, but one of these had died and the other had been outlawed for an unrelated murder.

70. His sickness was probably genuine rather than a ploy since he died soon thereafter.

land. Third, he gave an alternative story about the source of Henry's wounds. Henry, according to Stephen, had made love to the mistress of a priest and had received the wounds when the priest, finding them lying together, reacted violently. Thomas Lymer and John Hardy then corroborated Stephen's account throughout.

Thus, as often happened, the justices were presented with two plausible stories that were at complete variance with each other. Because Malger was not present, the justices turned to local jurors to discover the truth of the accusation against the defendants. These jurors denied all the charges made against Malger. The justices, however, apparently grew suspicious and pushed harder, whereupon the jurors acknowledged that the three accused were Malger's men, that John Hardy, in fact, was his seneschal, and that they had gone forth from Malger's house to commit the crime, thus revealing that Henry de Irton's accusations against both Malger and his men were at least partly true. The jurors did not admit, however, that Malger was present at the attack. Later, Malger appeared in person. He denied the charges, despite the fact that the jury had admitted at least some of them, and offered to answer the charge by means of a duel against Henry.[71] The duel was not fought, for Malger was able to settle by agreeing to pay the royal government sixty marks for license to agree.[72] Henry, who withdrew his claim with the court's permission, perhaps also received compensation.

Several points in this story demand attention. First, there was the use of perjury discussed earlier. Malger and his men cleverly sought to obfuscate the issue by inventing a story that not only explained their opponent's wounds but discredited him as well. They also explained why Henry should want to make a false accusation, citing the enmity between Malger and Henry's lord and thereby incidentally revealing the reason for the attack. Such fabrications, intended to stymie an accusation, were not unique to this case. They were made more effective by the fact that people probably did sometimes make up false accusations. If one was willing to undergo a certain amount of trouble and expense, false accusations were a wonderful way of harassing an enemy.[73] In an ongoing dispute, a false accusation could be one way of gaining a tactical advantage over one's opponent.

71. Since Malger himself was infirm and past fighting age, he presented his nephew, Nicholas, as a champion.

72. *Yorkshire Eyre*, 268–70, 330; *Pipe Roll 3 Henry III*, 330.

73. See *Pipe Roll 5 John*, 212, and *Pipe Roll 9 John*, 71, for claims that false accusations were being made through hatred of the accused.

A second key factor, and one that made perjury effective, is that Malger was able to suborn the jury. Though the power of the gentry could in no way compete with that of magnates, nevertheless many of them were powerful and influential figures in their own regions. They could use their power and influence to intimidate or subvert jurors and witnesses. In another case, the royal justices amerced the villagers of Oulston because they did not present a killing for which an important local landowner was subsequently outlawed.[74] In yet another case, in which the knight Alan de Follifoot was suspected of the murder of John Cote, found dead in the fields of Adwick, the villagers of Adwick first said that they knew nothing and then stated that a certain Dawe had killed him. They claimed that Dawe's lord, who unfortunately was not identified, had told them this. A shepherd who was apparently present at the killing refused to speak. The villagers were clearly under pressure, and it seems likely that this pressure was coming, directly or indirectly, from Alan.[75] As wealthy and powerful individuals, gentry could influence those around them who were less powerful, perhaps though bribes and favors, perhaps through threats, and thus attempt to protect themselves from the consequence of their misdeeds.

In Malger's case, the royal justices saw through the attempts to subvert justice and Malger suffered a heavy fine. One cannot be certain that this always happened. Had the royal justices not probed further or had the jurors remained firm in their perjury, there would have been no way for the historian to know that it was Stephen Carter's version of events that was the fabrication. As it was, the jury never admitted that Malger was present at the attack, nor that he was responsible for wounding one of Henry's companions. In light of the truth of Henry's other accusations it seems likely that Malger was present and did wound the companion and that the jury simply continued to protect him from the worst of the charges against him.

Several cases involving gentry have suspicious aspects and one in particular may show a member of the local gentry literally getting away with murder, though once again the evidence is problematic. In 1199, Richard son of Ralph accused a prominent local knight, William de Sancton, of murdering his father, Ralph. According to Richard, William had led Ralph into his chamber and struck him feloniously. Afterward, Ralph had intended to go to court to complain to the justices, but William, accom-

---

74. *Yorkshire Eyre*, 366–67. For a similar case see *Yorkshire Eyre*, 194.
75. *Yorkshire Eyre*, 204–5.

panied by his brother and several others, pursued Ralph into Lincolnshire and there killed him in a wood. Richard offered to prove this by means of a duel against William. William, as one would expect, denied the charge, and then went on to explain that a certain malefactor who had been hanged had confessed to the crime. William was immediately acquitted and Richard was amerced for false accusation. William's identification of the murderer as someone who was conveniently dead seems extremely fishy, while the circumstantial detail provided by Richard adds plausibility to his account. Without more information there is no certain way to tell who was speaking the truth and who was lying. However, there must be the strong suspicion that William frustrated a charge of battery through murdering the victim and then escaped punishment for murder through a successful cover-up.[76]

Participation in the administration of justice may not have given the gentry a firm commitment to the law but rather the connections, influence, and knowledge to circumvent it. Indeed, it may have given some of them the knowledge to escape justice not through perjury, bribery, or intimidation, but through the increasingly fixed rules and procedures of the royal courts themselves. On one occasion, for instance, the wife and sons of the knight Hugh de Verly, along with some companions, were accused of entering the courtyard of Stephen de Ottringham, killing Stephen and burning his house down. A woman named Lece, claiming to be Stephen's wife, accused one of that company, William de Warder, of giving Stephen his mortal wound. William replied that Lece was Stephen's housekeeper, not his wife. Since women were allowed to bring accusations on their own only for rape and for the murder of their husband, William's reply, if substantiated, would have invalidated the accusation.[77] As procedures came to depend more on fixed rules, gentry used their knowledge of the rules to promote their own ends.

Some gentry adapted so well that they were able not only to protect themselves from the consequences of their misdeeds, but to use the law courts as yet another tool in the pursuit of vendettas. When a set of seemingly unrelated cases from a plea roll of 1208 is investigated, some interesting patterns emerge. In this roll, William de Bolton was charged with the rape of Sibba daughter of William. At the same time William's cousin, Geoffrey de Fitling, was accused of robbery and Gilbert son of Marmaduke, who may also have been a relative, was appealed as the

76. *RCR* 1:309, 314, 412; *RCR* 2:12–13.
77. *RCR* 2:103. Unfortunately, the outcome of the case is unknown.

accomplice in a wounding.[78] What is interesting about these cases is that Sibba, who was awarded compensation of twenty shillings, won her case partly because immediately after the rape she went into Wheldrake and showed the evidence to two members of the gentry, Alan Malecake and Walter de Beauvais. In the two other cases, Alan acted as pledge to the accusers. This is significant because Alan and Walter both had ties to Richard Malebisse, who had earlier been involved in a dispute with the Boltons and Fitlings, heirs through marriage of a branch of the Darel family, over their refusal to perform homage to him.[79] Insufficient details survive to understand exactly what all these connections mean, and further complications are added by a fourth case in the same roll in which William de Bolton's brother Geoffrey accused William de Anger, who by his name may have been Sibba's father, of wounding him. Nevertheless, something was clearly going on behind the scenes. Perhaps all the people involved were associated with either Malebisse or the Darel heirs and the earlier legal dispute had developed into a violent feud. Malebisse and his followers may have sought out independent victims of the violence of the Darel heirs as a form of harassment. It could be that the initiative lay with the victims, who turned to the Malebisse camp, hoping to use a gentry feud to win justice for themselves. Whatever the case, it is clear here that the royal court was being used as another battleground for a wider feud or series of feuds.[80]

Power, status, and influence clearly mattered in royal courts and as any medievalist might expect, Angevin royal justice fell far short of the high standards expressed in the treatise called *Glanvill*. Justice could be circumvented and the royal courts could even be used as a tool of harassment and oppression by the powerful and influential. After all, this was a system in which the lawbreakers could be identical to the law keepers.[81] Richard Malebisse became a royal justice and Malger Vavasour heard pleas in county court.[82] From the standpoint of power and influence, the shortcomings of

---

78. *Pleas* 4:114–15. The name of Gilbert's father, Marmaduke, was uncommon but was used by several members of the Darel family. This may suggest a connection. However, Gilbert's position in the Darel genealogy, if he was in fact a member of that family, cannot be determined.

79. Alan was associated with Richard in the pogrom of 1190 and served him as an attorney on one occasion. Walter, in a charter witnessed by Alan, received a grant of land from Richard; *Pipe Roll 4 Richard I*, 221; *CRR* 2:277; *EYC* 3:466. For this dispute see *CRR* 5:77–79, *Rot. Obl & Fin.*, 379.

80. Interestingly, none of the cases was pursued very vigorously. There could have been an agreement between the feuding parties that led to an easy settlement of the court cases.

81. This was also true in later periods; Wright, *The Derbyshire Gentry*, 121–22.

82. Crook, *General Eyre*, 64; *CRR* 6:214–25.

royal justice made it all the more important that the gentry gained a role in its administration, for in that position it was easier to manipulate and influence royal justice to their own ends.

However, to present only the evidence of injustice, influence peddling and corruption would be to present a lopsided, overly simplistic, and unfair picture of both the Angevin legal system and the gentry. The ideals expressed in *Glanvill* were not written in a vacuum. Christian beliefs in justice and the duty of protecting the poor were widely preached, if less widely practiced, and local gentry were not unaffected by ideals of justice and fair play. For instance, one gentry litigant, in the 1218–19 eyre, withdrew his appeal against another man because he felt that his opponent had a genuine grievance.[83] Sometimes such ideals could appear in the most surprising of contexts. During King Stephen's reign a band of robber-knights inhabited a castle at Selby. According to one miracle story, after this band had strung up one of their squires for theft within the group, a member of the band had qualms and expressed the opinion that it was not right to execute someone without judicial sentence or proof.[84] As with all miracle stories, this one must be taken with more than a grain of salt, but it is interesting that the hagiographer thought his readers would believe it.

Such ideals of justice and proper procedure are reflected in the royal judicial records by cases in which less powerful people won cases against more powerful ones. It was by no means unknown for minor tenants to win cases over land against the gentry. A case from the 1218–19 eyre revealed that a certain Eudo had held a tenancy for eight shillings a year from Hugh de Cliff but that Hugh disseised Eudo's daughter Lecia after her father died because she would not pay twenty shillings to have the land. Hugh was apparently trying to offset the effects of inflation on a fixed rent by charging a large entry fine, but Lecia was awarded seisin notwithstanding her refusal to pay and Hugh was amerced.[85] In another case, Ranulf de Novo Mercato was amerced for disseising a tenant even though that tenant was seven years in arrears on his rent.[86] The amount of protection for tenants against gentry lords, in short, was surprisingly high.[87]

83. *Yorkshire Eyre*, 258–59.
84. Fowler, "Selebeiensis Monasterii Historia," 42–43.
85. Perhaps his demand was considered unreasonable or not customary; *Yorkshire Eyre*, 162.
86. *Yorkshire Eyre*, 21–22. For other instances in which gentry lost to less powerful people, see *CRR* 3:91; *Yorkshire Eyre*, 15, 79–80.
87. See also Sutherland, *Novel Disseisin*, 48–50.

That tenants, many of them peasants, could win such victories makes it seem likely that there was a genuine concern for law and justice that could be extended even to the lower classes. A concern for law and justice may also be revealed in certain procedural details in several cases. When jurors were chosen, the court records sometimes specified that they were not to be the men of one of the parties or of some local magnate.[88] As Ralph Turner has remarked concerning a similar case in the 1220s, this was probably an attempt to prevent any undue influence from being brought to bear.[89] In another case a juror was dismissed because he himself was involved in a lawsuit with one of the parties.[90]

A villeinage case shows that concern for fair procedure could help even those far down on the social scale. In this case, Richard de Brearton, who claimed Siward de Lindley as a villein, twice imprisoned Siward and seized his goods. Because Siward's status was unclear, the royal courts conscientiously, if not always effectively, protected him against the arbitrary treatment accorded to villeins, demanding that Richard follow proper procedure until Siward's true status was determined.[91] There was clearly a concern to protect the rights of free persons even if they were poor.

A comparison of the individual cases discussed above does not produce any simple patterns. In some, extraordinarily blatant subversions of justice occurred. In others, contemporary ideals of justice probably triumphed. However, to move from individual cases to a broader evaluation of the characteristics of Angevin justice and the degree to which it lived up to contemporary ideals is almost impossible. For one thing, contemporary ideals may have varied. More important is the lack of evidence. Even in the cases discussed above, more evidence might shed a very different light on the verdict. In most cases sufficient evidence to evaluate the quality of justice does not exist at all. It could be that corruption was rare and that, as in Malger's case, royal justices sought to stop it whenever they could. It is also possible that many more seemingly straightforward cases conceal corruption and injustice. Unfortunately, one simply cannot be sure which of

---

88. *CRR* 4:162; *Yorkshire Eyre*, 76.
89. Turner, "William de Forz," 245.
90. *CRR* 1:125.
91. *Pleas* 3:153. It should be noted that Siward claimed to be a free tenant of Malger Vavasour. If Malger was in any way involved, his influence may have motivated the courts more than ideals of fairness, but there is no way of knowing whether this was so. Unfortunately, the eventual outcome of this dispute over status is also not known. For a similar case in an earlier period, in which Osbert de Thorp was amerced because he imprisoned a man whom he claimed but could not prove to be his villein, see *Pipe Roll 21 Henry II*, 178.

the examples discussed above followed the norm and which were exceptions.

However, the evidence does permit some more positive conclusions. First, for all its shortcomings, Angevin royal justice did make a difference. Violence had been more widespread and on a much larger scale in Stephen's reign than late in the Angevin period, even accounting for exaggeration by the monastic chroniclers of the former period.[92] Although royal justice certainly did not eliminate illegal violence by the gentry or any other group for that matter, it did set limits on it. Malger did not escape scot free from his assault, for he had to pay the crown sixty marks as a result.[93] This was not a unique instance. One knight, William Gramary, gave the king £100 for the right to settle peacefully with Adam de Beeston after putting Adam in stocks and battling with Adam's men.[94] Another, William de Rocheford, also had to pay £100 and two palfreys to the king for license to settle with John de Harpham, whom he had struck in the eye.[95] A number of gentry had to pay the king as a result of the York pogrom.[96] The sums involved in these settlements were not small. £100 probably represented several years' landed income for most gentry.[97] Given the size of the amercements, any large scale act of illicit violence likely to attract the attention of the royal courts involved heavy financial risk. A member of the gentry might escape penalty, but if he did not the fiscal consequences could be serious. The royal government did not root out lawless violence, but it did keep the lid on, preventing disorder and lawlessness from getting too far out of hand. Violence did not disappear, but the lamentations of the chroniclers about Stephen's reign do not continue for Henry's. If the new or renewed rule of law did not always restrain the gentry, at least it made them cautious.

However, at the same time as the royal courts limited the lawless violence of gentry and others, there was a marked reluctance to pursue justice in its full rigor when it came to the upper classes. As far as the

---

92. For some local accounts of or references to lawlessness in Stephen's reign, see J. C. Atkinson, *Cartularium Abbatiae de Whiteby* 2:517–18; Fowler, "Selebeiensis Monasterii Historia," 33–44; Clark, "Fundacio Abbathie de Kyrkestall," 176; Hugh of Kirkstall, "Narratio de Fundatione Fontanis," 101; Greenway, *Mowbray Charters*, 75–76; *EYC* 3:190, 240–41.

93. *Pipe Roll 3 Henry III*, 203; *Yorkshire Eyre*, 330. It is not clear whether or not Malger also had to pay compensation to his victim as was sometimes required.

94. *Rot. Obl. & Fin.*, 138.

95. *Pipe Roll 5 John*, 213; *CRR* 3:37.

96. *Pipe Roll 4 Richard I*, 221; *Pipe Roll 6 Richard I*, 161.

97. It might be noted that the payments for these amercements were spread out over a number of years.

surviving records show, gentry malefactors almost never suffered more than a monetary penalty. One minor member of the gentry, it is true, was outlawed at the end of the Angevin period, but his victim had been a prominent knight, and the status of the victim made a difference, just as it did with Gilbert de Plumpton.[98] Some of the perpetrators of the York pogrom were also forced to go into exile. Not only had they committed multiple murders, but what was far worse in the eyes of Richard I and his officials, they had affronted the king's dignity by attacking those under his protection, and had also temporarily destroyed a valuable source of royal revenue. Even so, all those involved were able to gain reconciliation for a price, and Richard Malebisse, who was apparently the ringleader of the lot, went on to become a royal servant and royal justice in John's reign. Common people by the dozen may have been put to the ordeal of water,[99] and executed, exiled, or outlawed for even relatively minor crimes, but the gentry could clearly commit even the greatest crimes without much fear of more than a heavy financial penalty. *Glanvill* may have spoken forcefully of "crushing the pride of the unbridled and ungovernable with the right hand of strength," but when it came to deeds, the royal government was very restrained.

This may have resulted in part from the continuing influence of earlier ideas concerning dispute settlement. Van Caenegem, concentrating on land law, has described the tendency of early twelfth century courts towards compromise and agreement rather than clear-cut decision. The Angevin legal reforms began a shift towards the latter kind of decision, but as van Caenegem himself points out, the many final concords which brought about compromises in the royal courts show that the shift was a slow one.[100] The continuing tendency toward compromise and settlement may be seen in cases of gentry violence. In some of the payments to the crown, gentry were buying the right to settle up themselves. Of the £100 William Gramary paid, twenty marks were to go to his victim, Adam de Beeston.[101] The emphasis on dispute settlement over justice continued and this benefitted the gentry. The amercements did serve as a penalty, but one that was

98. *Yorkshire Eyre*, 366.

99. See *Pipe Roll 12 Henry II*, 43–45, *Pipe Roll 22 Henry II*, 118–19; *Pipe Roll 23 Henry II*, 79, for the large numbers of people put to the ordeal in Yorkshire after the assizes of Clarendon and Northampton. Most had chattels worth only small sums and none is recognizably a member of the gentry, although a few, such as Sigar Aguillun (*Pipe Roll 23 Henry II*, 79), may have been related to prominent gentry families.

100. Van Caenegem, *Royal Writs*, 41–50.

101. *Rot. Obl. & Fin.*, 138.

limited and could lead to the restoration of peace and the local status quo.[102] Compromise could continue to serve the mighty.

Why was the royal government unwilling or unable to impose its new or renewed norms of absolute justice on the powerful as well as the weak? Part of the explanation lies in patterns of elite solidarity. Members of the gentry had widespread ties of marriage, lordship, and friendship which extended throughout the upper ranks of society. In his account of Gilbert de Plumpton's brush with Ranulf de Glanvill and royal law, Roger de Howden emphasized Gilbert's high birth, calling him a "miles nobili prosapia ortus" and a "juvenis quidam nobili exortus prosapia."[103] The fact that Gilbert de Plumpton's case could become a cause célèbre is an indication of how such ties could be utilized even in a case in which heavy pressure was being exerted by the other side. Sellar and Yeatman wrote that one of the baronial demands in 1215 was that "Barons should not be tried except by a special jury of other Barons who would understand."[104] This comic statement may well provide an accurate reflection of an unpleasant aspect of Angevin elite thought.

Another factor is that the royal government needed the support of the powerful, and not only the magnates, but also the gentry. Because the gentry played such a crucial role in royal justice, the royal government could not bear down on them too hard. Because the gentry formed a large part of the feudal host, even in its decline, the royal justices could not alienate them by executing individuals who were lawless, but were also in the midst of a web of ties based on kinship, friendship, and neighborhood.

Finally, there was widespread acceptance and glorification of violence among the upper ranks of society as a whole. To punish illegal acts of violence impartially would cost the powerful in society one of their most important tools in maintaining their power. Few members of the elite, even among the royal justices involved in the Angevin legal revolution, might have wanted to see such an important source of power removed and therefore they were not willing to let elite violence be crushed, but only limited. Accustomed as elites of the Angevin period were to violence, they probably did not view lawless violence as a serious threat except when it got

102. See Rowney, "Arbitration," 367–76; Wright, *The Derbyshire Gentry*, 122–27; and Pollard, "The Richmondshire Gentry," 50, for the use of arbitration to achieve compromise and peace in later periods.
103. Roger of Howden, *Chronica* 2:286; Benedict of Peterborough, *Gesta Regis* 1:314–16.
104. W. C. Sellar and R. J. Yeatman, *1066 and All That*, 34.

too far out of hand, and even then they clearly regarded it with a tolerant eye.

Royal courts brought important changes to local areas and to the gentry, but there were limits to the impact. Kings and royal justices could not, and probably did not want to, create a system in which the power and status of local individuals was completely neutralized within the bounds of the judicial system. Royal justice did not fundamentally challenge local power structures, but included and to a degree was coopted by them. Though the Angevin legal reforms created a revolution in law, in social terms the revolution was blunted. For the gentry, the change was not overwhelming. The gentry already played an important part in the local courts and continued to do so in the royal courts, albeit with more outside supervision. Lawless violence was an important source of power for the gentry and though royal justice limited this source, it did not stop it altogether. Royal influence undoubtedly grew in important ways, but increasingly independent gentry, alongside their baronial neighbors, remained figures to be reckoned with on a local level, whether within or without the law. Both lawlessness and law gave them power, prestige, and authority and this would remain true for the gentry throughout the Middle Ages, despite the growth of royal justice.

3. Land and Economic Development Among the Gentry

Lawless violence and the legal system were both props for gentry power, but ultimately the greatest foundation of gentry power was landholding. One of the most frequently stated characteristics of medieval society, or indeed of almost any pre-modern civilization, is that wealth derived primarily from land and in talking about elite society and about local power structures, one cannot avoid talking about land. Thus, the control and transfer of land are pervasive themes in this book, from the endowment of gentry within the honorial system, to legal and extra-legal battles over land, to inheritance and donations of land. This chapter concerns the exploitation of land by the gentry and in particular the development of new sources of gentry income. The improving landlord is a stock figure in the history and literature of England of later periods. In this respect, as in others, the gentry of Angevin Yorkshire were very similar to their successors.

The study of gentry landholding in this period is often frustrating, for the evidence, and particularly the charter evidence, is plentiful, yet stingy in the sorts of information it reveals. One can see that the Yorkshire gentry of the Angevin period were typical medieval English landlords, deriving incomes from demesne farms, rents, and seigneurial dues, but it is difficult to gain a more nuanced picture. One can learn much about what gentry gave away to monasteries but little about what they kept, and it is generally impossible to reconstruct the demesne holdings of an individual or family.[1] The evidence is generally anecdotal; one can find instances of gentry home farms ranging in size from three bovates (probably about forty-five acres) to five hundred acres, but there is insufficient evidence to determine the average size of home farms on gentry estates.[2] One can see that many

---

1. A rare exception are the lands of the Grimthorpe family, recorded in something like the later inquisitions post mortem because the family heirs were in the custody of Robert de Ros after the Magna Carta revolt, but should have been in royal custody; *Yorkshire Eyre*, 326.
2. *EYC* 8:168; *Meaux Chronicle*, 220.

Yorkshire gentry had access to extensive pastures, but one cannot develop any meaningful figures about average herd sizes. In short, fundamental questions about gentry farming must remain unanswered. Despite the inadequacies of the evidence, however, one facet of gentry landholding does shine through, namely the interest of gentry in expanding and improving their incomes.

Yorkshire gentry possessed many opportunities to develop lands in part because of the history of their region. Yorkshire was relatively underdeveloped in the Angevin period. Underdevelopment was especially characteristic of certain areas within Yorkshire. Hallam in *Rural England* describes the West Riding in particular as "in many ways the supreme new-settlement county."[3] Not only was settlement in northern England later than elsewhere, but it received a severe setback with the harrying of the North under William I and even before that disaster settlement may have been receding somewhat, at least in the West Riding.[4] The late eleventh and early twelfth centuries were important for resettlement and expansion, but expansion would continue into the Angevin period.[5] The late settlement pattern gave room for population growth, the development of new arable lands and the creation of new sources of income.

It also meant that many of the Yorkshire gentry had access to nonarable resources in amounts that gentry in more heavily settled areas might have envied. Because of the primary importance of cereals in medieval diets, and therefore of arable land, it is all too easy to underestimate the profits that could be drawn from uncultivated land. A twelfth-century Selby historian stressed the richness of the woods and waters in the unsettled area around Selby at the time of its foundation and the modern historian D. J.

---

3. Assarting and settlement in the North and East Ridings were slower than in the West Riding, but clearly there was a great deal in those ridings as well; H. E. Hallam, *Rural England, 1066–1348*, 187–92.

4. See Hallam, *Rural England*, 189–90, for the decline in settlement even before William's attacks.

5. See H. C. Darby and I. S. Maxwell, eds., *The Domesday Geography of Northern England*, 14–15, 98, 175–76; Edward Miller, "Farming in Northern England during the Twelfth and Thirteenth Centuries," 5–7; and T. A. M. Bishop, "Assarting and the Growth of the Open Fields," 13–29, for resettlement and new settlement after the Conquest. For theories about the reorganization that accompanied resettlement, see T. A. M. Bishop, "The Norman Settlement of Yorkshire," 1–14 and William E. Kapelle, *The Norman Conquest of the North*, 158–90. For the possible creation of planned village sites by the new lords, see June Sheppard, "Medieval Village Planning in Northern England: Some Evidence from Yorkshire," 3–20; "Metrological Analysis of Regular Village Plans in Yorkshire," 133–35. For a different view of the planned villages, see Mary Harvey, "Planned Field Systems in Eastern Yorkshire: Some Thoughts on Their Origin," 91–103.

Siddle argues that in that period Holderness drew its wealth largely from its nonarable resources.[6] Wild or relatively wild areas could produce an abundance of useful products such as timber and provide extensive pasture. Such areas were far less valuable on a per acre basis, but to someone with a lot of land, they could be very valuable indeed, particularly as the market for such products as wool and lumber grew with the expansion of the economy throughout Europe in the central Middle Ages.

Late settlement and the devastation by William the Conqueror's armies not only left the possibility for later development but also forced tenants-in-chief to give out unusually large amounts of land to their vassals. When the new Norman lords of Yorkshire began rewarding their followers, they were handing out lands in an area that was already poor and had recently suffered appalling devastation. According to Donkin, the collective *Domesday Book* valuation of the North Riding fell between 1066 and 1086 by eighty percent, that of the East Riding by seventy-two percent, and that of the West Riding by forty-seven percent.[7] Although the *Domesday Book* description of lands as wasted cannot always be taken literally, the widespread use of this term in the Yorkshire folios illustrates the level of destruction.[8] To provide their followers with incomes which were commensurate with those of vassals in other areas of the country, lords in this devastated and impoverished area had to give out unusually large fees. In southern England an equation between five hides and a knight's fee was occasionally made, and although this was more honored in the breach than in practice, often enough, as at Peterborough, knights' fees could be smaller rather than larger.[9] In Yorkshire, though fees as small as three or four carucates existed on the honor of Conisborough, the vast majority of knights' fees were far larger, with some number of carucates in the teens being most typical. On the honor of the counts of Aumale, knights' fees

6. Fowler, "Selebeiensis Monasterii Historia," 12–13; D. J. Siddle, "The Rural Economy of Medieval Holderness," 40–45.

7. R. A. Donkin, *The Cistercians: Studies in the Geography of Medieval England and Wales*, 56–57.

8. W. E. Wightman argues that the effects of the harrying of the north were not so severe as traditionally thought and that much of the waste recorded in *Domesday Book* was the result of administrative reorganization and other factors; "The Significance of 'Waste' in the Yorkshire Domesday," 55–71. Given the massive drop in values recorded in 1086, however, and the comments of later chroniclers on the continuing effects of the devastation, it seems likely that Wightman greatly underestimates the amount of damage inflicted by William and his troops.

9. Edmund King, "The Peterborough 'Descriptio Militum,'" 90–91; *Peterborough Abbey*, 15–17.

were larger still, consisting of forty-eight carucates each.[10] Moreover, in some areas these carucates might provide rights of access to hundreds of additional acres of under-utilized marsh or moorland. After the Conquest Yorkshire gentry were rich in lands, though probably not in income. The access to such large amounts of land put the vassals of the Norman period and the gentry of the Angevin period in a prime position to take advantage of the opportunities available in Yorkshire.

Of course, the gentry's access to uncultivated or under-utilized land would vary widely according to geography, for Yorkshire was a huge county and encompassed many different landscapes. Those with estates bordering the marshy areas of Holderness and the Vale of York that could be drained or used for pasture, those with properties in the parts of the West Riding in which abundant land was available for assarting, and those with access to the extensive upland pastures of the Pennines, North Yorkshire Moors, and the Wolds had many more opportunities than their counterparts located in more heavily settled and populated areas. Despite the variation, however, Yorkshire as a whole was a county providing much opportunity for economic expansion and development.

The use which new monastic orders and particularly the Cistercians made of these opportunities is well known, but they were not alone.[11] All groups, from magnates to peasants, were involved. There are even references to assarts or clearings made by priests and to an assart held by a priest's "woman."[12] The gentry, however, were among the most closely involved.[13]

10. Forty-eight carucates, the standard for the honor of Aumale, was unique, but fees of ten to twenty carucates were extremely common. For some descriptions of the sizes of fees, see *EYC* 1:412, 413, 431, 433, 450, 501; *EYC* 2:22, 23, 25, 44, 50, 64, 68, 79, 80, 124, 165, 172, 345, 351, 414, 422, 457, 460, 461–62, 475; *EYC* 3:204, 258, 268, 310, 314, 341, 348, 351, 372, 410, 412, 417, 419, 425, 480; *EYC* 5:29–30, 46, 104, 112, 117, 118, 153, 160, 191–92, 209, 217, 218, 232, 252–53, 263, 265, 280, 310, 321; *EYC* 6:76, 258; *EYC* 7:94–95, 158, 160, 186, 189, 190, 220, 252; *EYC* 8:155, 170; *EYC* 9:140, 152, 160, 174; *EYC* 10:92–93, 95, 96; *EYC* 11:91, 99, 125, 133, 135, 160, 162, 163, 165, 250, 265, 272, 281, 344, 349, 250, 351. For a discussion of the size of fees in Yorkshire, see English, *Lords of Holderness*, 142–43.

11. See Donkin, *The Cistercians*, 57–59, 107–15, and Bryan Waites, "The Monastic Grange as a Factor in the Settlement of North-East Yorkshire," 627–56, for the contributions of monks.

12. *EYC* 3:332; *Pipe Roll 13 Henry II*, 94.

13. It is notable that two of the knights most extensively involved in draining the fens in Lincolnshire, Fulk de Oiry and Conan son of Elias, also had Yorkshire lands; for their involvement in Lincolnshire and their participation in the attack on the Precinct of Crowland, see H. E. Hallam, *Settlement and Society: A Study of the Early Agrarian History of South Lincolnshire*, 25–26, 28–30 and K. Major, "Conan Son of Ellis, an Early Inhabitant of Holbeach," 10.

Development came in a variety of ways. The most important of these was the expansion of arable through the assarting, or clearing, draining, and cultivation of forests, moorland, and marsh and it is not surprising that the fullest evidence for development by gentry comes in the area of assarting. Indeed, one knight who was an early benefactor to Fountains was called Robert de Sartis, or Robert of the assarts.[14] Members of the gentry frequently mention assarts in their grants, sales, and agreements.[15] A few examples will suffice to show the degree to which they were active assarters. The trouble between Alan de Ridale and Roger de Mowbray discussed in the first chapter began when Alan plowed up land in a moor in which Roger had granted common pasture to Rievaulx Abbey. Several other eager gentry developers had to be restrained from assarting lands shared with monasteries too, or forced to promise recompense.[16] In a less competitive vein, Robert de Hessle promised Guisborough Priory two thirds of the tithes from land he had cultivated "de novo" in Hessle since he had acquired it and in lands he or his heirs would cultivate in the future.[17] The possibility of members of the gentry assarting land is mentioned in a number of grants and agreements and several knights purchased from King John the right to make assarts in royal forests.[18] Generally, gentry assarters created new arable land, but there are references to new gardens and the creation of meadows.[19] The gentry saw the advantages of assarting just as clearly as the monks or anyone else.[20]

14. Hugh of Kirkstall, "Narratio de Fundatione Fontanis," 54–55; Robert was identified as de Sarz in his own charters and as de essartis in a royal confirmation. The editor suggests Sarz comes from Sars-sur-Cauches in Artois, but both the Fountains chronicler and the royal scribe were clearly translating the name as "of the assarts."

15. For mentions of assarts, riddings, or newly cultivated land held or alienated by gentry in *Early Yorkshire Charters* alone, see *EYC* 1:56–57, 59, 61–62, 327, 421, 431; *EYC* 2:65, 357, 424, 425–26; *EYC* 3:121, 224, 227, 253, 288, 309, 338, 340, 357, 362, 370–71, 381–82, 388, 403–4; *EYC* 5:29, 49, 76, 107–8, 170; *EYC* 6:256; *EYC* 7:130–31, 206; *EYC* 8:217; *EYC* 10:94, 103–4; *EYC* 11:183–84; *EYC* 12:72.

16. *EYC* 9:238–39; *EYC* 2:83; *EYC* 3:414; Brown, *Pedes Finium Ebor.*, 160–62; *Sallay Cartulary* 2:40; Egerton MSS 2823:36v. Such prohibitions could go the other way, with gentry protecting their rights against monastic assarters; Egerton MSS 2827:6.

17. *EYC* 12:64.

18. *EYC* 1:398–99; *EYC* 2:345; *EYC* 7:258; *Yorkshire Deeds* 6:54; J. T. Fowler, *The Coucher Book of Selby* 1:379; Holmes, *Chartulary of Pontefract* 1:280; *Rot. Chart.*, 42b, 122b; *Rot. Obl. & Fin.*, 55; *Pipe Roll 12 John*, 40.

19. *EYC* 1:383–84; *Yorkshire Deeds* 6:23; Egerton MSS 2827:39; *Meaux Chronicle*, 218. Trevor Rowley suggests that some assarting was not for arable but to provide for sheep; "Medieval Field Systems," in Leonard Cantor, ed., *The English Medieval Landscape*, 40.

20. The gentry, of course, would not have done the labor of assarting themselves and one novel disseisin lawsuit suggests how gentry assarts might have been made. In this case, the defendant stated that he claimed no fee in the land except that he should hold for two years that which he assarted through the grant and will of the plaintiff; *CRR* 3:89–90. Perhaps, then,

Georges Duby has argued that knights and other lay lords in the Mâconnais and France in general, whose demesnes were being eaten away by gifts to the Church, reconstructed these demesnes by assarting, by the end of the twelfth century often shifting their home farms away from the anciently cultivated lands to the fringes of cultivation.[21] A similar process may have been going on in Yorkshire, and although the evidence does not allow the historian to see what percentage of gentry demesne was made up of old lands and what percentage of assarts, newly cultivated land was obviously very important in the home farms of some landlords. John de Crigglestone, possibly a relative of the gentry family of that name, made an agreement with the Bishop of Durham about the estate he had built up in Howdenshire, an area where much land was being reclaimed from the marshes. John's estate consisted of ten bovates of what was probably anciently cultivated land, but it also included over 350 acres of arable in parcels ranging from three to 120 acres. One of these parcels is specifically identified as land that had been reclaimed; since newly cultivated land tended to be measured in acres rather than bovates, it is very likely that the rest of the parcels had been reclaimed as well, although not necessarily by John. Thus a very large percentage of John's estate was made up of new arable land.[22] Another document mentions one hundred acres assarted by Roger, brother of the Constable of Richmond, and this would have given him a good core around which to form a home farm.[23] Most assarts were smaller, containing five, ten, or twenty acres, but a few assarts of that size could make a healthy addition to any gentry demesne. Generalizations are difficult because the amount of assarting varied widely from area to area within Yorkshire, but assarting clearly contributed greatly to the construction or reconstruction of gentry demesnes in Yorkshire.

Other ways in which the gentry exploited more intensively the marshes, moorlands, and forests of Yorkshire are harder to trace. For instance, it is clear that there was a market in wood.[24] It is also clear that some members of the gentry had access to valuable tracts of timber and

---

gentry landholders granted out land for short terms in return for the labor of clearing it. They could also have relied on the labor of their famuli or on wage labor.

21. Georges Duby, *Rural Economy and Country Life in the Medieval West*, 82–83, 182–83; Duby, *La société mâconnaise*, 73.

22. The exact percentage would depend on the size of the bovates. Even if one assumed large bovates of twenty acres each, nearly two thirds of John's arable lands would have been in these parcels; Brown, "Pedes Finium Tempore Ricardi," 187.

23. *Yorkshire Deeds* 7:51–52.

24. See below for a discussion of gentry and the market in Angevin Yorkshire.

could exploit these. One member of a prominent family, Roger de Birkin, made a special agreement with the head of another prominent family, Thomas de Horbury, to cut down eighty oaks from their common wood. The agreement involved an exchange of land, showing how valuable these oaks were.[25] However, one cannot be certain whether the cutting of timber by gentry increased as gentry sought to exploit their land more intensively or decreased as more land was cleared for arable.[26] The odd pieces of evidence do not allow the creation of a coherent picture.

There is more evidence, however, for the increase of pastoral activities by the gentry. Cattle and sheep were very important sources of wealth, producing meat, hides, wool, milk, cheese, and manure, the most important fertilizer in medieval agriculture.[27] A lease granted by the dean and chapter of York to two farmers, one of them a knight, shows how valuable pastoral activities could be. This lease gave the farmers the manor of Cottam at a yearly rent of £12 but stated that the rent was to be raised to £18 if the manor were to be stocked with six hundred sheep.[28] Presumably the sheep brought even more income than £6, since the farmers would have wanted a profit and in a period in which Henry II demanded that those with sixteen marks purchase what was basically the armor and weapons of a knight (admittedly before the onset of the inflation of the late twelfth and early thirteenth century), this was no small sum.[29] Gentry frequently gave large stints of scores of cattle and hundreds of sheep to monasteries and this shows just how large the potential for profit was.[30]

Although the records of the period tell us far less about moveable chattels than about land, there are clear indications that at least some gentry were building up the size of their herds. In one agreement Adam de Boltby

25. *EYC* 8:214.

26. Of course the cutting of timber could be combined with the clearing of land, but only on a one time basis.

27. A number of agreements about the droppings of herds pastured in common fields shows that landlords in Angevin Yorkshire were aware of the value of manure. For some examples, see *EYC* 1:301–2; *EYC* 2:63; Atkinson, *Cartularium de Rievalle*, 79.

28. Charles Clay, ed., *York Minster Fasti* 2:103–4. Farms of £1 or two marks per one hundred sheep may be seen elsewhere; J. H. Round, ed., *Rotuli de Dominabus et Pueris et Puellis*, xxxiv; G. T. Lapsley, "Introduction to the Boldon Book," in *The Victoria History of the County of Durham* 1:301.

29. William Stubbs, ed., *Select Charters and Other Illustrations of English Constitutional History*, 183.

30. Examples of the largest gifts of this sort by gentry, gifts of pasture for between five hundred and one thousand sheep, include *EYC* 2:57, 60, 156, 496–97; *EYC* 3:309; *EYC* 5:79, 121, 237, 307–8; *EYC* 7:238–39, 252; *EYC* 10:168; *Sallay Cartulary* 2:7; Cotton MSS, Claudius D.XI, 195v; *Meaux Chronicle*, 430. There are dozens of gifts of pasture for smaller but still substantial numbers of animals.

and Robert Fossard, member of a cadet gentry branch of that baronial family, promised not to cultivate any of the common pasture that they shared with the Templars without the Templars' permission, but retained the right to build bercharies, or sheepfolds, wherever they pleased and without permission. This suggests that they were contemplating increasing their herds of sheep.[31] An agreement between William de Mowbray and Adam de Staveley over the latter's rights in William's forest near Lonsdale was almost certainly made because Adam was developing pastoral activities there on a relatively large scale. The agreement allowed Adam to keep three vaccaries already in existence, but forbade him from building any more and similarly forbade him from enclosing any more meadow than he had already enclosed.[32] These two examples of pastoral development were probably duplicated throughout Yorkshire.

Indeed, on one occasion, an increase in pastoral activity led to the creation of an entirely new village, Bainbridge, which was on the edge of the pre-1066 limit of settlement and probably well beyond the limit of settlement after the harrying of the North.[33] Various pieces of evidence show the emergence of a settlement out of wilderness. Bainbridge was in upper Wensleydale, which was afforested by the earls of Richmond and which was infested with wolves in Stephen's reign, a sure sign of sparse or nonexistent habitation.[34] The Middleham family, the most important vassals on the honor of Richmond, received the hereditary forestership of the earl's forest in Wensleydale from Duke Conan. At some point a settlement of foresters was established and this expanded quickly.[35] During John's reign, the abbot of Jervaulx brought a lawsuit against Ranulf son of Robert de Middleham, claiming various rights in the forest of Wensleydale and stating that Ranulf had built within the forest three vaccaries, one pig farm (porkeriam), and twenty-nine homes[36] from which two thousand sheep went out to pasture, and that he had plowed up certain pasture, showing the extent to which Bainbridge had grown.[37] The Middlehams may con-

31. Brown, *Pedes Finium Ebor.*, 160–62.

32. *Pleas* 3:136.

33. The editors of the Phillimore edition of *Domesday Book* suggest that the Domesday vill of Brough Hill was renamed Bainbridge. I suspect the change came because of discontinuity in settlement; Margaret L. Faull and Marie Stinson, *Domesday Book, Yorkshire*, note to 6N77.

34. Dugdale, *Monasticon* 5:572.

35. Gale, *Registrum Honoris de Richmond*, 101.

36. The abbot's claim refers to twenty-nine "domos focarias cum duabus familiis." This is somewhat obscure; *CRR* 7:123–24.

37. *CRR* 7:98; 123–24, 270–72, 278; John Parker, ed., *Feet of Fines of the County of York From 1218 to 1231*, 2–4. Despite the arable land present in the settlement, Bainbridge in this

currently have been founding some of the Coverdale vaccaries that figured among their possessions in the later thirteenth century.[38] The Middlehams were no ordinary vassal family, and would eventually enter the nobility, but what they did on a large scale, others could and did do on a smaller scale.

Yet another form of development, and one that was impressive in its own right, consisted of the building projects which some members of the gentry undertook. For instance, John de Meaux cooperated with the abbot of Meaux and several local landowners in building a boundary ditch and waterway in Holderness.[39] Similarly, William Constable of Flamborough promised Selby to make a bridge to provide access to one of the monastery's holdings.[40] Mills were the most popular building projects, which is not surprising, given their profitability. Mills were complex projects, involving not only the building itself, but the damming or diversion of water; often complex negotiations were required with other landlords whose lands might be affected by the construction of a pond or sluice. Detailed agreements about mills built by the gentry reveal this complexity.[41] The building of mills could involve important alterations to the landscape and sometimes the results of gentry building projects can still be seen. Bishop Hugh of Durham, in a grant of land in Blacktoft and Hook to Gilbert Hansard, also granted him the right to build a mill. The channel which Gilbert built to bring the water needed to power the mill still exists and is still known as Hansardam.[42] Some gentry were even using the new technology of windmills, showing their willingness to adopt innovations when these were available.[43] Building a mill was no easy matter, but at least a few

---

period seems to have been devoted mostly to pastoral activities. In a late thirteenth-century survey, Bainbridge, with the associated vaccaries in the forest (which had multiplied in the meantime), was worth an astonishing £280 a year, though this was after control had passed back to the earls of Richmond; *Yorkshire Inquisitions* 1:225–26; *Calendar of Inquisitions Post Mortem* 2:213–14.

38. *Calendar of Inquisitions Post Mortem* 1:237–38; *Yorkshire Inquisitions* 1:114–15.

39. *Report on the Historical Manuscripts of the late Reginald Rawdon Hastings, Esquire* 1:165–66.

40. *EYC* 12:72.

41. For one of the best examples, see York Minster Library, XVI.A.1:230–31. In another example, Arnold de Upsall charged Ralph de Belvoir the surprisingly high rent of one half mark a year for the right to make and use a sluice for what was presumably a new mill on Arnold's land. Being no one's fool, Arnold developed an effective strategy to prevent dilatory payment; if the rent was not paid within forty days of the day it was due, Arnold had the right to cut off the water to the mill. *EYC* 9:182–83.

42. *EYC* 2:314; June A. Sheppard, *The Draining of the Marshlands of South Holderness and the Vale of York*, 15.

43. W. T. Lancaster, ed., *Abstracts of the Charters and Other Documents Contained in the Chartulary of the Priory of Bridlington*, 80, 206. It should be noted that these charters show only the possession of windmills by gentry, and not their construction, but since windmill technol-

members of the gentry were willing to do so in return for the profit mills could bring.[44] Their willingness and ability to build mills shows their eagerness to gain new income and their economic savvy.

A final form of development, the enclosure of parks for hunting, was one that had more than just economic purposes. The meat obtained by hunting would have been an important source of protein for at least some gentry households, though it must often have been the case that park lands could have been used more profitably for other economic purposes. For the upper classes, however, hunting was not just an economic activity, but also a sport, and a means of developing at least some of the skills needed in battle, such as horsemanship and the use of some weapons. In addition, it was a social activity and a source of prestige. For all these reasons, the gentry of Angevin Yorkshire, like the upper classes throughout Europe in the Middle Ages and into the modern period, were enthusiastic hunters. One indication of their enthusiasm was the willingness of gentry to buy rights of warren from the king and their eagerness to obtain hunting rights in the forests of their lords.[45] This enthusiasm is also indicated by the number of gentry families who had parks, at least some of which were new.[46] Thomas de Etton created a park in Henry II's reign and Alan de Wilton created one in John's reign, in both cases with royal approval.[47] Though this form of development cannot be seen simply in economic terms, it shows the willingness and ability of the gentry to alter their estates and shape the landscape around them to suit their interests and purposes.

---

ogy seems to have emerged in England around the middle of the twelfth century, it is almost certain that the mills would have been built in the Angevin period, either by the gentry donors who gave them away or by their immediate predecessors. For a full account of windmills in England in this period, see Edward J. Kealey, *Harvesting the Air: Windmill Pioneers in Twelfth-Century England.*

44. For other instances in which gentry were building mills, see W. T. Lancaster and W. Paley Baildon, *The Coucher Book of the Cistercian Abbey of Kirkstall*, 87; York Minster Library, Hailstone Collection, 3.24; BL Add. MSS 32,113:11–12; John Rylands Library, Latin MS 251:22v; *CRR* 3:125.

45. For purchases and grants of warren, see *Rot. Chart.*, 51b, 66b, 90a, 122b; *Rot. Obl. & Fin.*, 68, 481; Cotton MSS, Claudius B.III, 57–58. For gentry hunting in forests controlled by barons, see *EYC* 1:398–99; *Pleas* 3:136.

46. *EYC* 3:371, 381–82; Cotton MSS, Vespasian E.XIX, 22; *EYC* 1:299; *Sallay Cartulary* 1:72; *EYC* 4:127; J. W. Walker, ed., *Abstracts of the Chartularies of the Priory of Monkbretton*, 163; Parker, *Feet of Fines, 1218–1231*, 31–32; Purvis, *Chartulary of Healaugh*, 93. Charters in the archives of the Constable family show that the Constables of Flamborough had parks in Flamborough and Holme on the Wolds. The catalogue dates these charters to 1260, but I would date them to the early thirteenth century; Humberside Record Office, DDCC/135/2, 1–4.

47. *EYC* 2:398; *Rot. Chart.*, 127b; *Pipe Roll 6 John*, 189. John also gave Robert Vavasour permission to make a new park if he desired; *Rot. Chart.*, 122b.

Charters, the greatest source of evidence for the economy of Angevin Yorkshire, generally show little about change on estates, acting more as snapshots than moving pictures of the economic scene. Striking testimony of the widespread nature of this change is the fact that so much evidence about development and change under the gentry survives. The gentry of Angevin Yorkshire may have been, in their own fashion, as active improvers as their successors in the early modern period. Unfortunately, it is difficult to know whether this interest in economic development was new. Certainly it appears in the sources for the first time in the Angevin period, but given the sharp rise in documentation, an argument from silence for the earlier period would be dangerous. It seems fairly clear that land was being redeveloped on gentry estates in the Norman period, for villages that were unpopulated in *Domesday Book* were later producing revenue, but what is not clear is whether the gentry themselves were playing an active role in the earlier period or simply left it to their tenants. In any case, they were certainly actively improving their estates in the Angevin period. As the generosity of magnates declined, economic development was the best opportunity most gentry had to increase their incomes.

How much the gentry succeeded in improving their fortunes through development must remain unknown, given the nature of the sources. Undoubtedly it varied from family to family, depending upon availability of opportunity and individual skill and interest. However, some families probably did quite well out of development. It is probably no accident that some of the families that later entered the nobility such as the Middlehams, the FitzHughs of Ravensworth, and the Meinils, held estates in the Pennine dales or on the edges of the North Yorkshire moors; these upland pastures, of little worth when Yorkshire was underdeveloped, could provide remarkable opportunities for the expansion of pastoral activities. The families listed above held unusually large estates, it is true, but the same possibilities for expansion could also exist for lesser families. The Askes held only one knight's fee in Swaledale, but in the late thirteenth century, even after they had granted away a large section to found Marrick priory, their estate produced the sizable annual income of £40 10 shillings.[48] Many of the gentry of the Angevin period, like their successors of later periods, shrewdly enriched themselves by taking advantage of opportunities for economic advancement.

48. *Yorkshire Inquisitions* 1:235.

The comparison of the gentry improvers of the Angevin period with their later successors, however, raises several historiographical issues. First, did economic development by gentry landlords lead to a reconstruction of agricultural arrangements and to tension between landlords and peasants as it did in later periods? Second, did market forces play a role in encouraging gentry development? Third, does the active involvement of gentry in development suggest that the gentry practiced direct management techniques and if so, did gentry landlords follow the pattern of magnates in switching from leasing to direct management in the late twelfth century? Unfortunately, the evidence does not permit conclusive answers to these questions, but it does provide enough material for partial or probable answers.

In the early modern period, enclosure was an important tool which landlords used to improve the profitability of their land. However, enclosure was often a great source of tension, for in some cases it involved depriving tenants of important rights of common and sometimes it even led to depopulation.[49] Did such tensions result from gentry development in Angevin Yorkshire? The possibility is certainly there, for many of the traditional agricultural practices that could be disrupted by enclosure were used in Yorkshire. Though in some areas of Yorkshire, land was held in severalty, in many areas open field farming was practiced. Moreover, there was a widespread system of share holding in which all landholders in a village received access to the pasture, woodland, turbaries, and even fishing areas they needed to obtain grazing, fuel, building materials, and even food in proportion to the number of bovates or carucates they held.[50] Thus Eudo de Bentley gave the hospital of St. Giles, Beverley, two bovates in Bentley and specified that they were to have the common pasture and easements pertaining to any other two bovates in the village.[51] An agreement between William de Barthorpe and Meaux Abbey stipulated that William and his men should have pasture throughout Wharram according to the size of their tenancies.[52] Indeed, since bovates varied in the number of acres they contained, they should probably be seen less as measurements

49. See Joan Thirsk, *The Agrarian History of England and Wales* 4:200–255, for a discussion of enclosure and the tensions it caused in the sixteenth and early seventeenth centuries.

50. See D. J. H. Michelmore, "The Reconstruction of the Early Tenurial and Territorial Divisions of the Landscape of Northern England," 7, for the need for access to a variety of resources and therefore types of land.

51. *EYC* 10:102. For a similar clause, see *EYC* 8:168.

52. *Meaux Chronicle*, 322. Similarly, Ralph de la Hay gave nine bovates or one fifth of his arable land in Spaldington and with it he gave one fifth of his wood there; *EYC* 12:90.

of land than as shares in the resources and fiscal responsibilities of the village.[53] Many gentry demesnes were part and parcel of this system, differing only in size from the lands of peasants.

In improving their lands, gentry often worked not against the traditional share holding system but within it. Entire villages sometimes assarted land communally. Several charters and agreements exist in which the possibility of this happening is mentioned and these documents make clear that the newly cleared area was divided up in proportion to the number of bovates each landholder in the village held. Thus, William de Spaldington gave North Ormsby a bovate and stated that if the boundaries of cultivated land in the village were extended, their bovate would be enlarged as much as those of the other tenants in the village.[54] A gift by William son of Hervey to Pontefract consisted of two bovates and the assarts pertaining to them, while another gentry charter mentions a half carucate with sixty acres plus ten new acres; in each of these cases assarting had already taken place.[55] Any member of the gentry who held a large demesne in a village that assarted in common would receive a commensurately large increment to his home farm.

Most gentry assarters, however, seem to have been working alone. I suspect that gentry, when they were the chief lords of individual villages, had a free hand in the disposition of unused or under-utilized lands. Early in Henry III's reign, the Statute of Merton gave magnates freedom to exploit waste lands without interference from tenants, as long as the tenants had sufficient pasture, and Coss has pointed out that this statute was also applied to knights and other manorial lords.[56] I would argue that this statute may have made legal what was already customary for or, at least practiced by landlords of sufficient power to dominate a village in the Angevin period. Gentry gave blocks of land within specified boundaries, sometimes cultivated, sometimes not, to monasteries and in one case from

53. For the variation in the size of bovates and similar units in Yorkshire and elsewhere, see June A. Sheppard, "Field Systems of Yorkshire," 173; Faull and Moorhouse, *West Yorkshire* 2:240–41; Andrew Jones, "Land Measurement in England, 1150–1350," 10–18; F. M. Stenton, *Documents Illustrative of the Social and Economic History of the Danelaw*, xxviii-xxx. For the idea that units such as bovates, virgates, carucates and hides represented shares of a village's resources, see Paul Vinogradoff, *Villainage in England*, 233–36, 262–63, 317; Robert Dodgshon "The Landholding Foundations of the Open-Field System," 3–29, and *The Origin of British Field Systems: An Interpretation*, 34–41, 49–53, 151–52.
54. F. M. Stenton, ed., *Transcripts of Charters Relating to the Gilbertine Houses of Sixle, Ormsby, Catley, Bullington and Alvingham*, 62–63. For similar agreements, see *EYC* 1:380–81; *EYC* 11:270; *Fountains Cartulary* 1:182; *Yorkshire Deeds* 7:82–83; *Yorkshire Deeds* 9:169–70.
55. *EYC* 3:357; *EYC* 2:65.
56. *The Statutes of the Realm* 1:2; Coss, *Lordship, Knighthood and Locality*, 105–6.

just before the Angevin period the block was explicitly stated as being drawn from the waste.[57] They sometimes gave monasteries large stints in the common fields of their villages that were unconnected with holdings in the village, as when Thomas Boniface granted Kirkham pasture in Kirby Grindalythe for three hundred sheep *in addition* to the pasture pertaining to the monastery's ten bovates there.[58] In such gifts there is no reference to obtaining the permission of tenants, which one would have expected if such permission were required. If gentry lords could set aside land and pasture for monasteries in such fashion they could probably set aside land and pasture for their own home farms.

Independent development of waste lands by lords would not have seriously disrupted traditional agricultural institutions so long as lords left enough such land to supply the needs of tenants, as the Statute of Merton later demanded concerning pasture. The widespread existence of peasant assarts, indicated in the sources by the frequent identification of an assart with the name of an individual peasant, shows that peasants, far from facing an economic threat from gentry economic development, had room for expansion themselves. This may explain why although there are cases of struggle over common lands between gentry and other powerful landlords, there is little if any evidence of struggle between gentry lords and their own tenants over such lands.[59] Basically, there appears to have been enough land to go around. Gentry could get rents and payments from peasant assarts and could benefit indirectly from peasant development through increased use of mills and other seigniorial monopolies and were thus unlikely to challenge peasant land development.[60] As long as their own livelihoods were not being threatened, peasants were not likely to challenge powerful gentry lords over the exploitation of wasteland.

57. *EYC* 9:166. Dozens of grants of land in specific boundaries survive and though some may have been held in severalty long before the grant, I suspect that many others were recently carved out of unused lands. For some typical examples of such grants, in addition to the one given above, see *EYC* 2:86, 242–43, 351, 387–88; *EYC* 3:236, 248, 261, 309–10, 334, 369–70, 453–54.

58. *EYC* 2:386. Unfortunately, gifts of pasture for set numbers of animals are rarely so specific as this, but since the gifts of pasture are often far larger than the land given would seem to warrant (for instance, *EYC* 2:60, where a gift of thirty acres is accompanied by pasture in the common for one thousand sheep), it seems likely that Boniface was merely spelling out what was a common practice. See above, note 30, for references to some of the largest gifts of pasture land.

59. For examples of disputes between landlords, see *EYC* 9:155–56, 238–42; *Yorkshire Deeds* 6:54; *CRR* 1:379.

60. For rents and payments to gentry from peasant assarts, see *EYC* 3:121, 384; *Fountains Cartulary* 2:698.

Another controversial issue in the early modern period was engrossing, the practice of buying or otherwise obtaining small holdings and using them to create or enhance a large estate. Eleanor Searle argues that from the late twelfth century, knights, monasteries, and other lords had begun engrossing peasant holdings in the newly settled area of the Sussex Weald. In Yorkshire, gentry sometimes gained control of peasant assarts, for they often gave away assarts that were identified by the name of a person and while sometimes such assarts were tenanted lands, in other cases they were clearly part of the demesne. Thus Hippolitus de Braham, in a gift to the hospital of St. Peter, York, listed the assart of Warin within what was clearly part of his home farm.[61] However, there is no evidence of engrossing on a systematic basis in Yorkshire, and while this lack of evidence might stem from the nature of the sources, I suspect that it actually reflects the fact that in Yorkshire in the Angevin period there was still plenty of land to go around. Gentry landlords simply did not have to engross the lands of others.

More work needs to be done on the influence of assarting and other forms of development on agrarian organization and social structures in this period; the conclusions given here must remain tentative. That said, I would argue that development in this period went on either within the framework of traditional agrarian institutions or, when development was carried out independently of these institutions, without serious disruption to them. Access to large amounts of waste land allowed the gentry of Angevin Yorkshire to be as active improvers as later gentry without having to disrupt traditional agrarian institutions to the same degree.

The second major question raised by gentry economic development concerns the influence of market forces. Economic development can take place in the absence of such forces, for instance, through population growth, but economic historians have long stressed the importance of markets and commercial exchange in explaining how and why economies developed. Recently, Mark Bailey has done an excellent job of demonstrating the importance of market forces in the development of the East Anglian Breckland, an area, like large parts of Yorkshire, of late development.[62] Did market forces enable and inspire the gentry of Angevin Yorkshire to develop and more fully exploit their lands?

61. Hippolitus first listed six bovates of what was probably tenant land and then added his hall with its toft and croft, the assart of Warin and two bovates from his demesne; *EYC* 1:56–57.
62. Mark Bailey, *A Marginal Economy? East Anglian Breckland in the Later Middle Ages.*

The evidence does not allow this question to be answered directly, but it does show that gentry had access to and used regional and international markets for produce. York had been a center of international trade since at least the Viking age, and the settlement of a Jewish community there testified to its continuing economic importance. The growth of other towns throughout the county suggests the importance of regional and in some cases long distance trade at these centers as well. Members of the gentry had many interests in urban centers. At least twenty-seven gentry families held property in York.[63] The extent of gentry interests in York may be seen from the fact that two knights, John de Meaux and Robert Vavasour, could dispute the ownership of half the advowson of a church there.[64] Indeed, the street called Davygate takes its name from the fact that David Lardiner, the king's lardiner in York but also a knight, lived there and held land in the area.[65] Members of the gentry also held land in other smaller boroughs, including Richmond, Pontefract, Beverley, Doncaster, Ripon, Scarborough, Thirsk, and Hedon.[66] Chapter one has shown that these urban interests were not always economic in origin, but sometimes honorial. Nevertheless, urban property would have given many gentry families the urban contacts which could have exposed them to the wider commercial world within and beyond Yorkshire.

Such contact did not necessarily mean that the gentry would be involved in the selling of grain, wool, and other commodities, but despite the lack of surviving records for trade there are strong indications that they did produce for the market and that markets had permeated the Yorkshire countryside as a whole. The predominance of money rent in surviving charters shows the importance of cash and indicates the access of all levels of society to markets. The frequent use of pepper and cumin for the symbolic rents found in charters granting land to family members or others from whom the donor did not wish to draw a full economic rent shows how far into Yorkshire society the international spice trade reached.[67] Unfortunately, the evidence tells us little about specific production for the market by

63. See Appendix two for families holding property in York.

64. Brown, *Pedes Finium Ebor.*, 37.

65. *EYC* 1:197. Cotton MSS Nero D.III, a cartulary of St. Leonard's hospital, contains several references to property in "vico David le Lardiner" or "David gate Lardiner"; 113.

66. *CRR* 6:328; Egerton MSS 2827:252; *EYC* 3:217–18, 249–51, 294, 315; Brown, "Pedes Finium Tempore Ricardi," 177; *EYC* 2:336; Brown, *Pedes Finium Ebor.*, 21, 36; *Fountains Cartulary* 2:589; *EYC* 11:239–40, 344–45; Bodleian Library, Rawlinson MSS B455, 26v-27r; English, *Lords of Holderness*, 218–19.

67. For two examples of spice rents, see *EYC* 5:135; Brown, *Pedes Finium Ebor.*, 74–75.

members of the gentry, because no mercantile records or estate accounts from the period survive, but a few scraps of evidence can be found. In the pipe roll of John's fourth year, three men of Appleby, probably merchants, made a proffer to have royal help in collecting a debt of £100, fifty-two quarters of grain, and seventeen stones of wool from Jervaulx Abbey and several individuals, including the knight William Engelram; Helena daughter of Alan, heiress of a gentry family, the Allerstons; and the heirs (presumably Helena's children) of her husband, Hugh de Hastings.[68] In that same year, the widow and daughters of William le Tanur, who was probably a merchant as well as a tanner, also proffered money for certain debts in goods and money. These included six marks from Elias de Flamville for wool (presumably Elias had been given an advance and had not yet delivered the wool) and one hundred shillings from Robert de Meinil; both Flamville and Meinil were members of the gentry.[69] The prioress of Kirklees complained that the knight William Fleming had sold wood from woodland that his father had given to the Priory, and agreements about woodland generally included a clause about whether wood could be given away or sold by the parties involved.[70] Taken together, these fragments of information indicate that at least some members of the gentry were selling grain, wood, and wool to merchants. It is impossible to know how much of a role market forces were playing in gentry development, but it seems likely that it was an important one.

The third issue is that of management, that is, whether the gentry were directly managing their own demesnes in the system known as demesne or high farming or leasing them out to "farmers."[71] If the latter was the case, the question must be raised whether landlords or farmers were more responsible for improvements to gentry estates. The evidence clearly shows that both forms of estate management were available to gentry. The sources reveal a number of examples of gentry leasing land out, sometimes for lengthy terms of up to sixty years, but many of these leases consisted of small parcels rather than entire estates, and thus did not preclude the

68. *Pipe Roll 4 John*, 63–64.
69. *Pipe Roll 4 John*, 65.
70. *Yorkshire Eyre*, 176. Examples of agreements about selling wood include *EYC* 3:381–82; *EYC* 9:156; Holmes, *Chartulary of Pontefract* 1:280. In one case concerning the division of woodland, there was a prohibition against selling any wood before the division was made; *Pleas* 1:302.
71. In this context, the term farmer refers to a person who managed agricultural operations on a demesne farm and paid a fixed sum each year to the landlord, keeping any excess profits for himself.

possibility that the lessor was directly managing other lands.[72] The direct evidence for high farming by the gentry is spottier, but in this period before regular written accounts were generally kept one would *expect* to find less evidence for direct management among the gentry. Examples of gentry who managed their demesne farms can be found, however, such as the knight who in a gift of a voluntary second tithe from two estates made arrangements *in case* the estates were leased out to a farmer, indicating that he was managing them himself when he made the gift.[73]

In addition to such isolated examples, there is indirect evidence for high farming by the gentry. First, a number of gentry leased parcels and estates for specific terms of years from other landlords.[74] Their activity as lessees shows that at least some gentry had the skills and knowledge to run agricultural estates and indicates that it was socially acceptable for gentry to be involved in direct agricultural management. If these gentry were farming other people's estates, they were probably managing their own. Second, the evidence also shows that some gentry had small administrative structures to help manage their estates. Adam de Wennerville and Geoffrey Haget both referred in charters to payments from their "camera" or treasury.[75] Many references to the stewards, bailiffs, foresters, and reeves of gentry land-holders survive.[76] Nigel de Plumpton had both a steward and a marshal and may have had other officers as well.[77] Some gentry even had access to the services of a person capable of writing, though this may have been no more than the local priest.[78] Of course, agricultural affairs are not the only reason

72. For shorter terms of six, seven, eight, thirteen, or seventeen years, see *EYC* 10:132; *CRR* 1:392–93; *Fountains Cartulary* 1:11; Egerton MSS 2827:133; *EYC* 11:258. For longer leases, in which multiples of twenty years seem to have been common, see *EYC* 1:487–88; *Yorkshire Eyre*, 43; *Meaux Chronicle*, 231.

73. *EYC* 5:284.

74. *EYC* 2:131–32; *EYC* 5:109–11; *EYC* 7:248; *EYC* 8:215; *Pleas* 3:143; *CRR* 3:6–7; Humberside Record Office, DDCC/141/68, 14, 19; *Report on Hastings Manuscripts*, 167–68. See *EYC* 11:136, in which an agreement was made that if Sallay leased land, it would do so to Robert Vavasour. A few gentry held some or all of their lands in fee-farm; for some large hereditary farms, see *EYC* 1:292, 348; *EYC* 3:379; *EYC* 12:42, 50. These families undoubtedly at least started out managing the lands themselves, though there is no guarantee that they continued to do so over the course of generations. See Du Boulay, *The Lordship of Canterbury*, 99–100, for some contemporary or near contemporary examples of gentry as lessees and Searle, *Lordship and Community*, 334–36, for a later example.

75. *EYC* 1:193; *EYC* 3:262–63.

76. *Meaux Chronicle*, 303–4; *CRR* 6:120; *Yorkshire Eyre*, 145, 149, 161, 269, 371–72; *CRR* 1:392–93; *EYC* 1:169–70; *EYC* 12:92; *Fountains Cartulary* 1:18–19; Atkinson *Cartularium de Whiteby* 1:209–10; Cotton MSS, Claudius B.III, 57–58; *CRR* 1:379.

77. *EYC* 11:271–72; Dodsworth MSS 148:3.

78. Evidence survives that gentry were using written documents to convey messages, but there is no indication who was writing these documents; Cotton MSS, Claudius D.XI, 58;

for having administrative officials. Nevertheless, direct management would have greatly increased the demand for estate officials and the frequent use of such officials points to the employment of that practice.

Unfortunately, the evidence for both leasing and demesne farming is scanty, anecdotal, and often indirect in nature, and there is insufficient evidence to determine which predominated. Moreover, there is too little evidence to see whether or not a chronological shift occurred in management practice. It is well established that in the late twelfth century magnates moved from a system of leasing to direct management.[79] However, one cannot assume that because such a shift occurred among magnates, it necessarily occurred among the gentry, or indeed that the gentry relied on leasing earlier in the twelfth century. Even in later periods that were unfavorable to demesne farming, gentry families often directly exploited at least one demesne farm, and Edward Miller suggests that knights used direct management from the time they ceased to be professional full-time warriors.[80] More information is needed to provide certain answers about how gentry generally managed their lands in this period but sufficient evidence will only be obtained by casting the net more widely than one county.

To the extent that farmers managed gentry estates, they undoubtely had some role in improvements on those estates, but ultimately, of course, the gentry would have been involved to some degree in improvements on their lands whether they used direct management or leasing. Farmers would have needed permission to make any large scale changes, and at the very least gentry would have had to make any arrangements involving other landlords or the royal government. Moreover, though farmers might make minor changes that would pay off quickly, few would have had the capital or sufficient hope for long term profit to carry out large scale projects independently. For such projects as the building of mills or large increases in pastoral activities, the gentry landlords must have been closely involved. Leasing might reduce the direct involvement of gentry in improving their lands, but it could not eliminate it.

Humberside Record Office, DDCC/141/68, 14; York Minster Library, Registrum Magnum Album, L 2/1, 1:404.

79. Reginald Lennard, *Rural England, 1086–1135*, 105–212; Edward Miller, "England in the Twelfth and Thirteenth Centuries: An Economic Contrast?" 1–14; P. D. A. Harvey, "The Pipe Rolls and the Adoption of Demesne Farming in England," 345–59; A. R. Bridbury, "The Farming Out of Manors," 503–20; M. M. Postan, "A Note on the Farming Out of Manors," 521–25; *The Cambridge Economic History of Europe*, 585–87.

80. Susan Wright, *The Derbyshire Gentry*, 14–16; Bennett, *Community, Class and Career-ism*, 86; Miller, "An Economic Contrast?" 12.

The gentry were clearly not passive players but rather active participants in the economic changes and developments of their time. Many
improved their fortunes through clearing land, increasing herds, and building mills. Some, at least, were active managers of their own lands or the
estates of others. The evidence collected in this chapter suggests that the
gentry as a whole were economically quite active. This raises questions
about the postulated "crisis of the knightly class" and the theory that the
knightly class underwent this crisis because it was not able to adapt to
changing economic circumstances. However, other factors such as the
alienation of land to cadet lines and to the church also played a role in the
economic fortunes of the gentry. As a result, a full discussion of gentry
prosperity, and of the postulated crisis of the knightly class in the thirteenth
century, must wait until chapter six. The intervening chapters will discuss
the family life and piety of the gentry and the resulting shifts in the
distribution of land in Angevin Yorkshire.

4. Family and Household Among the Gentry

Not long after the murder of Thomas Becket, according to two Canterbury hagiographers, the house of Jordan son of Essulf, ancestor of an important gentry family, the Thornhills, was visited by a serious disease which afflicted many members of the household. The nurse of one of Jordan's sons died and the son himself, a boy about ten, was thought dead and laid out for burial. The family kept vigil over the body throughout the night, awaiting a priest. "Concerning the immoderate grief of the relatives," wrote one Canterbury monk, Benedict, "I will remain silent, for even the simple could imagine it." When the priest did come, however, Jordan postponed the burial, hoping to use water which pilgrims had just brought from Becket's shrine to bring about a miracle. He bid the rather skeptical priest pour the water into the boy's mouth. When hours more of waiting produced no result, the priest, who was beginning to doubt Jordan's sanity, urged him to let the burial take place, but Jordan did not give up. Jordan pried the boy's teeth apart with a knife and poured more of the holy water into his mouth, whereupon his faith was rewarded and the boy revived. Whatever one makes of the precise truth of this story (see Appendix three for a discussion of this issue), it provides a rare and vivid image of the powerful emotions that might be roused by the death of a family member.[1]

Neither the power of these emotions nor the fact that family and household were key elements in gentry society is likely to surprise many historians. In any society, ties of kinship and family are of paramount importance. Human beings, unless separated from their kin at an early age, are shaped by the emotional relations, intellectual perceptions, structure, and status of their families. Larger households and followings that contain non-relatives are less universal, but among elites these too have their importance. Thus, it is not surprising that medievalists as well as historians of

1. Robertson and Sheppard, *Materials* 1:160–62, 2:229–34. See Charles Clay, "The Family of Thornhill," 286–321, for a summary of the story and an account of Jordan's family.

other periods have shown increasing interest in family and household in recent decades. This chapter discusses these institutions among the gentry of Angevin Yorkshire.

This chapter begins with an overview of family and household among the Angevin gentry and continues with a discussion of the support that both heads of household and all family members received from these institutions. It follows with an analysis of the patterns of gentry alienation to non-inheriting family members and to followers and ends with a discussion of the effects of this on the structure of landholding and on local society in general.

The family structure predominant among the gentry of Angevin Yorkshire fits the broad patterns found among medieval elites in the later centuries of the Middle Ages. There is a widespread perception among historians of the Continent that in the tenth, eleventh, and twelfth centuries there was a movement, at various times in various places, from a relatively amorphous kinship structure to lineages that were structured around castles and patrimonies.[2] J. C. Holt has argued convincingly that the Norman Conquest brought this change to England.[3] It is true that in terms of the passage of land from one generation to the next, the gentry of Angevin Yorkshire differed both from the continental patterns, especially those reconstructed by Georges Duby, and from the patterns found later in England, a point that will be discussed below. In other respects, however, the structure of Yorkshire gentry families of the Angevin period was similar to later patterns, with an emphasis on what is now called the nuclear family and a firm sense of lineage.

The emphasis on lineage can be seen from the use of surnames, in many cases adopted during this period, from patterns among the use of forenames, and from the frequent reference to *antecessores* and *successores* in donations to the church. It would be an oversimplification to describe surnames simply as a symbol of the importance of lineage, and historians may sometimes be too eager to point to the adoption of surnames as a sign of changing family structure, but clearly surnames do point to a sense of family and lineage, whether or not it was new.[4] So too does the common

2. For a good overview on this in English, see David Herlihy, *Medieval Households*, 82–98.

3. J. C. Holt, "Feudal Society and the Family in Early Medieval England: I. The Revolution of 1066," 193–212.

4. When the Malebisse family adopted its name, as discussed in chapter two, it was not simply expressing its sense of unity, but also creating an image of itself. The many cadet branches of the Percys which retained the name of Percy were not focusing on their own

practice of naming eldest sons after paternal grandfathers and second sons after their fathers.[5] As their references to *antecessores* and *successores* show, the Yorkshire gentry perceived themselves as part of a kin group or lineage that extended both backwards and forwards in time.

The nuclear configuration of the family can be seen, in the absence of any surveys or censuses which would give exact statistics for family structure, from a mass of incidental evidence. Husbands, wives, parents, children, and siblings constantly appear together in documents, but more distant relatives are rarely linked. Time and time again, it was members of the immediate family who acted together or for one another, whether in feuds, religious matters or other aspects of life.[6] The nuclear family was the key kinship grouping in this society. Moreover, though ties between parents and children continued after the latter became adults, married children lived apart. A set of two distinct but related documents allow us to see a new gentry household being established at the time of a wedding. In one, the couple received a typical marriage portion for the gentry of one half carucate from the bride's brother, Roger Scot of Calverley. The bride and the groom, Geoffrey de Arthington, also received one carucate with four agricultural tenants from the groom's father Peter, whose heir he was. Clearly he was being given an advance on his inheritance so that the couple could set up a household of their own.[7] Thus, in each generation a new nuclear family was created.

Of course, the predominance of the nuclear family did not prevent wider kinship ties from having some importance. Uncles could be particularly influential, especially in the absence of a father, and instances can be found of uncles advising nephews, raising them even though the father

specific lineage and patrimony but were rather calling attention to their connection with their distant but powerful cousins. These cases show that surnames could have more than one purpose. See also Newman, *Anglo-Norman Nobility*, 38–39, for problems in using names to identify family structure.

5. See Constance B. Bouchard, "The Structure of a Twelfth-Century French Family: The Lords of Seignelay," 47–49. Newman does not see the use of such naming patterns in the Norman period; Newman, *Anglo-Norman Nobility*, 39. However, they certainly existed among the gentry of the Angevin period in Yorkshire, and apparently in Lincolnshire as well; Wales, "The Knight," 231–33.

6. In view of the use of the *Libri Vitae* as one of the chief sources to demonstrate the widespread nature of kinship ties in early medieval Europe, it is interesting that the Yorkshire knight, Roald son of Alan, appears in the *Liber Vita* of Durham with his nuclear family, consisting of his wife, son and daughter. Unfortunately, the appearances in this volume of Yorkshire gentry of the Angevin period are far too few to make any broad or systematic study; *Liber Vita Ecclesiae Dunelmensis*, 45.

7. *EYC* 3:310; Dodsworth MSS 92:55. See *Meaux Chronicle*, 359, for a more generous provision made so an heir could grant dower lands to his bride when he married.

was alive, or purchasing their wardships after their fathers' deaths, presumably to prevent greedy strangers from doing the same and exploiting their position to the harm of the nephew.[8] More distant kin could also have ties, especially when kinship and service were mixed, as when William de Bosville served his gentry kinswomen Denise de Tilly and her husband Henry du Puiset as steward and frequently as an attorney.[9] Occasionally, wider kin groups could act in concert; one example from a more elevated social group than the gentry comes from the dispute over the Archbishopric of York in Stephen's reign, when Fountains Abbey, which supported Henry Murdac, was attacked by a large band of knights from the "cognatione" of Henry's rival, William FitzHerbert; given the size of the band it presumably included more than FitzHerbert's immediate family.[10]

Connections by marriage could also have influence. At the very least marriage could make peace between families. When a settlement was arranged by friends and relatives between two members of the gentry, Arnold de Upsall and Adam Fossard, who had been disputing possession of some woodland, part of the agreement involved Arnold marrying a sister of Adam. Thereafter, apparently, the two lived in peace.[11] It was clearly believed that marriage bonds could sharply alter the relationship between two families.

Undoubtedly, were our sources fuller, we would see other types of connections beyond the nuclear family, such as the sorts of social introductions, visiting, and exchanges of favors so common among the aristocratic in-laws and relatives of later periods.[12] Undoubtedly the gentry valued good connections to powerful people by blood or marriage and found them useful in their affairs. Nevertheless, distant ties of kinship were far less important than those within the nuclear family. One might occasionally

8. For an uncle influencing his nephew, see *Meaux Chronicle*, 311. For an uncle raising his nephew, see *EYC* 5:318–19; For the purchase of wardships, see *Pipe Roll 7 Henry II*, 37; *Pipe Roll 11 Henry II*, 48; *Pipe Roll 14 Henry II*, 92; *Pipe Roll 2 Richard I*, 67. For the importance of uncles, and particularly maternal uncles, in the Norman period, see Newman, *Anglo-Norman Nobility*, 51–52.

9. *CRR* 1:104, 331; *CRR* 3:93, 113; *EYC* 8:148. William also acted as attorney for Denise's mother, Mabel; *CRR* 2:234. For a similar case of a member of the gentry acting as steward for a powerful kinswoman, see *EYC* 1:413, 416, 431.

10. Hugh of Kirkstall, "Narratio de Fundatione Fontanis," 101. The importance of kin groups in the invasion of Ireland can be seen clearly from Gerald of Wales' account of that invasion and of the role of his own kindred in it; Gerald of Wales, *Expugnatio Hibernica: The Conquest of Ireland*.

11. *EYC* 9:155. For a similar instance in which a dispute was settled partly by marriage, see *EYC* 2:422.

12. See Wales, "The Knight," 242, for his argument that marriage among knights strengthened extra-feudal bonds among neighbors and the class as a whole.

receive favors and benefits from distant kin, but one could really rely only on parents, siblings, and children. Thus, the gentry of Angevin Yorkshire conform to kinship patterns associated with the later Middle Ages, and were not members of the widespread clans or kindreds historians have described for earlier periods.

In many ways the gentry had closer though very different bonds to the chief members of their households than to cousins and in-laws.[13] After all, they interacted with their household on a daily basis. The closeness of these bonds will be seen from the evidence for household cooperation and for generosity to followers seen later in the chapter. Gentry households would have been composed of a variety of people in addition to the family. The greater part of the household would have consisted of ordinary servants such as maids, carters, and laborers. Above them would have been the estate officials, such as stewards and bailiffs, mentioned in chapter three. Some prominent members of the gentry also seem to have had squires, sergeants, and even knights in their following.[14]

A final aspect of family and household in Angevin Yorkshire worth noting is that they were patriarchal and that male heads of household ruled firmly. This is illustrated most forcefully in the Canterbury miracle story concerning Jordan son of Essulf and his family. Jordan is the central figure throughout the story and indeed is described as paterfamilias. It is he who makes all the decisions, not only to seek the miracle, but later to delay a pilgrimage which he had sworn in thanksgiving and, after illness struck his household a second time (a sign of the saint's displeasure), to fulfill his vow. When Jordan finally decided to go to Canterbury, he overruled his wife's protests that she was too sick and said, "Living or dead, we will both come to the martyr. I will either go living or be carried dead. My wife will either be led alive or brought deceased." An even more interesting indication of Jordan's standing comes from some of the apparently unconscious assumptions of the hagiographers. Not only were Jordan and his wife struck by the second round of disease for failure to fulfill his vow, but most of his household were as well. The Canterbury hagiographers saw nothing odd

13. I am including estate officials and military followers in my discussion of the household although one cannot always be certain that they lived with their lords. Most of them *would* have lived with their lords and even those who did not would have been closely involved with the household. When I speak of military followers I am not referring to all those who held by knight's service of gentry, but only to those who actively served with a member of the class.

14. For the sergeants of Torfin son of Robert, see *Pipe Roll 21 Henry II*, 165. For the squires of Richard Malebisse and William de Percy of Carnaby, see *Pipe Roll 4 Richard I*, 221. For the knights of Ranulf son of Robert, see *CRR* 2:237; *CRR* 4:202.

about this; just as an entire kingdom could be punished for the sins of a king, so too could a family and household be punished for the sins of its head. Just as a king had a special relationship to his people, so too a lord had a special relationship with his household.[15] That Jordan, as depicted by the hagiographers, was not unique in ruling over his family can be seen from the control by fathers over the marriages of their children and also by their extensive rights over the lands of their wives. A vivid illustration of pa-triarchal power comes from a statement by Walter de Percy in which he disputed a gift made by his mother, Agnes de Flamville, saying that if it had been made at all, it had been made only on her deathbed, when she was "under the rod" of her second husband, Walter's stepfather, John de Bir-kin.[16] John probably did not mean this literally, for the phrase was very common; but even so, the use of a phrase so redolent with violence is striking and anyway this case, similar cases, and the related laws, show the power of husbands over wives.[17] Families varied and obviously much depended on the personalities involved; a couple described in one of the *curia regis rolls* as "Herbert de St. Quintin and Sir Agnes his virago" (Sire Agnetem suam viraginem) may have had a more equal relationship than the average gentry couple, but the very fact that a writer of the normally terse records of royal justice was moved to provide such a description shows that "Sir" Agnes was hardly typical.[18] This was a society that gave authority to the paterfamilias, and that authority in turn gave gentry heads of house-holds power that could be used outside of as well as within the household.

In fact, the descriptions of family and household given above include little if anything that is surprising. The Angevin period was not a time of revolutionary change in family structure. The lack of change in families and households, however, should not be allowed to conceal the importance of these institutions. Honorial ties may have disintegrated but family ties did not. This meant that family and household continued to be among the key elements in society.[19] Of course, much of the importance of the family and household would have rested in the mundane and everyday, the raising of

15. Robertson and Sheppard, *Materials* 1:160–62, 2:229–34.
16. *Yorkshire Eyre*, 407.
17. For similar cases, see *Yorkshire Eyre*, 69, 178; for law see Hall, *Glanvill*, 60, 64–65, 76. In practice, the ability of husbands to alienate the land of wives varied; Pollock and Maitland, *History of English Law* 2:410–11.
18. *CRR* 2:323.
19. For the importance of family connections and also their limitations, see J. C. Holt, "Feudal Society and the Family in Early Medieval England: III. Patronage and Patrimony," 1–25.

children, the performance of daily chores, and the sharing of shelter and food. These institutions were so important simply because they were so ordinary and so pervasive. Such ordinary aspects of household life, however, were not generally deemed to be worth recording in a period in which writing was a rare and special skill, though one can get glimpses of the everyday economic services of the household. Evidence for the importance of family and household in other areas is more likely to come from moments of crisis. When gentry were involved in violent disputes or when death threatened or the passage to heaven needed to be eased, family and household support came to the fore.

An important source of gentry power was violence, as the second chapter has shown, and the gentry of Angevin Yorkshire lived in a violent milieu. In such a setting, well-armed family members and household members could prove very useful. Family cooperation can be seen in a number of disputes against outsiders. For instance, the knight Hugh de Verly and his two sons assaulted one man and burned his house down and the same sons, with their mother, led a band that murdered another unfortunate.[20] If family members did not actively participate in lawless acts, they might help relatives face the consequences of such acts by giving them shelter, helping them in legal difficulties, standing as pledges for them, or, as Nigel de Plumpton did for his brother, Gilbert, purchasing their freedom from jail.[21] Family members, in short, often went to great lengths to look after their own.

When members of the gentry turned to violence, they also called upon members of their households. A dispute over woodland between two Yorkshire worthies, Adam de Beeston and William Gramary, led to William putting Adam's forester in the stocks. When Adam rode to William's house to arrange for the forester's release, he met with the same fate, whereupon Adam's man Liulf, along with Adam's brother Alan, rode to the rescue, only to be assaulted by William's relatives (perhaps brothers) Ralph and Robert Gramary, the latter of whom was a priest, and by Lucas, David son of Durand, and Gilbert Carter. The last three cannot be identified, but they were probably servants of William (a carter, for instance, would have been

---

20. *RCR* 2:98, 103; *CRR* 1:49. For other acts of violence in which gentry were aided by family members, see *RCR* 2:12–13; *CRR* 1:379; *CRR* 7:340; *Pleas* 4:103–4; *Rot. Litt. Claus*, 396.

21. For a father giving a son shelter after the son committed murder, see *Yorkshire Eyre*, 194; for a brother securing the release before trial of another accused murderer, see *Yorkshire Eyre*, 370; for relatives standing as pledges after crimes, see *Yorkshire Eyre*, 95, 169–70, 377; for the Plumptons, see *Pipe Roll 2 Richard I*, 66.

useful in a gentry household).[22] Thus a dispute between two men came to involve not only members of their family but retainers as well. There are a number of other instances where men identified as followers or with names suggesting they were officials or servants of gentry landlords became involved with their lords in disputes. For instance, when Ralph Mauleverer and his brother Nicholas were accused of killing Ralph Follifoot, two of their four accomplices were Gilbert Carpenter and Reiner Forester.[23] In a number of novel disseisin cases, gentry landholders were accused as the first in a group which included both kinsmen and servants.[24] Perhaps the most blatant example, however, is the case discussed at length in chapter two of Malger Vavasour who led or sent his steward and others out to ambush the followers of an enemy.[25] The ability of gentry to coerce others came not just from their possession of arms or military training, but also from their ability to call upon bands of family members and retainers to back them up.

In the religious sphere, it was the family alone that played a prominent role in protecting and advancing the salvation of the souls of the gentry.[26] For medieval believers, one's relationship with God and the saints was a grave and immediate concern, affecting both life and afterlife. As the story of Jordan son of Essulf's sickness showed, contemporaries believed that one's health could depend very heavily on supernatural favor or disfavor. Even more important than pleas for one's health and prosperity, however, were pleas and prayers on behalf of the dead, who according to religious teachings faced either salvation or an eternity of punishment and whose fate their kin hoped to influence. It was widely believed that the prayers of the living, and especially of monks, nuns, and regular canons, could help the souls of both the living and the dead. Donors often gave land to religious houses for this purpose, and while they usually requested prayers for their own souls, they often requested prayers or other benefits for the souls of their relatives as well. Such requests were frequently couched in very general terms, stating that the gift was for the benefit of the donor's ancestors, successors, or relatives (*antecessores, successores,* or *parentes* respectively). In some cases, however, the donor specified one or more relatives by name and sometimes a gift was closely connected with the death of a

22. *CRR* 1:379; *Pipe Roll 3 John*, 160.
23. *CRR* 7:340.
24. *CRR* 6:331–32; *Yorkshire Eyre*, 15, 25.
25. *Yorkshire Eyre*, 268–70. See also chapter two.
26. The household might, however, worship with the gentry in the private chapels of the latter. See chapter five.

relative. On the day that Robert de Lascelles was buried, for instance, his brother John gave a bovate of land to Selby Abbey, in return for which the monks were to perform the same sort of anniversary service they would perform for a monk every year.[27] Thus family solidarity lasted even beyond the grave, and individuals could expect support from their close kin from the cradle to the afterlife.

If the family dominated in the religious sphere, retainers had a central role in management and production. As seen in chapter three, many members of the gentry had a rudimentary administration, and this would most likely have been centered in the household. Moreover, the household probably provided much of the manual labor, not only in the household garden but also in the demesne fields, given the lack of substantial labor services in Yorkshire.[28] A gift by the magnate Roger de Mowbray to his vassal, Roger Daiville, included three carucates "in demesne and in ploughmen's lands," and the term ploughmen's lands almost certainly refers to a practice Postan has shown was common in the twelfth century of setting aside part of the demesne for agricultural workers in the *familia*.[29] This is a unique reference to the practice in the surviving documentation from Yorkshire, but I suspect the practice itself was quite common. Much of the work of turning agricultural products into food or saleable goods was undoubtedly also done by the household. For instance, the prominent landowner Conan son of Elias referred to the cheeses produced in his homes at East Cowton and Hornby; this sort of production must have been common.[30] The economic clout of the gentry came from their land, but to exploit that land they relied heavily on their households.

27. *EYC* 3:226–27. For other gifts for the souls, or the health of the souls of immediate family members, whether parents, siblings, or children, who were specified by name, see *EYC* 1:42, 193, 490; *EYC* 2:53, 93, 125–26, 144–45, 241, 425–26, 465; *EYC* 3:47–48, 219, 221, 248, 262–63, 264–65, 265–66, 270, 293–94, 304, 315, 326, 354, 365, 366, 367, 375, 385; *EYC* 5:79, 130, 149, 150, 161; *EYC* 6:156, 225, 227–28, 231–32; *EYC* 7:147, 180, 206; *EYC* 9:189; *EYC* 10:96–97, 103, 131, 134; *EYC* 11:125, 182–83, 193, 281–82; *EYC* 12:34–35, 107–8; *Cartularium de Rievalle*, 250; Purvis, *Chartulary of Healaugh*, 119; Egerton MSS 2827:46r; Cotton MSS, Nero D.III, 88r; Rawlinson MSS, B455, 228–29; Fairfax MSS 9:34v, 56r, 81r; York Minster Library, XVI.A.2:18r; *Meaux Chronicle*, 317. In addition, in many charters parents are included but not named. In contrast, only very occasionally are gifts made for the souls of people outside the nuclear family. See *EYC* 2:57–58 and *EYC* 5:121, 150, for gifts for the souls of uncles and *EYC* 3:327 and *EYC* 6:260, for gifts for the souls of in-laws.

28. E. A. Kosminsky showed that labor services were generally light in later thirteenth-century Yorkshire and there is no evidence that this was different in the Angevin period; *Studies in the Agrarian History of England in the Thirteenth Century*, 254.

29. M. M. Postan, *The Famulus: the Estate Labourer in the Twelfth and the Thirteenth Centuries*, 12–13, 35–37; Greenway, *Mowbray Charters*, 231.

30. *EYC* 5:284.

The solidarity of family and household was of value to all involved. Family members and followers received sustenance and, as shall be seen, many received land for their service. Gentry heads of households received valuable economic and strong-arm help from their dependents. Undoubtedly they also received the luxuries and comfort that household servants could supply and the prestige that large households or followings generally provided in medieval society. Thus the gentry received support of all sorts from their families and household and the solidarity of these institutions was an important factor in gentry life.

Inevitably, of course, tensions and disputes arose, especially within families. Ignald de Furneaux's murder of his brother-in-law for mistreating his sister has been mentioned in chapter two, and on another occasion, in 1208, John de Harpham's wife fled for the murder of her husband.[31] The court rolls of the Angevin period are filled with cases of relatives squabbling over land, though often the disputes were between relatives outside the nuclear family or between a widow seeking her dower and a stepson or a brother-in-law who inherited from her husband; in such cases the ties of family were more fragile.[32] Any institution that was as crucial to both the emotional and practical lives of people was bound to foment discord as well as solidarity. This was bound to weaken the support the gentry could draw from household and especially family, but nevertheless these institutions were far more a source of strength than of weakness.

Ironically, the generosity of gentry landlords to daughters, younger sons, and followers, an important aspect of family and household solidarity, posed a far greater threat to gentry prosperity than did discord, and it is to gentry generosity that the chapter must turn next. Both the support that gentry heads of households had from their dependents and the strong emotional ties that would often have existed make it easy to understand why the heads of households were so willing to give land away. Yet it must also be stated that this generosity does not accord with what is found later in England, or in many areas on the continent. The manner of distribution

31. For Ignald, see Cotton MSS, Claudius D.XI, 142r. For the date of this, see chapter two, note 36. For Harpham's murder, see *Rot. Obl. & Fin.*, 423.

32. In many disputes, the only surviving evidence concerns uninformative procedural matters or consists of a final concord which tells little about the dispute and may even at this early date have been the result of collusive litigation. However, for a number of disputes, sufficient evidence survives to determine the causes of litigation, which were numerous and varied; *Rolls of the King's Court in the Reign of King Richard the First*, 21; *RCR*, 145, 438; *CRR* 1:189; *CRR* 3:71; *CRR* 4:290–91; *CRR* 6:76, 143–44, 235, 297, 299, 363–64; *CRR* 7:19; *Yorkshire Eyre*, 44–45, 143, 408; Dodsworth MSS 94:36 and Brown, "Pedes Finium Tempore Ricardi," 179–80; Brown, *Pedes Finium Ebor.*, 3–4, 7, 21–22.

of lands and the reasons it differed from the practice of other groups must therefore both be explored.

The place to start is inheritance and provision for family members. Laws and customs of inheritance went far in determining which child or children got land and whether or not family estates remained intact from generation to generation. Inheritance, however, posed a difficult choice in a society such as this in which elite families relied almost completely on land for wealth and power: whether to divide the land among their children or keep the family lands intact from generation to generation. By dividing up the land, parents could provide for all their children and allow them to found new landed families. Unless there was a constant supply of new land, however, this division of resources could lead to the impoverishment of every branch of the family after a few generations and could result in a loss of power for the family as a whole. Georges Duby has shown the ill effects this had on many aristocratic families in the Mâconnais in the immediate post-Carolingian period.[33] By directing all the property to one child, in contrast, parents could ensure that the family's power would not be dissipated. Under such an arrangement, however, non-heirs were left out in the cold.

Part of the widespread perception among historians of the Continent that the tenth to twelfth centuries saw a shift from amorphous kinship structures to lineages is based on changes in inheritance patterns. The new structure required that the family lands be kept together. In the Mâconnais, families began to do this by exercising tighter communal control over family lands and by restricting the marriage of offspring. By preventing a proliferation of descendants, families could prevent the dissipation of their estates.[34] In Lorraine where a variety of inheritance customs held sway, primogeniture took on an increasing importance.[35] In some parts of Europe, it is true, division of inheritance continued to be the norm.[36] Nevertheless, there was a growing tendency to preserve family inheritances intact at the expense of those children who did not inherit.

When the Normans brought this new aristocratic emphasis on lineage and on preserving family lands to England, as Holt has argued, they also

---

33. Duby, *La société mâconnaise*, 57–65.

34. Duby, *La société mâconnaise*, 263–81, 418–42. See also Bouchard, "Lords of Seignelay," 49–51, for the use of this practice outside the Mâconnaise.

35. Parisse, *Noblesse et chevalerie*, 161–91.

36. In the German lands, for instance, division between sons was predominant among the ministerials, who held roughly the same position in society as English knights; Arnold, *German Knighthood*, 180–83.

brought new rules of inheritance.[37] As a result, the rules of descent governing tenure by knight's service, the tenure by which most gentry held land,
normally funneled all the land to a single male heir, thus keeping family
lands together and preserving the wherewithal that allowed vassals to
provide service for their lords. By these rules, land inherited by a father
passed on only to his eldest son. In the absence of sons, the daughters
divided it evenly among themselves. In the absence of any children at all, it
went to the eldest brother, or was divided among sisters if there were no
brother, and in the absence of siblings it went to more distant relatives,
with the eldest male in any given degree of relationship being given preference.[38] In *Glanvill* so strong were the rights of the male heir that a father
could not give land he had inherited to a younger son without his own
heir's permission, although he could so dispose of land he had acquired.[39]

As a result, in the normal course of inheritance, daughters and younger
sons received no land. If a landholder had only daughters or sisters, of
course, they would all receive equal shares of the inheritance, but otherwise
no one but the eldest son or brother could hope to inherit land. Through
inheritance laws and customs, the interests of the lineage and particularly
the male lineage were carefully protected, ensuring that land would remain
in the family. Individual property holder's rights were subordinated to
family interests. In theory, at least, the future of younger sons and of
daughters who had brothers was sacrificed to the concerns of the lineage.

One way to get around the unhappiness this would have provoked in
loving parents was to provide for non-heirs, and especially sons, from
sources other than the family estates. This was done among other groups
and in later periods and could also be done among the gentry in the
Angevin period.[40] For instance, a younger son might be introduced into
the retinue of a magnate with whom the family had contact in hopes that he
would eventually be rewarded with land.[41] Marriage was another option

37. Holt, "Revolution of 1066," 199–200.

38. There was still doubt about who should succeed when the eldest son predeceased the
father, the eldest son's son or the eldest son's brother, a situation described late in the period as
the *casus regis* because of King John and Arthur. For a recent discussion of this, see J. C. Holt,
"The *casus regis*: the Law and Politics of Succession in the Plantagenet Dominions 1185–1247,"
21–42. For two Yorkshire gentry cases involving this problem, see Dodsworth MSS 94:36 and
Brown, "Pedes Finium Tempore Ricardi," 179–80.

39. Hall, *Glanvill*, 70–71. Moreover, if a father had only acquired land, he could not
disinherit his heir by giving it all to a younger son.

40. For near contemporary families who adopted this practice, see Charlotte A. Newman, "Family and Royal Favor in Henry I's England," 295–96.

41. For example, Roger Daiville on the Mowbray honor, Greenway, *Mowbray Charters*,
231; Jollan de Hallay and possibly Hugh son of Fulk and Marmaduke Darel on the Percy

for younger sons and brothers, since husbands gained control of the property of their wives. Roger de Birkin, younger son of the knight Adam de Birkin, received a marriage portion of one manor with his first wife and received not only a marriage portion of unknown size with his second wife but another entire manor she held in dower from her own first marriage.[42] Other younger sons of Yorkshire gentry found careers as clerics and in two instances surviving documents show parents arranging for this.[43] Another option for children or siblings of both sexes was entry into a monastery. The placement of sons in monasteries can be documented in a handful of instances; the placement of daughters in nunneries was somewhat more common.[44] Marrick Priory, in fact, was founded by a Richmondshire knight who placed his daughters there, and the nunnery was enriched by the gifts that other local knights and landowners granted when their own close kinswomen joined the nuns there.[45]

However, this reference to gifts raises a caution. The evidence for the placement of children in monasteries and nunneries survived because it was recorded in charters concerning gifts of land. If religious houses regularly expected gifts of land with gentry children, which may well have been the case, then this method of providing for younger sons and daughters would have caused a drain on family resources. Moreover, the options of service or marriage described above were limited. The decline of baronial generosity meant that few younger sons could hope to find their fortunes and establish lineages through service in noble households. There were far fewer heiresses than younger sons and as often as not heiresses married heirs. Moreover, at least some gentry heiresses came into the royal patronage network, and few local gentry were in a position to compete for royal patronage. Even fewer would have had the courage and ruthlessness to emulate Gilbert

honor, *EYC* 11:211, 264, 336–37; Hugh de Stapleton and William de Longvillers on the honor Pontefract, *EYC* 3:204, 293, 305; Wimar son of Warner and Walter son of Acaris on the honor of Richmond, *EYC* 4:62–63, 82; *EYC* 5:24, 317–18.

42. *EYC* 3:375–76; Brown, *Pedes Finium Ebor.*, 114–15. It is not certain whether Roger had children by his first marriage. If not, the manor of Over Shitlington returned to his wife's family upon her death. If Roger and his first wife did have children, however, Roger would have been legally entitled to hold the manor for his lifetime.

43. *EYC* 5:318–19; *Pipe Roll 28 Henry II*, 46.

44. *EYC* 1:300; *EYC* 2:355; *EYC* 3:83, 479–80; *EYC* 7:187–88; *EYC* 11:276, 296; *EYC* 12:112–13; Greenway, *Mowbray Charters*, 179; Holmes, *Chartulary of Pontefract*, 147; Stenton, *Transcripts*, 62–63; Cotton MSS, Vespasian E.XIX, 80v.

45. *EYC* 4:53–54; *EYC* 5:29–30, 76–78, 122, 325, 327.

de Plumpton and kidnap an heiress.[46] Women with marriage portions and dower lands were more common, but their estates were generally less valuable and often temporary in nature.[47] Even the church had its limitations, and in any case, some younger sons may not have wished to become clerks. Only a minority of non-heirs could have been well provided for without cost to the family estates.

In fact, however, many families were perfectly willing to diminish the family patrimony in order to provide for younger sons and daughters. Since they could not do so through inheritance, they did so by gifts "inter vivos." Fathers often gave a portion of their lands, whether acquired or inherited, to their younger sons.[48] If a father not make such a grant, moreover, the eldest brother frequently did. For instance, one document describes how Alexander de Rawcliffe gave two and one half of his six carucates in Cracoe to his brother William; Alexander's son Richard later gave one and one half of the remaining three and one half carucates to his brother, Ralph.[49] Sometimes widows provided for younger sons from their own inheritances or marriage portions.[50] Occasionally uncles or other relatives might provide for younger sons, though usually their gifts were small.[51] Thus grants could come to younger sons from a variety of sources, a fact that underlines how important families considered such grants. These grants were not always made gratis. Roger Peitevin, for instance, gave land to his brother Hugh because Hugh had made a journey to Jerusalem on his behalf, perhaps fulfilling a pilgrimage or more likely a crusading oath.[52] Occasion-

46. Roger of Howden, *Chronica* 2:286; Benedict of Peterborough, *Gesta Regis* 1:314–16. See chapter two for a discussion of this incident.

47. Dower lands would return to the heirs of the previous husband after the death of the wife; marriage portions might also go to the children of a first marriage. It might be noted also that marriage portions consisting of land depended on the endowment of daughters with land, which will be discussed below.

48. For gifts from fathers to sons not discussed elsewhere in the chapter, see *EYC* 3:492; *EYC* 5:232; John Rylands Library, Latin MSS 251:11–12.

49. *EYC* 7:163. For other examples, see *EYC* 1:381, 510–11; *EYC* 3:283–84, 341, 374; *EYC* 11:157; *Yorkshire Deeds* 5:92; Brown, *Pedes Finium Ebor.*, 96; *Meaux Chronicle*, 102; *Fountains Cartulary*, 1:164, 430; Cotton MSS, Claudius D.XI, 64r; Rawlinson MSS, B455, 103. On one occasion, a younger son himself provided for yet another younger son; *EYC* 11:344.

50. Ralph Pudsay Littledale, ed., *The Pudsay Deeds*, 95; *EYC* 3:277; Martin, *Percy Cartulary*, 80–81.

51. For provision for nephews, see *Meaux Chronicle*, 319; *EYC* 1:327, 429; *EYC* 2:172, 422; *EYC* 5:158. It should be noted that the word nepos, which I take in these examples to mean nephew, could also mean grandson. For gifts to other kin, see *EYC* 2:245; *EYC* 12:54, 79; Lancaster and Baildon, *Coucher Book of Kirkstall*, 144; *Yorkshire Deeds* 2:119; Charles Clay, "The Family of Longvillers," 43.

52. *EYC* 3:248.

ally such transactions were at least partially sales.[53] Nevertheless, these grants generally seem to have been made for the purposes of giving non-heirs the wherewithal on which to live.

Grants to younger sons and brothers varied a great deal in size. Some could be quite generous. Hippolitus de Braham gave his younger son Hugh a total of four carucates for one quarter knight's fee.[54] This was a comfortable estate, especially considering that Hugh could expect at least a marriage portion when he married and could always hope to acquire other land. It is not surprising that Hugh was able to assume knightly rank.[55] More typical was the estate of nine bovates that John Manuvilain held from his brother, Serlo, or the half carucate that William de Areyns gave his second son, Thomas.[56] Though one can never be sure that an individual gift represents the entire share of the family lands given to a younger son, some gifts seem to have been very small. For instance, Baldwin de Bram-hope, who had many sons, gave one of them two bovates.[57] Especially small were the gifts granted to younger sons of younger sons. Hugh son of Hippolitus was only able to give his own younger son, Nicholas, a toft and two pieces of assarted land.[58] Even if Nicholas received other bits of land, which he may well have, he and others like him probably had no more land than a prosperous peasant. Nevertheless, such younger sons of younger sons did get a share in the family estates.

Daughters could also expect land from their fathers or elder brothers. Sometimes the head of the family would simply grant them land, as when Thomas de Horbury purchased one sixth of a knight's fee and gave it to his daughter Josiana.[59] Simple grants to daughters, however, were extremely rare.[60] A far more common method by which fathers, brothers, and occasionally other relatives provided for a female relative was to find a husband for her and grant some piece of land to the couple as a marriage portion.[61]

53. See note 54 for an example.
54. *EYC* 10:92–93. Hugh paid both his father and his brother for this gift, but not the full market value.
55. In 1201, Hugh was one of four knights sent to check an essoin; *CRR* 2:13.
56. *EYC* 2:79–80; *Meaux Chronicle*, 306–7.
57. *EYC* 11:278–79.
58. *EYC* 10:94; for a similar example, see *EYC* 3:341.
59. *EYC* 8:156.
60. But see *Fountains Cartulary* 1:92–93, and Lancaster, *Abstracts of Bridlington*, 105, for two other grants and *CRR* 5:166–67, for a lawsuit that turned partly on whether a woman was given land as a marriage portion or for homage and service. Another woman claimed to have been given an advowson and land by her father; *CRR* 4:75; *EYC* 2:82.
61. For provisions by fathers and brothers not mentioned elsewhere in the chapter, see *EYC* 1:232–33; *EYC* 2:79, 106, 373–74; *EYC* 3:254–55, 273, 420; *EYC* 5:68–69, 116; *EYC* 7:159, 212–13; *EYC* 11:232, 250; *EYC* 12:33–34, 116–17; *Yorkshire Deeds* 2:88; *Fountains Cartulary* 1:347;

The granting of marriage portions was an integral part of marriage, and so ingrained was the practice that according to *Glanvill*, marriage portions were exempt from the rule that a father could not make a grant of inherited lands without the consent of the heir; indeed, a father could grant a marriage portion against his heir's will.[62]

Marriage portions, like grants to younger sons, varied widely in size, depending upon the wealth of the family, the number of daughters or sisters, and the position of the woman in relation to her sisters, for the eldest generally got the biggest marriage portion, the second a slightly smaller one, and so on. A common size for the marriage portions of gentry families was between one half and one and one half carucates. They could be much larger, encompassing entire manors, and when Alan, Constable of Richmond, married his daughter to Jollan de Neville, the new couple received fifteen librates (i.e., land producing a yearly revenue of £15) with a promise of five librates more. This gift was a handsome one in a time when Henry II had ordered that all landowners with land producing sixteen marks (£10 13s. 4d.) or more of revenue should possess the basic equipment for knightly warfare.[63] Even when there was a male heir, more than a token part of the family lands went to the women of the family, their husbands, and their own heirs.

Enfeoffments and gifts of property to younger sons and daughters were extremely common.[64] Indeed, such grants were so common that they possibly constituted the norm rather than the exception. Younger sons and daughters, in other words, might not only have hoped but have expected to receive a portion of the family lands. It may have been normal to divide off parts of one's estates for non-heirs even if it meant a reduction of the patrimony. There is no way to prove this from the spotty documents that survive; gifts to younger sons and daughters generally survive only if the

---

Fowler, *Coucher Book of Selby*, 1:379; Humberside Record Office, DDCC/135/51, 11, 13; Dodsworth MSS 62:32r; Dodsworth MSS 117:1v, 156r; Dodsworth MSS 126:85r; Dodsworth MSS 139:57r; Dodsworth MSS 148:20r; *Yorkshire Eyre*, 82; *Meaux Chronicle*, 310; T. Walter Hall, *Etton: An East Yorkshire Village*, 7. For marriage portions given by uncles, see *EYC* 11:240, 272. For marriage portions provided by female relatives, see *EYC* 7:164–65; *Meaux Chronicle*, 364.

62. Hall, *Glanvill*, 69.

63. *EYC* 5:153–54; Stubbs, *Select Charters*, 183. For examples of entire manors given as marriage portions, see *EYC* 1:498; *EYC* 2:312–13; *EYC* 3:375–76; *EYC* 10:162; *Fountains Cartulary* 2:666; Dodsworth MSS 129:110.

64. This was true not only of Yorkshire; Holt, "Patronage and Politics," 15–16; Edward Miller, "The State and Landed Interests," 112–14; King, *Peterborough Abbey*, 52; Sidney Painter, "The Family and the Feudal System in Twelfth-Century England," 208–11; Scott L. Waugh, "Marriage, Class and Royal Lordship in England under Henry III," 187–88; Wales, "The Knight," 229–30.

land passed to monasteries. Nevertheless, a brief survey of four families for which ample evidence does exist strongly suggests that there was a standard practice of providing each and every family member with some share in the family estates.[65]

The first family, the Vavasours, was an extremely prosperous one, which traced its descent from a Percy tenant who held land in 1086, and which profited from service to the crown and to the Percys. The head, early in the Angevin period, was William, who served at times as a judge and royal servant.[66] The family tree, including William's generation and the two following, is shown below.

One small gift by William to Richard is recorded, consisting of two tenants and their lands, but it is likely that Richard received other, more generous gifts as well, for his son, Hugh, was later a knight.[67] Malger, William's younger son, did very well. Despite making a very profitable marriage, Malger also received land from his father, including part of the Vavasour patrimony; Malger received a quarter of the village of Bolton in Bolland, and the land that Malger held in Sharlston and Hazelwood probably came from similar gifts, for he later held them of his brother.[68] Robert was William's heir, and he in turn had a son and a daughter. In arranging an extremely prestigious marriage to Theobald Walter for his daughter, Robert provided her with an unusually large marriage portion consisting of another quarter of Bolton and the estates of Narborough, Shipley, Ragil, and Edlington.[69] Malger, the younger son of William for whom generous provision had been made, himself had two younger sons, Robert and Walter, and both of these received healthy grants of land.[70] Thus, not only William's heirs, but all his descendants (with the barely possible exception of his daughters), as well as his brother Richard and Richard's descendants, obtained a share in the family fortune.[71]

65. Baildon has detailed the provision for younger children late in the Angevin period for a fifth family, the Leathleys. These provisions were extremely generous; W. Paley Baildon, "The Family of Leathley or Lelay," 24.

66. See chapter seven for William's activities in the service of the king.

67. *EYC* II:126; *Yorkshire Eyre*, 87, 119.

68. *Sallay Cartulary* 1:68; *Yorkshire Eyre*, 129–30; *EYC* 7:172; *EYC* II:123. Bolton in Bolland was a new acquisition by William but the Vavasours had held Hazelwood, which was the chief manor of the family, since 1086.

69. *EYC* II:129; Meisel, *Barons of the Welsh Frontier*, 98–99, 153–54. She subsequently married Fulk fitz Warin, whose family ultimately gained these lands.

70. Robert received Malger's land in Elslack and William, his land in Sharlston and six bovates in Oxton. *EYC* 7:220–21; *Sallay Cartulary* 2:146.

71. There is no record of land being given to William's daughters, but they almost certainly received marriage portions and given the spotty survival of evidence, the fact that gifts can be found for all the other family members is significant.

Vavasour Genealogy (c. 1160–c. 1230)

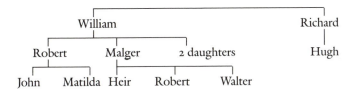

Information for the other three families, the Anlabys, Kneetons, and Ettons, mainly concerns the provision for one generation, and is charted in Table 4. William de Anlaby, who died in the first decade of the thirteenth century, held land in Anlaby from St. Mary's Abbey and also held other estates. Alan de Kneeton, who also died early in the thirteenth century, held twelve librates in Kneeton and Middleton and also held land by knight's service in those villages. Thomas de Etton, who probably died late in the twelfth century, held land in Etton, Skerne, and Cranswick.[72]

From this table a clear pattern emerges. Sons were favored over daughters and within each sex, certain children over others, probably on the basis of their order of birth.[73] In each of these cases, the eldest son still received the lion's share of the father's land, but a large chunk was redirected toward the other children.[74] The lands received by some of these children were minuscule, but nevertheless they all received shares.

It cannot be proved from the surviving evidence that every family provided for each of its members as a matter of course or followed the patterns described above, but I strongly suspect that most or all did. At the

72. For the Anlabys, see Dodsworth MSS 8:301, 314; *EYC* 12:25–26. For the Kneetons, see *Calendar of Inquisitions Miscellaneous* 1:166; *Yorkshire Inquisitions* 1:267; *EYC* 4:143. For the Ettons, see *Meaux Chronicle*, 318–19. The land granted by Alan de Kneeton was held by drengage tenure and at least some of the land granted by Peter de Anlaby and his son and heir William, actually the one who gave his sisters their marriage portions, was held at rent, but that does not really change the picture, for the distribution of lands was made by grants rather than inheritance. In other words, the distribution was not the result of inheritance laws differing from those governing knights' fees.

73. The unusually large grant by Thomas de Etton to his fourth son, the first child of his second marriage, was the result of an agreement with his second wife's father.

74. Unfortunately, it is almost impossible to estimate what percentage of land remained to the eldest son in any of these cases. The record that describes the alienations to William de Anlaby's younger sons and daughters states that a descendant of William who was his heir after several generations held only twenty-two bovates in Anlaby. The record also reveals several small alienations in addition to the ones mentioned above, but it is impossible to tell whether all the alienations between William and this descendant were mentioned and whether the twenty-two bovates in Anlaby constituted the descendant's entire holding.

Table 4   Distribution of Land by Three Families

Children of William de Anlaby (measured in bovates)

son 2	son 3	daughter 1	daughter 2	daughter 3
16	12	6	2	1

Children of Alan de Kneeton (measured by value)

son 2	son 3	son 4	daughter 1	daughter 2
28s	10s	6s	20s	26s

Children of Thomas de Etton

First marriage

son 2	son 3	daughter 1	daughter 2
12 bov	8 bov	4 bov	1 toft and some land

Second marriage

son 1	son 2	son 3
16 bov	pieces of land	pieces of land

very least the provision for non-heirs was extremely common. It should be noted that inherited land as well as acquired land was often given, despite *Glanvill*'s rule that the father needed the permission of the heir to alienate such land, at least to younger sons.[75] Perhaps heirs gave their consent as a matter of course, a possibility bolstered by the fact that it was often the heir who provided for his siblings after the death of the father. Perhaps *Glanvill*'s rule did not have much effect in actual practice.[76] In any case, gifts "inter vivos" strongly modified the descent patterns of land in many and indeed I suspect almost all gentry families. In effect, a system of modified primogeniture came into being whereby one member of the family got the bulk of the lands while the remainder of the land was used to help establish the other members in society.

75. For instance, some of the land given to Malger Vavasour, as mentioned earlier, was from the Vavasour patrimony. The lands given out by Thomas de Etton were also inherited lands.

76. A passage in the Meaux Chronicle shows that shortly after the Angevin period one father decided not to deprive his heir of land he himself had inherited, tried to provide for younger sons and the Church with acquired land, and wrestled between his desire to provide for these sons and for the Church; *Meaux Chronicle*, 422–23. It is striking, however, that in disputes between gentry siblings over land the issue of the heir's consent was never raised, at least in the surviving records for Yorkshire.

The frequent practice of endowing non-heirs with land may be contrasted with what is found in England in the later Middle Ages. Gentry families always tried to provide for as many children as possible, but in later periods they generally attempted to do so without any distribution of the family lands. In the late Middle Ages, marriage portions normally consisted of money rather than land.[77] Younger sons occasionally received heritable grants of land, but more often they received annuities, grants of land for life, lump sums of money, or training in a profession.[78] Much more care was taken to preserve the family lands intact, and new legal devices, such as the entail, were created in part to protect the interests of the lineage even more strongly. The practice of the gentry of Angevin Yorkshire may also be contrasted with what was found on parts of the Continent in the period, where land was divided among sons and sometimes daughters, but most children were discouraged from marrying and thus the dispersion of estates was prevented. In Angevin Yorkshire, there was no attempt to restrict marriage or reproduction, and younger sons and daughters routinely had their own families. On the other hand, gentry families did not divide their land equally, but normally left most of the patrimony in the hands of one son. The gentry of Angevin Yorkshire, in other words, struck a balance between the desire to conserve the patrimony and the desire to provide for every member of the family.

The giving of land, however, was not restricted to family but also extended to important members of that second crucial institution, the household. Lords expected loyalty and good service, especially from their closest and most important followers. In return, loyal retainers expected to be rewarded. Walter Map, the great satirist of the period, complained bitterly about the expectations of his servants and the members of his household.[79] Rewards often took the form of grants of land, as when Warin de Vescy and Robert Constable of Halsham made grants of one and four bovates respectively to men described as *servientes*.[80] Gentry gifts can be found to men described as squires, stewards, marshals, cooks, hunters, and

---

77. One fine from John's reign mentions what may have been a marriage portion consisting of money; Brown, *Pedes Finium Ebor.*, 76–77. Nevertheless, marriage portions consisting of land were overwhelmingly predominant in the Angevin period.

78. Wright, *The Derbyshire Gentry*, 46–50; Carpenter, "Fifteenth-Century English Gentry," 51–52; Payling, *Political Society*, 70–73; Peggy Jefferies, "The Medieval Use as Family Law and Custom: the Berkshire Gentry in the Fourteenth and Fifteenth Centuries," 66.

79. Walter Map, *De Nugis Curialium*, 16–25.

80. *EYC* 3:494; Humberside Record Office, DDCC/141/68, 4, 18–19, 21. See also *EYC* 3:223. Serviens may be translated either as servant or as sergeant.

carpenters, and even to a woman described as a nurse.[81] Many of these followers would have settled down as prosperous peasants, but a few very important retainers could end up as minor landowners in their own right. Nigel de Plumpton's steward, Robert son of Huckman de Plumpton, received several gifts from Nigel and from other lords; by the end of his life he had built up a large enough holding to become a lesser member of the gentry himself.[82]

How can the extreme willingness of the gentry of Angevin York to hand out land, including portions of their patrimony, to non-heirs and followers be explained, when this differed from the practices of their counterparts on the continent and their own descendants in England? The explanation lies, I think, in the unique circumstances of England, and especially Yorkshire, in the aftermath of the Norman Conquest. As a result of the Conquest, enormous amounts of land passed into the hands of great nobles who in turn passed much of it on to their vassals. The amount of land that passed down the honorial pipeline made this a bonanza period, in which knights and other followers could hope and perhaps expect that their estates would continue to grow. Moreover, given the economic growth in this period, the return from their holdings would grow even as the holdings themselves grew. One can imagine how such a situation could engender generosity towards younger sons, daughters, and followers. Since under these circumstances a landowner could make such provisions without necessarily condemning his heir to a less valuable patrimony than the landowner himself had started with, it was only natural to provide for everyone. The receipt of lands from lords and the growth of the economy meant that a balance could be struck between the interests of the heir and those of others without anyone losing out.

It is possible that during the Norman period restrictions by lords on alienation could have limited the generosity of vassals. Certainly, few gifts appear in the earlier period. Once again, the problem of telling real from apparent change arises, due to the rising curve of documentation. I suspect the change is only apparent. However, even if lords did restrict alienation earlier, the decline of the honor, as seen in chapter one, lessened the ability

81. *Meaux Chronicle*, 317; Cotton MSS, Claudius D.XI, 190v; *EYC* 11:271–72; Dodsworth MSS 148:3; *EYC* 3:64; *EYC* 7:173–74, 242; Martin, *Percy Cartulary*, 59–60.

82. *Yorkshire Deeds* 10:76–77, 133; Dodsworth MSS 148:3–4, 15; Add. MSS 32,113:9–11, 29, 40; York Minster Library, Hailstone Collection, 3.21; *Rot. Chart.*, 181; *Yorkshire Deeds* 4:64; Thomas Stapleton, ed., *Plumpton Correspondence*, xiii–xiv.

of lords to do so, and thus in the early Angevin period, the opportunity would have arisen to disperse the accumulation of several generations.[83]

It might be pointed out that later in the Angevin period, circumstances had become much less propitious for this sort of generosity. The honorial land bonanza had basically dried up by the middle of the century and from the 1180s on the effects of inflation may have been counteracting the benefits of economic growth.[84] However, once the widespread practice of giving land to non-heirs and followers had become established, it would have been very hard to stop it. It would have been difficult for a father to tell a beloved younger son that he could not receive the same sort of provision that the father's own brothers had received or that other youths were receiving, or for a family to provide good marriages for their daughters if they did not provide the land expected for a marriage portion. A gentry landlord could not hope for good service from his chief followers if he did not provide the expected reward. Eventually, the gentry had to restrict these practices, but it must have been a painful process and it was certainly one that took place after the Angevin period, for such gifts continued throughout the period covered in this work.

Since for all practical purposes the parceling out of land through grants, though not strictly inheritance, did alter the passage of land from one generation to the next, the later decline of gentry generosity should make historians wary of assuming that a change in inheritance practices *necessarily* reflected a change in family structure, for the family structure of English gentry in the Angevin period was little different from that seen later. Other factors, such as economic growth, conquest, and the availability or lack of new land and income could affect inheritance patterns without necessarily affecting family structure.[85]

In any case, the widespread practice of parceling out family estates to younger sons, daughters, and followers had several important consequences for the gentry and for society at large. First, it meant that gentry

83. Another factor that must be pointed out is that the larger fees and greater opportunities for development in Yorkshire might have given a greater impetus for generosity. However, other scholars have found similar generosity in other counties, so if there was a difference, it was only one of degree; see above, note 64.

84. See chapter six.

85. In relation to this it should be noted that Duby finds a certain relaxation of family control over marriage and property in the late twelfth century. He attributes it to the growing prosperity of the period, which gave some leeway to parcel out estates without impoverishing the family; Georges Duby, *Medieval Marriage: Two Models from Twelfth-Century France*, 102–5.

families tended to create a series of cadet lineages. One of the younger sons of the Etton family probably became the progenitor of the Ettons of Gilling and Malger Vavasour founded the line of the Vavasours of Denton.[86] Many other examples could be cited. This multiplication of lineages, however, is often difficult to trace, since family names were only just coming into vogue among the gentry and many younger sons adopted new names from their own chief residence rather than that of the head of the family. Moreover, younger sons usually ended up as small landowners and therefore they and their descendants rarely appear in the surviving records. Nevertheless, it is clear that the number of families of gentry descent, though not necessarily of gentry status, expanded steadily during this period.

Another consequence was the continued downward devolution of property. The Conquest had led to the concentration of vast amounts of land into relatively few hands. From the beginning, however, the tenants-in-chief handed out land to their vassals, thus making landholding widely diffused. The gifts by gentry to non-heirs and followers carried this process of diffusion much further, creating many minor landlords throughout the countryside.

A closely related consequence was the creation of a broad spectrum of landownership. In the later Middle Ages, though various ranks such as knight, squire, and gentleman had developed, society lacked any sharp breaks of status from the division separating free from unfree to the division separating parliamentary nobility from the rest of the elite. At each level, from free peasant to knight, there was overlap with other groups, and England lacked the sharp social or juridical distinctions that existed between nobles and non-nobles on the continent. In Yorkshire after the Norman Conquest, however, there must have been a great gap between peasants, with their small plots of land, and vassals, with knight's fees of three or more (usually far more) carucates. Moreover, there would have been little in between, except perhaps for the remnants of the old thegnage and drengage of Anglo-Saxon times and a few holders of fractional fees. Even in southern England, where fees were smaller, there must have been a similar gap.[87] More than one factor prevented that gap from becoming

86. Charles Clay and D.E. Greenway, *Early Yorkshire Families*, 25–26, 95; *EYC* 7:172–73.
87. Sally Harvey's theories about the small size of knights' fees, if accepted, would argue against the existence of such a gap. However, I find Donald Fleming's recent critique quite convincing and think that the gap described did in fact exist; Harvey, "The Knight and the Knight's Fee," 15–19; Fleming, "Landholding and *Milites*," 83–98. The gap would have been smaller in areas where the size of knights' fees was smaller, but there would nonetheless have been a gap.

permanent and a different hierarchical structure from developing. The rise and fall of individual families, both among the vassals and peasants, would have narrowed this gap, for instance. But a large factor must have been gifts to non-heirs and followers, which created a whole range of landowners between the tenants of individual knight's fees and the most prosperous peasants, thus creating a spectrum of landholding.

Finally, a hypothesis can be advanced concerning the relationship between the parcelling out of gentry estates and the status of free peasants. One result of the Angevin legal reforms was that free peasants received a surprising amount of support and protection from the law, at least in theory. Free peasants could, and often did, use the new assizes such as novel disseisin and mort d'ancestor, which protected property rights. The royal courts soon began hearing cases between free peasants and members of the gentry, even between peasants and gentry landholders who were their lords.[88] Frequently enough, peasants won such cases.[89] The fact that the English royal government was able to reach down to the level of the free peasant is remarkable and is partly a testimony to the strength of that government. Another factor, however, may have been the existence of free peasants who were also the descendants of the gentry. Most younger sons of gentry landholders would have received enough land to give them tenants of their own and to keep them above the level of peasant, but in especially large families this may not always have been the case. Moreover, the younger sons of younger sons, as mentioned earlier, could easily have ended up as prosperous peasants. Thus many gentry would have had first and second cousins, and possibly even brothers or nephews, who were hardly distinguishable from peasants. Moreover, they must have known that some of their own descendants could end up in that position as well. This situation undoubtedly contributed to the strong distinction that the upper classes and therefore the royal courts made between free and unfree peasants. The gentry would have been anxious that none of their descendants suffer the arbitrary treatment often meted out to villeins, and would have been more willing to allow the royal government to protect the rights of free peasants. Theoretically, and to a large degree practically, no descendant of a member of the gentry would end up unfree, and therefore the royal government was less willing and less free to intervene on behalf of serfs. Unfortunately, there is no direct evidence, at least among the York-

---

88. Milsom, of course, would argue that the assizes were in fact designed for the latter sort of case, the dispute between tenant and lord; Milsom, *Legal Framework*, 8–25.

89. See chapter two.

shire sources used for this work, to prove this hypothesis. Nevertheless it seems likely that the presence of descendants of gentry among the ranks of free peasants greatly enhanced the legal standing of the free peasantry as a whole.

Thus the large number of grants to non-heirs and followers, and what I suspect was a widespread if not universal custom of providing every member of a gentry family with some parcel of land, had fundamental long-term effects in shaping the patterns of English society. The downward devolution of property, the creation of a spectrum of landholding, and the protection of free peasants all involved complex processes, but clearly the succession practices of the gentry in the Angevin period and their concern to provide for younger sons, daughters, and followers had much to do with them.

In the short term, these succession practices also had the obvious effect of placing a strain on the finances of many gentry families. If parts of the patrimony were being parceled off at the same time as honorial sources for new land dried up and as inflation at least partially counteracted the benefits of economic growth, clearly gentry prosperity was going to be adversely affected. Thus succession practices form another factor that must be counted in a discussion of the knightly crisis of the thirteenth century which is posited by some scholars. However, another factor that must also be included was the giving of land to monasteries and churches. Therefore, before turning to the question of a knightly or gentry crisis, it is necessary to explore the religiosity of the gentry and their relationship with and generosity to the Church.

5. The Gentry, Piety, and the Church

The central Middle Ages was a time of remarkable vitality for the Church in Western Europe. The rise of the papacy, the development of scholastic thought, the creation of new monastic orders, and the development of the Crusades profoundly influenced not only the religious life of the period, but all other aspects of life as well. For the Yorkshire gentry, two movements had particular impact. The first was the Crusades, which had existed since the late eleventh century, but first drew widespread English participation only in the Angevin period. Second, and more important, was the rise of new monastic orders in the twelfth century. In 1066 Yorkshire was devoid of monasteries and even in 1100 there were only a handful of foundations, all of them Benedictine. In the course of the twelfth century there was an explosive expansion of monasticism in Yorkshire, with the foundation of numerous Augustinian, Cluniac, Savigniac, Gilbertine, Premonstratensian, and above all Cistercian houses, a few of which grew to be among the greatest monasteries in England. The work of the monks in the new houses literally changed the landscape of the county, as they cleared lands, sent great flocks out to pasture and occasionally rooted up entire villages to create the isolation that some orders required. The impact of the new monasteries on the economy and the structure of society was profound.[1] They also offered new religious opportunities to Yorkshire people, whether as lay brothers, monks, nuns, or patrons. Yorkshire gentry reacted enthusiastically, to say the least, to these new monastic movements throughout the late Norman and Angevin periods. All classes, from magnates to peasants, were involved in the monastic revival in the north, but in the post-Benedictine stage of this revival the gentry were in the forefront.

Many scholars have been interested in the notoriously difficult question of the motivation for gifts to monasteries and for participation in the

---

1. For a discussion of this northern revival, see David Knowles, *The Monastic Order in England*, 164–71, 227–66; L. G. D. Baker, "The Desert in the North," 1–11. Janet Burton estimates that by 1200 there were over fifty religious houses in Yorkshire; "Monasteries and Parish Churches in Eleventh- and Twelfth-Century Yorkshire," 39.

Crusades.[2] Charter after charter asserts the pious motives of the donor in grants to religious houses but such assertions cannot always be taken at face value. Crusades were ostensibly religious in character, but secular concerns had a way of making their presence felt. Clearly non-religious as well as religious motives could inspire both participants in the Crusades and supporters of monasteries. However, in my discussion of the Yorkshire gentry as supporters of the Crusades and of the monastic revival of the North, I will concentrate on religious motivation.

I focus on religious motives not because I think the Yorkshire gentry were uniquely pure in their dedication to these causes. This was far from the case and I will briefly return to the subject of non-religious motives later in the chapter. I concentrate on religious motives in part because I believe their importance is sometimes underemphasized and in part because I believe that other scholars have done an excellent job of describing the secular motives for crusading and supporting monasteries; there is little to add to their discussions of the political, economic, and social factors that might lay behind ostensibly religious actions.[3] My main reason for focusing on religious motives, however, is that I wish to place the support Yorkshire gentry gave these religious movements in the context of their wider religious lives. All too often, grants to monasteries and crusader vows are discussed in isolation, without regard to the role Christianity played in the ordinary lives of donors and crusaders. Yet to understand and assess the role of religious motivation in the Crusades and in the support for monasteries, it seems to me useful to look, insofar as is possible, at the religious background of those involved. How active were the gentry as Christian worshipers? To what degree did they embrace Christianity as part of their lives? To what extent did they place themselves in a position to be influenced by and reminded of Christian teachings on a regular basis?

2. For English crusaders, the best discussions are Simon Lloyd, *English Society and The Crusade, 1216–1307*, 93–112, and Christopher Tyerman, *England and the Crusades, 1095–1588*, 176–86; there is extensive literature on the general question of crusade motivation. Discussions of patronage by knights and magnates of religious houses in the eleventh and twelfth centuries include C. Harper-Bill, "The Piety of the Anglo-Norman Knightly Class," 63–77; Victoria Chandler, "Politics and Piety: Influences on Charitable Donations During the Anglo-Norman Period," 63–71; Bennet D. Hill, *English Cistercian Monasteries and their Patrons in the Twelfth Century*, 42–79; Emma Mason, "Timeo Barones et Donas Ferentes," 61–75; Richard Mortimer, "Religious and Secular Motives for some English Monastic Foundations," 77–85; Barnes, *Kirkstall Abbey*, 22–29; Janet E. Burton, *The Yorkshire Nunneries in the Twelfth and Thirteenth Centuries*, 17–27; and Joan Wardrop, *Fountains Abbey and its Benefactors, 1132–1300*, 235ff.

3. For discussion of secular motives, see the works cited in note 2. Many of these works also discuss religious motives, of course, but there is still more work that needs to be done in the area of religious motivation.

In the absence of diaries, letters, and devotional tracts, answering these questions is not easy. Obviously, the evidence necessary to probe the inner thoughts and beliefs of members of the gentry is lacking. Nevertheless, there *is* evidence to show that many gentry sought to make Christianity an integral part of their daily lives. Much has been written about the deep piety of many gentry in later periods and I would argue that deeply pious gentry existed in the Angevin period as well. I would further argue that a large measure of the gentry support for monasteries and crusades must be seen in the context of the psychological strains and stresses that piety created in members of a violent and wealthy elite.

The evidence for the religious lives of gentry is scattered, and not always straightforward, but when gathered together makes a convincing picture of gentry piety. One set of evidence concerns pious individuals or individual acts of piety outside a monastic or crusader setting. Within this set, one of the most interesting pieces of evidence comes from a vision of the afterlife experienced by a Yorkshire boy during the early twelfth century and recounted to a local priest. Among the figures seen in Paradise, according to the account, was the daughter of a local knight. Like Christina of Markyate, this daughter wished to live chastely and devote herself to God, but was being pressured to marry. In this case, however, the girl died, supposedly in answer to her prayers. As always, with accounts of the miraculous, extreme caution must by used in interpretation, but it is at least possible that such a pious woman existed. Even if the story was concocted, it was certainly meant to be believable, and this believability would depend on the presence of pious women among the aristocracy.[4]

A similar example of piety among gentry remaining outside of monasteries concerns a woman named Matilda de Rouellé who made a vow of chastity "in facie ecclesie" after her husband entered a monastery.[5] Pilgrimage to Compostella could be yet another expression of lay piety.[6] Scattered references also show members of the gentry supporting hermits and lepers. William de Percy of Dunsley founded a hermitage which he subjected to Whitby.[7] The life of St. Robert of Knaresborough, a noted hermit of the Angevin period, states that he received aid from a "certain

4. Hugh Farmer, "The Vision of Orm," 79. The parallels of this story with that of Christina of Markyate who was living at the time it was written, are remarkable.

5. *EYC* 6:193.

6. Ralph de Palling, related by marriage to a gentry family, the Caytons, went to Compostella in 1191; Lancaster, *Abstracts of Bridlington*, 289; before the Angevin period, in the early twelfth century, Richard Mauleverer had made the same pilgrimage; *EYC* 2:74.

7. *EYC* 2:242–43.

noble matron named Helena" who lived in the area, and though I have not identified this woman, it is more likely than not that she was from a gentry family.[8] In the story of the miraculous revival of Jordan son of Essulf's son discussed in the last chapter, Becket, wishing to convey a warning about Jordan's delay of his promised pilgrimage, appeared to the leper Gimpe and asked if he knew Jordan. Gimpe replied that he knew him well because of the knight's generosity toward him.[9] A legal case shows that the important landholder Roger de Rosel was disseised of a "maladaria" in which he maintained a leper.[10] These references show gentry who were living ordinary lives in the world carrying out ongoing acts of Christian charity. With a gift to a monastery, one could simply be a donor without any further involvement. These incidents show a continuing relationship between members of the gentry and individuals who were believed to have a special relationship with God and the saints: hermits because of their self sacrifice and devotion to God, lepers because of the many New Testament stories concerning the disease. The desire to have such a relationship and the evidence for ongoing concern may be indicative of a deep and continuous piety.

Another piece of evidence for gentry piety concerns a young knight, Ralph Haget. Ralph was a regular visitor to Fountains abbey, and had a lay brother, Sunulf, as an informal religious advisor.[11] Ralph clearly desired to embrace Christianity as an important part of his life. This piece of evidence also reveals a close interaction between a member of the laity and an inmate of a religious house, despite the supposed isolation of Cistercians from the secular world. The Cistercian chronicler who recorded this interaction seemed to find nothing unusual in it and it is therefore quite possible that the members of powerful gentry families, whether patrons or potential patrons, had regular access to monasteries. This could both encourage piety among gentry in the world and allow its expression.

That other gentry living in the secular world might share Ralph's closeness to and interest in the inhabitants of a monastery is suggested by

---

8. P. Grosjean, "Vitae S. Roberti Knaresburgensis," 369. The names of women of magnate families generally survive and since there is no possible candidate from any local baronial family, it is probable that Helena was a member of the gentry. Admittedly, there are no clear candidates from that class either, but there are some possible ones, and moreover, the names of women of the gentry class are more likely to be lost.

9. Robertson and Sheppard, *Materials* 2:230–31.

10. *CRR* 3:90.

11. Hugh of Kirkstall, "Narratio de Fundatione Fontanis," 118.

some gifts to monasteries which show an interest that went beyond secular motivation or even the simple purchase of prayers for salvation. Although most donors simply handed over their gifts, leaving those in charge of such matters within the monastery to allot the income as they pleased, some charters specified that the gift was to be used for a specific purpose. Relatively common specifications were for the purchase of wine for mass, for the support of the poor by the monastery, for building purposes, for perpetual lights at altars, for lights during the saying of mass, or for lights at night in the cloisters.[12] Less common gifts of this sort were made by William de Percy of Dunsley to Whitby to support the making and writing of books, by Malger Vavasour to Sallay so that pepper and cumin could be administered in the infirmary, and by Adam de Birkin to Pontefract of oak for burning at Christmas.[13] Such gifts suggest a genuine interest in the affairs and well-being of the inhabitants of religious houses. It is possible that some of the gifts were solicited for the stated purposes by the monks, but even if this was so, it shows that monks could appeal to lay interest in specific aspects of monastic life and activity. Clearly, some gentry desired to have the same sort of ongoing and personal relationship with the inmates of religious houses that others had with hermits. Again, this is suggestive of a continuing and deep piety. These gifts also show a devotion to saints and an interest in the ceremony and ritual of the Church.

The best evidence for widespread gentry piety, however, comes from agreements which show the eagerness of many of the gentry to have their own chapels. Despite the potential of close contact with monasteries, the normal focal point of religion for members of the gentry would have been the local church or chapel. It is there that they would have attended mass and there that they would have had their everyday religious needs ministered to. In later periods, pious members of the gentry directed much of their patronage to the local churches.[14] Relatively few charters of gifts to

12. For gifts for purchasing wine, see *EYC* 3:357–58, 365; *Meaux Chronicle*, 222; York Minster Library, XVI.A.2:18r. For gifts to support the poor, *EYC* 7:261–62. For gifts for building and rebuilding, see *EYC* 2:38, 466; *EYC* 3:320–21, 460–61; *EYC* 5:115. For lighting, see *EYC* 2:125–26, 383–84; *EYC* 3:227; *EYC* 12:50–51; *Sallay Cartulary* 1:116–17; Lancaster, *Abstracts of Bridlington*, 178, 302; *Meaux Chronicle*, 361; Cotton MSS, Claudius B.III, 26. One cartulary of Meaux abbey devotes a section to gifts for specific purposes and this section includes the gifts of approximately a dozen gentry of the Angevin period; Cotton MSS Vit. C.VI, 47–50.

13. *EYC* 2:241; *Sallay Cartulary* 2:60; *EYC* 3:371.

14. Nigel Saul, "The Religious Sympathies of the Gentry in Gloucestershire, 1200–1500," 99–112.

parish churches survive from the Angevin period, but local churches did not keep cartularies and thus the evidence may simply be missing.[15] The importance of local churches and chapels to the gentry can be seen instead from gentry creating chapels in their own households and in hamlets lacking churches.

In discussing the foundation of chapels, it must be stressed that profit was not a very likely motive. There had been a time when the tithe system had made it profitable to found churches, but by the Angevin period the Gregorian reform, the growth of local ecclesiastical courts, and the crystallization of the system of tithes and parishes had largely removed this possibility. Although many places lacked churches, a wealthy landholder who wished to found a chapel faced entrenched and powerful interests from the incumbents of existing churches and the owners of advowsons.

In order to build a chapel one had to obtain a license from the patrons and incumbents of the parish or mother church and a large number of these licenses survive from Angevin Yorkshire or the early part of Henry III's reign.[16] In issuing such licenses, patrons and incumbents made agreements carefully designed to ensure that the mother church would not lose its superior status or any of its rights or prerogatives and that the licensee would be responsible for the full cost of the new chapel. The superior status of the mother church was protected by various sorts of provisions such as the demand that those worshiping in the chapel attend the parish church on important feast days. Its rights might be protected by demanding oaths of chaplains, patrons of chapels, or both not to infringe upon these rights. Occasionally the patrons or incumbents of the mother church demanded some sort of control or at least veto over the appointment of the chaplain. By such means, chapels could be kept subordinate and parish churches could prevent any poaching of tithes or other rights.

Other aspects of the agreements were more directly designed to pro-

15. Surviving gifts to local churches or chapels include *EYC* 2:314–15, 468; *EYC* 3:221, 462; *EYC* 6:193–95; Cotton MSS Vespasian E.XIX, 68v. Usually these gifts survived because a monastery owned the advowson. Interestingly, two of the donors were Ralph Haget and Matilda de Rouellé, for whose piety the evidence has been discussed above.

16. *EYC* 1:115; *EYC* 2:295–96, 376, 495; *EYC* 3:264–65; *EYC* 4:141; *EYC* 5:61; *EYC* 8:195–96; J. T. Fowler, ed., *Memorials of the Church of SS. Peter and Wilfrid, Ripon* 1:199, 201; 4:37–38, 40–41, 81; Walker, *Abstracts of Monkbretton*, 222–23; Fowler, *Coucher Book of Selby* 2:144; BL, Harley MSS 236:38; Cotton MSS, Vespasian E.XIX, 40; Egerton MSS 2827:168; Dodsworth MSS 62:9; York Minster Library XVI.A.1:223v. Some of these agreements may have taken place slightly after the Angevin period. See also Burton, "Monasteries and Parish Churches," 49, and Dorothy M. Owen, *Church and Society in Medieval Lincolnshire*, 16, for discussion of this sort of agreement.

tect or even improve the revenues of the mother church. In return for the license, the founder of the chapel almost invariably gave some land, ranging from two acres to two bovates, to the mother church. In addition, the agreements often stipulated that the founder should provide for the chaplain and for the costs of the chapel, and in certain agreements the founder set apart additional land for this purpose.[17] Some agreements stated explicitly that all the tithes and other revenues were to go to the mother church and this condition was almost certainly implicit in the other agreements. Occasionally, a chaplain might be allowed to have certain free-will offerings and minor dues. The income lost from these, after all, would be more than replaced by the founder's gift to the mother church.

In protecting their own interests, the patrons and incumbents of mother churches placed the financial burdens of founding a chapel squarely upon the founder alone. Despite this, nearly twenty of the licenses listed in note 16 were obtained by gentry. This is an impressive number when one realizes that agreements were likely to survive only if a monastery held the advowson and that most gentry would have had regular access to a parish church, and thus little need to found a chapel. Clearly many gentry were very concerned to have ready access to Christian worship, sufficiently concerned to pay well for the privilege when necessary. This concern is also reflected in a number of disputes between gentry and monasteries over control of chapels in which the gentry showed a strong interest in ensuring that the chapels would be staffed and services heard; in some cases the gentry litigants relinquished rights of patronage in return for guarantees to this end from the monasteries.[18] Many gentry wished to make religion part of their daily life; indeed, in some chapel licenses it was stipulated that mass could be heard in the chapel as frequently as every day.

Unfortunately, the evidence discussed above does not open windows into the inner religious life of the gentry of Angevin Yorkshire. It does suggest, however, that the deep religiosity of many gentry of later periods, revealed by the fuller sources for those periods, may have been nothing new. Given the scantiness of documentation for things not directly related to monasticism or the royal government in this period, the cumulative evidence discussed above strongly indicates that many gentry of the An-

17. In at least one case, there was a charter endowing the chapel which was separate from the original agreement; *EYC* 11:182–83; Fowler, *Memorials of Ripon* 4:81.

18. *EYC* 1:499–501; *EYC* 3:66, 495–96; *EYC* 9:143; Brown, *Pedes Finium Ebor.*, 34; Brown, *Cartularium de Gyseburne*, 2:147–48.

gevin period embraced religion as an ongoing part of their lives, which in turn gave the Church many opportunities to influence them.

This influence did not lead the gentry to become perfect Christians. Many sins, especially more ordinary ones, would not, of course, appear in the sources, but one can occasionally find breaches in the marriage laws of the Church, as when two gentry women claimed dower rights from the estate of one knight; one wife had apparently been set aside for another, clearly a violation of the prohibition of divorce.[19] The most plentiful evidence for irreligious behavior on the part of the gentry can be found in the arena of violence. Chapter two has shown how extensive gentry violence was and how brutal some members of that class could be. On some occasions that violence was directed against monks, clerks, or members of those powerless social groups the Church was urging the upper classes to protect.[20] The surnames discussed in chapter two, such as Malebisse or "Evil Beast," are suggestive of a warrior ethos and of attitudes far out of harmony with Christianity. Chivalry, particularly in the later Middle Ages, represented in part an attempt to reconcile Christian virtues with aristocratic warrior virtues. This attempt, still in its infancy in the Angevin period, could never be entirely successful and in any case the laws of chivalry were as widely ignored as the rules of the Church. Neither stopped the lawless violence of aristocratic thugs.

Often enough, pious and irreligious behavior could exist side by side, a point that can best be illustrated from a story in the chronicle of Selby Abbey. This chronicle tells how a group of knights during Stephen's reign, using a castle outside the abbey as a base, terrorized the countryside, plundering and taking many prisoners to hold for ransom. The chronicler recorded this not only because it affected the monastery, but because St. Germanus, the patron of Selby, was believed to have taken a hand in protecting some of the victims. On one occasion, for instance, the saint was thought to have freed a prisoner. The chronicler, however, mentions a telltale detail. St. Germanus was helped, it seems, by the fact that all the knights and their followers had left the castle to hear mass.[21] Being practicing Christians did not prevent these knights from being bandits. Con-

19. *CRR* 5:125; *CRR* 6:256, 262, 284, 295, 301, 391–92; *EYC* 7:223. For another case over the validity of a marriage, that between Nigel de Plumpton and Juliana de Warwick, see *CRR* 6:363–64.

20. See chapter two.

21. Fowler, "Selebeiensis Monasterii Historia," 40–41.

versely, being bandits did not prevent them from being practicing Christians.

That the Yorkshire gentry should fall short of the ideals of their religion is hardly surprising; hypocrisy is common enough in most human societies. More important, even when people try to live up to ideals they often fail. However, the gap between belief and practice could produce psychological strain. Christopher Harper-Bill, writing of the Anglo-Norman period, said that "Orderic Vitalis, like most historians who have followed him, found it difficult to reconcile the predatory and pious instincts of the upper echelons of Norman society," and the same difficulties apply to the gentry of Angevin Yorkshire and most other medieval elites.[22] What is more important for our understanding of gentry participation in the Crusades and the monastic revival of the North is that the gentry themselves may have found it difficult to reconcile their pious and predatory instincts. For the introspective, the sensitive, and the deeply pious among the gentry, the dissonance between Christian teachings and warrior ideals and the gap between Christian ideals and human behavior must have been extremely troubling. Human beings, of course, are remarkably capable of sincerely holding to contrasting and conflicting beliefs, and of rationalizing or ignoring their own shortcomings. It helps, however, if no one points out the contradictions and shortcomings. Unfortunately for the gentry, members of the clergy and monks were clearly eager to point out the contradictions and shortcomings of the laity, if the religious writings of the period are any indication. Given this, even the least sensitive and introspective among the gentry must have been aware that something was not quite right.

Moreover, monks and priests would also have pointed out that failure to assiduously follow church teachings could have serious consequences. We cannot know precisely what members of the gentry heard in sermons or conversations with the religious, but we can get a general idea from surviving religious writings. One of the things the gentry would have been told was that sinfulness and disobedience could result in temporal misfortunes, particularly when a saint was involved and was offended. Examples could have been drawn from miracle stories concerning local gentry. The knight Thomas de Etton, according to the Canterbury hagiographers, upon hearing rumors of Thomas Becket's sanctity, expressed his doubts forcefully,

22. Harper-Bill, "Piety of the Knightly Class," 63.

and as far as the hagiographers were concerned, blasphemously. Since Thomas de Etton had known Becket early in the latter's career, his doubts are hardly surprising, but in the tradition of the miracle story the expression of these doubts brought swift retribution in the form of illness, after which Thomas repented.[23] Gerald of Wales described an encounter in nearby Lincolnshire between a knight on the way to see to his plows and Saint Peter and the Archangel Gabriel, who gave the knight certain instructions. When the knight failed to follow through on one of the minor instructions, he was punished.[24] The message of these stories was not subtle; one should not trifle with the saints (and often by extension with the religious bodies under their protection). One never knew, after all, when St. Peter and the Archangel Gabriel might appear in the middle of one's field.

More serious still, of course, was the threat of eternal damnation. This is a threat that appears again and again in religious writings and almost certainly appeared with similar frequency in religious sermons and conversations. Moreover, religious teachers could produce graphic and terrifying "eyewitness" accounts of the afterlife, such as the vision of Orm mentioned earlier, which was only one example of an extensive medieval genre, close in space and time to Yorkshire gentry of the Angevin period.[25] Since sin could lead to eternal damnation, sin was not something to be taken lightly.

It is hard to know to what degree the words of the religious affected the thinking of the gentry. To draw an example from outside Yorkshire and the gentry, William Marshal felt sanguine about disappointing some of the expectations of clerks on his deathbed. On the other hand, he made careful religious preparations, such as becoming a Templar, as he approached death.[26] Given the eagerness with which many Yorkshire gentry embraced religion in their life, as has been shown, it is highly unlikely that they ignored the perils of their irreligious behavior.

The rise of the new monastic orders in Yorkshire and the appeal of the Crusades to Yorkshire gentry must be set firmly in the context of widespread gentry piety, conflicts between religious and warrior ideals, and deep fears of the consequences of sin. Both the new monastic movements and the Crusades offered the hope of achieving salvation and provided

23. Robertson and Sheppard, *Materials* 1:153, 2:92. Similarly, when Jordan son of Essulf failed to fulfill his thanksgiving vow of a pilgrimage to Canterbury after the revival of one son, sickness struck his household again and he lost another son as a consequence; *Materials* 1:162, 2:232.

24. Gerald of Wales, *De Principis Instructione Liber*, 183.

25. Farmer, "Vision of Orm," 76–82.

26. Paul Meyer, ed., *L'Histoire de Guillaume le Maréchal* 3:304–5.

opportunities for the pious to resolve the conflicts between religious and warrior ideals.

For the very pious, entry into a monastery or nunnery provided the most drastic answer to their inner conflicts. The rapidly expanding Yorkshire religious houses offered what monasteries had always offered to the deeply Christian: a way to escape the temptations of the secular world, a stern external discipline to aid in the task of self-discipline, a chance to devote oneself entirely to God, and the opportunity to begin one's life anew. Houses of the new orders offered more: a vigor sometimes lacking among the Benedictines, an even sterner discipline, and sheer novelty. Moreover, in their early days the Cistercians, the most successful of the new orders, offered new or at least long-absent rigors, the flight into the wilderness and the practice of manual labor, that would have appealed to the most determined.[27]

Through their use of military imagery, the Cistercians also offered a special appeal to the gentry, particularly to knights. Military imagery was nothing new in Christianity, but St. Bernard, himself of aristocratic background, and many of his followers used it with insistent frequency. "In your country there is a prize of my Lord's and yours which I am resolved to seize by sending our force of knights," wrote Bernard in a letter to Henry I on behalf of the monks founding Fountains Abbey.[28] Hugh of Kirkstall, the historian of Fountains, referred to this passage in his own work and in another section of that work compared Gervase, a monk who had left Fountains under pressure and then gone back, to a knight who fled battle and then returned to the fray.[29] The chronicler of Selby monastery, who was heavily influenced by Cistercian thought and writings though his house was Benedictine, wrote that Benedict, Selby's founder, served the abbot of St. Germain's, Auxerre, for a long time in secular garb and was offered one of two choices as a reward, "either the belt of knighthood in the secular world or the military service of a monk in a monastery."[30] Benedict chose the latter and explained his decision by saying "There is an infinite

27. Cistercian chroniclers may have exaggerated how far their early members went into the wilderness, but they were often at least on the edges of settlement.

28. J. Leclercq and H. Rochais, *S. Bernardi Opera* 7:241. Translation from Michael Clanchy, *England and its Rulers, 1066–1272*, 104. Bernard often used such imagery and was a strong supporter of the Templars; see G. R. Evans, *The Mind of St. Bernard of Clairvaux*, 24–36.

29. Hugh of Kirkstall, "Narratio de Fundatione Fontanis," 3, 31.

30. Fowler, "Selebeiensis Monasterii Historia," 6; ". . . ut scilicet quod mallet e duobus eligeret, vel militiae cingulum in saeculo, vel militiam monachatus in Monasterio."

multitude of knights in the world, but, shameful to say, they serve vices rather than virtues." In contrast, Benedict speaks of monks as God's knights, whom God "strengthens with virtue, gladdens with calm, and crowns with glory and honor."[31]

This sort of rhetoric is extremely important. It did not erase the line between monks and knights, for knights were still violent, greedy and disobedient; in short, they served vice. What the rhetoric did do was help resolve the tension between a warrior ethos and religious ideals for those considering entry into the monastic life. Monks, it proclaims, shared courage, hardihood, and a heroic status with knights. Like knights, they were involved in difficult and perilous struggles. By becoming a monk, one did not sacrifice knightly virtues. Instead, one shed the vices and adopted new virtues. Monks were to be seen as warriors in a greater and more spiritual cause. Such rhetoric may well have been used to counter the taunts of knights against "soft" or "cowardly" monks. It was certainly designed to appeal to members of warlike elites.

Many members of the Yorkshire gentry responded to this and the other appeals of the monastic life in the Angevin period. Our most complete account of a conversion to the monastic life, drawn from the work of Hugh of Kirkstall, is that of Ralph Haget, member of an important gentry family who went on to be abbot of Kirkstall and later of Fountains. Ralph, as described above, often visited Fountains as a youth and as a young knight. One night, when he was about thirty years old, he rose from his bed for the sake of prayer. He went into a nearby chapel dedicated to the Virgin Mary. There, weeping, he prayed before the cross for guidance, for he was weary of the world and was considering entering a life of religion. He prayed that God would direct him "for God's praise and glory and for his own salvation." A voice spoke. "Why do you not come? Why do you delay so long?" Ralph threw himself to the ground and cried, in a tearful voice, "Behold, lord, behold I come." Shortly thereafter, Ralph became a monk at Fountains Abbey. In doing so, in the words of Hugh of Kirkstall, "he did not untie the belt of knighthood but changed it into a better one."[32]

The emotional intensity of the experience described here is remark-

31. Fowler, "Selebeiensis Monasterii Historia," 6; "Infinita est in saeculo militantium multitudo, verum quod pudor est dicere, vitiis potius quam virtutibus servientum. . . . Illi Domino militabo, qui suos milites virtute corroborat, quiete latificat, gloria et honore coronat." See also William of Newburgh, *Historia Rerum Anglicanum* 1:53, for his description of monasteries as castles and monks as knights.

32. Hugh of Kirkstall, "Narratio de Fundatione Fontanis," 117–20; "militiae cingulum non solvit, sed mutavit, in melius."

able, with sleeplessness, nocturnal prayer, voices, and tears. It is, perhaps, what one might expect of a pious person, given the tensions discussed earlier in the chapter. Derek Baker, however, has pointed out the similarity of this story to the story of Bernard of Clairvaux's conversion.[33] It may be that Hugh of Kirkstall drew on the latter account to describe what he thought Ralph's conversion must have been like, or to strengthen Ralph's reputation through an implicit comparison with the great saint. It may be, however, that Ralph's earlier visits to Fountains as a pious layman and his conversations there prepared him for the possibility of such experience. Certainly Ralph's visits and his piety paved the way for his conversion. Interestingly, Ralph may have come from an unusually pious family, for the Hagets, as shall be seen, were among the greatest monastic patrons among the Yorkshire gentry. With such an environment, it is not surprising that Ralph made the transition from secular to spiritual warrior.[34]

Ralph was by no means alone among the Yorkshire gentry in embracing a religious life. Indeed, one of the three monks who began the northern monastic revival in the eleventh century, the converted knight Reinfrid, was ancestor of a prosperous Yorkshire gentry family, the hereditary stewards of the Percys.[35] Among the earliest converts to join Byland Abbey during King Stephen's reign were "veterani et emeriti" knights from Roger de Mowbray's household.[36] The entry of gentry into monastic houses continued during the Angevin period. Meaux Abbey drew novices and monks from many of the important local families, including the Harphams, Meauxs, Octons, and Suttons.[37] Numerous gentry charters survive recording the granting of land to a monastery in conjunction with the entry of the donor or a family member.[38]

Entry into a religious house, however, was a solution only for a minority, if a sizable one. Most members of the gentry did not wish to or could not bring themselves to break away from the world and from the

33. L. G. D. Baker "The Foundation of Fountains Abbey," 32.

34. It might be noted that one of the important figures of the Northern revival, Gilbert de Sempringham, came from a typical knightly background, although unlike Ralph Haget he seems to have been prepared for the church from an early age; Raymonde Foreville and Gillian Keir, eds., *The Book of St Gilbert*, 11ff.

35. Atkinson, *Cartularium de Whiteby* 1:1–2; *EYC* 11:92–99.

36. Dugdale, *Monasticon* 5:350.

37. *Meaux Chronicle*, 83–84, 96, 100–102, 221, 321, 359. Many of these joined in their old age.

38. See, for instance, *EYC* 2:104, 387–88; *EYC* 3:265–66, 398–99, 475; *EYC* 6:226; *EYC* 11:114, 123, 142–43; *Fountains Cartulary* 1:244, 296, 332. See also the documents cited in chapter four, notes 44–45.

luxuries and privileges to which they had access. Many would have refused to undergo the privations demanded by the most vigorous new houses. Others may have felt obligations to family or to lords. Yet for the pious the fears and tensions inspired by Christianity would have remained. What options lay before them? One option was to enter a religious house, but to put it off as long as possible, perhaps until one's final illness, hoping, as it were, to slip through the gates of Paradise just before they banged shut. Indeed, in some donations arranging for the donor's eventual entry into a monastery, special stipulations were made in case the donor died suddenly before entering the monastery.[39]

There were other options, however, for those who did not wish to enter a monastery. After 1095, one of the most significant for knights was the Crusades. Guibert of Nogent, after the First Crusade, wrote that

> God has instituted in our time holy wars, so that the order of knights and the crowd running in their wake . . . might find a new way of gaining salvation. And so they are not forced to abandon secular affairs completely by choosing the monastic life or any religious profession, as used to be the custom, but can attain in some measure God's grace while pursuing their own careers, with the liberty and in the dress to which they are accustomed.[40]

For members of a warrior elite, the Crusades had a number of advantages as a path to salvation. As Guibert pointed out, they allowed knights to seek salvation without giving up the world. Moreover, the Crusades resolved the tension between knightly and religious ideals even more effectively than did Cistercian rhetoric.[41] As historians have pointed out so often, the Crusades gave knights what was seen as a positive way to exercise their violent skills. They also provided relief from the fear of damnation and from the weight of sin. For these reasons, among others, the Crusades, despite their dangers and expenses, were extremely popular among the military elites of Western Europe.

The gentry of Angevin Yorkshire were no exception. No comprehensive list of participants survives, but evidence of the popularity of the Crusades, and particularly the Third and Fifth Crusades, can be drawn from a number of sources. In the pipe roll of Richard's second year, Robert de

---

39. For instance, *EYC* 2:387–88; *Fountains Cartulary* 1:296.

40. Guibert of Nogent, *Gesta Dei per Francos*, 4:124. Translation from Louise and Jonathan Riley-Smith, *The Crusades: Idea and Reality, 1095–1274*, 55–56.

41. See Tyerman, *England and the Crusades*, 165, for the ways in which crusade preachers could appeal directly to knightly ideals.

Lacy received a pardon for scutage owed by those of his knights who had gone on crusade.[42] Various charters show that members of the Hessle, Peitevin, Touche, Bosville, and Sancton families went on crusade at one time or other, and a charter of John de Lacy, issued at Damietta during the Fifth Crusade, was witnessed by a number of Yorkshiremen, including several knights.[43] Other sources show members of the gentry leasing and selling land to raise money to go on crusade.[44]

One can rarely learn more than the names of ordinary knights on crusade, but in the case of Yorkshire knights we are fortunate that the Yorkshire cleric, Roger of Howden, went on the Third Crusade, where he witnessed a charter of his Yorkshire gentry neighbor, John de Hessle, giving land to the Templars.[45] Roger took an interest in other neighbors on that Crusade and recorded their exploits. He described how on one occasion at the siege of Acre, Walter de Oiry, member of a family that held lands in Holderness, helped fight off an attack on the camp of the crusaders. On another occasion, the Muslims made a sortie, taking a siege engine from the Germans and driving the English into the trenches they had dug. Tying ropes around an English siege engine, the besieged tried to pull it into the city, but three Yorkshire knights, Ralph de Tilly, Humphrey de Veilly and Robert de Lalande, along with Roger de Glanvill, ran to its defense, braving the Greek fire that the Muslims were pouring down on the siege engine. Ralph de Tilly, running closest to the enemy, finally cut the ropes and thus saved the engine.[46] Ordinary knights such as these formed the backbone of crusading armies and made possible their victories.

The Crusades, however, were not an easy path to salvation. First of all, they were expensive. One prominent Yorkshire knight, Robert Constable, gave five hundred acres in Tharlesthorpe and leased the rest of that village as well as his village of Halsham to Meaux Abbey to raise money to go on the Third Crusade.[47] Crusades were also extremely dangerous, as Roger of Howden's anecdotes reveal. Indeed, many Yorkshire gentry paid for remission of their sins with their lives. A note by the antiquary, Dodsworth,

---

42. *Pipe Roll 2 Richard I*, 73.

43. *EYC* 3:248, 375–76; *EYC* 8:152; *EYC* 12:57–58; *Yorkshire Deeds* 7:83; Holmes, *Chartulary of Pontefract*, 1:36–37.

44. William de Cornborough leased land in order to go on the Third Crusade; *Pipe Roll 3 Richard I*, 76; *Pipe Roll 7 Richard I*, 92; Henry de Octon and William de Sancton sold land to go crusading; *Meaux Chronicle*, 102; *Yorkshire Deeds* 7:83. See below for Robert Constable.

45. *EYC* 12:57–58.

46. Roger of Howden, *Chronica* 3:73.

47. *Meaux Chronicle*, 220.

reveals that Hugh Malebisse died on crusade.[48] Among the long lists in
Roger of Howden's chronicles of those who died at the siege of Acre and
thereafter were many Yorkshire and Lincolnshire worthies, including
Robert Constable, the seller and lessor mentioned above, Robert Scrope of
Barton, Walter Scrope, Henry Picot, Ranulf de Tang, Osmund de Stuteville, Robert le Venur, and Walter de Kyme, all members of gentry families
that held land in Yorkshire.[49] One could make no greater sacrifice for one's
religion, but according to the beliefs of the time, these crusaders would
have been more than repaid in the afterlife. Crusading was a difficult,
dangerous, and all too often fatal road to salvation, but it was embraced
with fervor in Yorkshire and throughout Christendom by knights and
others. After all, as a relative of the Welsh prince Rhys ap Gruffyth is
reported to have said, "What man of spirit can hesitate for a moment to
undertake this journey when, among the many hazards involved, none
could be more unfortunate, none could cause greater distress, than the
prospect of coming back alive."[50]

What of those who could not or would not go on crusade, or for
whom participation in crusade alone was not a sufficient act of piety? For
these, patronage of a religious house was another, if less sure, road to
salvation and it is this road to salvation that concerns us most, for it led to
massive transfers of land from the gentry to monasteries. Ailred of Rievaulx's biographer stated that Ailred was willing to take land from knights
because

> he had realized that in this unsettled time such gifts profited knights and
> monks alike, for in those days it was hard for any to lead the good life unless
> they were monks or members of some religious order, so disturbed and
> chaotic was the land, reduced almost to a desert by the malice, slaughters and
> harryings of evil men. And so he desired that that land, for which almost all
> men were fighting to the death, should pass into the hands of the monks for

48. Dodsworth MSS 63:64.
49. Roger of Howden, *Chronica* 3:89; Benedict of Peterborough, *Gesta Regis* 2:149–50.
The question of the authorship of the *Gesta Regis*, attributed to Benedict of Peterborough, is a
vexed one. Doris Stenton argued that it was written by Roger of Howden whom she further
identified with the Roger of Howden who witnessed a charter at the siege of Acre. Antonia
Gransden has expressed reservations about these identifications, but states that the question
remains open. Recently, David Corner has presented compelling arguments to support
Stenton's view. The strong interest in the actions of local Yorkshire and Lincolnshire knights
evinced in both chronicles adds further weight to the identification of Roger of Howden, the
crusader, as the author of both works. Doris M. Stenton, "Roger of Howden and 'Benedict',"
574–82; Antonia Gransden, *Historical Writing in England, c. 550 to c. 1307*, 227–30; David
Corner, "The *Gesta Regis Henrici Secundi* and *Chronica* of Roger, Parson of Howden," 126–44.
50. Gerald of Wales, *Itinerarium Kambriae*, 15. Translation from *The Journey through
Wales*, trans. Lewis Thorpe, 76.

their good; and he knew that to give what they had helped the possessors of goods to their salvation, and that, if they did not give, they might well lose both life and goods without any payment in return.[51]

If one could not earn salvation, which was no easy thing to do, one's best chance was to hope for mercy, which could be more easily obtained through the intercession of holy men and women.

When the gentry made gifts to religious houses they had very definite ideas about the spiritual benefits they would receive in return.[52] First, the donation itself was an act of charity that would be weighed upon their side of the scales on Judgment Day. More important, they expected the recipients of their generosity to actively intercede on their behalf. The foundation narrative of Jervaulx Abbey states that when a congregation was formally sent out of Byland to the new abbey, the first founder Acaris and many other noble men greeted them, promising help and comfort to the monks and requesting that they be included in the prayers and spiritual benefits of the house.[53] The exchange of gifts for prayers was, of course, standard.

Some donors were not content with a vague request for prayers but stated explicitly what spiritual services were to be performed in return for their gift. Adam de Birkin stipulated in gifts to Kirkstall and Haverholme that he and his wife would be given the services normally accorded to a monk, canon, or nun upon their deaths and this was not an uncommon request.[54] In a sense, this was taking the practice of delaying entry into a religious house to an extreme, by making the donors quasi-members of the community posthumously. Other donors demanded that anniversaries be performed for them or for relatives.[55] Still others required that masses be said a certain number of times each year for their souls or for the souls of others.[56] That spiritual services could be specified in detail shows that

51. Walter Daniel, *The Life of Ailred of Rievaulx*, ed. Maurice Powicke, 28; Powicke's translation. As Powicke points out, the passage was written about King Stephen's reign, when disorder was especially bad.

52. White, *Custom, Kinship, and Gifts*, 26–28.

53. Dugdale, *Monasticon* 5:571.

54. *EYC* 3:479–80. For other examples of this sort of stipulation, see *EYC* 1:482; *EYC* 2:387–88; *EYC* 3:47–48; *EYC* 6:192, 251; *EYC* 7:187–88; *EYC* 11:265; *Fountains Cartulary* 1:296–97. Sometimes this stipulation was made when the donor hoped to join a religious house before his death but feared that death would overtake him before he had the chance.

55. *EYC* 3:47–48, 227, 266–67, 293–94, 398–99; Walker, *Abstracts of Monkbretton*, 222–23; Holmes, *Chartulary of Pontefract* 1:275.

56. For instance, *EYC* 3:357, 398–99; *EYC* 11:246; Cotton MSS, Claudius D.XI, 70v; in some of these instances, the priests within the monastery were expected to say mass and the rest of the monks to chant psalms.

donors expected a definite if intangible return on their investments. Prayer and other forms of intercession were as real a form of service or payment as any other and in some agreements between monasteries and members of the gentry concerning rights of patronage over churches, the latter accepted spiritual rather than monetary compensation in giving up their claims.[57]

One way to ensure that prayers and masses would be said on behalf of the donor was to create a position within a religious house for someone who would perform those duties. In return for a very generous gift, Ralph de Chevercourt and his sister Beatrice expected Pontefract to "make" one monk for each of them and one for their mother.[58] Roald son of Alan, early in Henry III's reign, gave a large manor to Easby for the sustenance of ten canons whom Roald and his heirs would nominate to the house.[59] A similar practice was to create a position for a chaplain to serve at a specific altar in a religious house.[60] The practice of creating positions for monks and chaplains foreshadowed and eventually led to the common late medieval practice of setting up a formal chantry devoted to saving the donor's soul.[61] When it came to giving land to monasteries, the gentry were not indulging vague or spontaneous feelings of generosity. They had a specific goal, salvation, and wanted to be sure that they got a proper return on their investment.

Gifts could assuage the guilt and fears of damnation for those conscious of their own sinfulness. Ironically, when it came to this sort of religious act, sinful tendencies were not a discouragement but rather an encouragement. The more sinful one was, the more one needed the intercession of the religious. In the middle of the twelfth century, Hugh Malebisse lived up to his surname by harassing Byland abbey, yet elsewhere he was described as a devoted patron of that monastery.[62] For many members of the Yorkshire gentry, impiety and piety, rather than being entirely opposing tendencies, were inextricably linked by the beliefs in forgiveness and the efficacy of intercession that were so predominant in this society.

Gift giving was the easiest way to ease the strain caused by the gap between religious ideals and human behavior. One might diminish the

57. *EYC* 1:351; Brown, *Pedes Finium Ebor.*, 169, 171. See Wardrop, *Fountains Abbey*, 257–60, for a similar point.

58. *EYC* 3:393–94. Presumably, the donation was used to provide for three new monks, who would then pray for the three family members.

59. Egerton MSS 2827:166–68.

60. For instance, Cotton MSS, Nero D.III, 88; *EYC* 2:125–26; Brown, *Pedes Finium Ebor.*, 34.

61. K. L. Wood-Legh, *Perpetual Chantries in Britain*, 8.

62. Dugdale, *Monasticon* 5:351–52.

family's wealth by giving land to monasteries, depriving oneself and one's heirs of actual and potential income, but what was the loss of a small proportion, or even of a large proportion of the family estates, when measured against eternal damnation? The thousands of gentry donations from the Angevin period recorded in surviving charters indicate that many members of the gentry found the reasoning of Ailred of Rievaulx and other religious figures who urged them to make donations to be sound.

Several gentry families even acted as the secular founders of small religious houses. During the Angevin period, the hereditary constables of Richmond founded the Premonstratensian house of Easby and William son of Peter de Goodmanham founded a house of Gilbertine canons at Ellerton.[63] Another knight, Bertram Haget, first tried to make a foundation at Healaugh Park in Henry II's reign, but it was not until 1217 that his granddaughter Alice and her husband Jordan de Sancta Maria firmly established a house of Augustinian monks there.[64] All of the above were foundations for men, but the gentry were far more likely to found nunneries. Though Bertram Haget's plan for a religious establishment for men may not have gone far in his lifetime, he was able to found Sinningthwaite for women. Indeed, the great majority of the twenty-four nunneries founded in Yorkshire in the twelfth century were founded by members of the gentry.[65] This preference for founding nunneries derived not so much from a special interest in female piety (though several of the founders were women) as from the relative cheapness of founding a nunnery. Nunneries were generally on a smaller scale than houses for men and more gentry families were able to afford the initial endowment.

Only a small percentage of gentry families were both willing and able to finance their own foundation, but almost all contributed gifts, sometimes very large, to houses founded by others. Ralph de Chevercourt and his sister Beatrice gave Pontefract the village of Barnsley and Hugh Malebisse gave Byland the village of Murton.[66] Other donors preferred to give

63. *EYC* 2:426; *EYC* 5:132; *The Victoria History of the County of York* 3:245, 251; David Knowles and R. Neville Hadcock, *Medieval Religious Houses: England and Wales*, 188, 198. Earlier in the century, Richard Mauleverer founded a Benedictine priory at Allerton Mauleverer and Acaris son of Bardulf acted as the first founder of the Savigniac house of Jervaulx, although later the earls of Richmond took over the patronage; Dugdale, *Monasticon* 5:568; *EYC* 2:74; *Victoria History of the County of York* 3:387, 138–39; Knowles and Hadcock, *Religious Houses*, 198, 119.

64. Purvis, *Chartulary of Healaugh*, 1, 6–7, 9; *Victoria History of the County of York* 3:216; Knowles and Hadcock, *Religious Houses*, 159.

65. Burton, *Yorkshire Nunneries*, 24, 38–43.

66. *EYC* 3:393–94, 447.

pasture rather than arable but they sometimes gave it in large amounts. Walter Engelram gave Rievaulx pasture for one thousand sheep, and gifts of pasture for five hundred sheep or more were not uncommon.[67] At a time when one hundred sheep could produce revenue of £1 or two marks a year, such gifts were extremely valuable.[68]

Most gifts were smaller: a few bovates; pasture for 100 sheep; a serf and his family; a mill. Some gifts were smaller still; a few acres or the right to collect firewood in a small wood. Small gifts, however, could quickly add up if there were enough of them. Between 1160 and 1218, John de Hessle and his son Robert made over a dozen gifts to the Templars' establishment at North Ferriby. Most of these gifts consisted of a toft or two, a few acres, a half bovate, or a serf, but together, they added up to a healthy estate for the Templars.[69] Most monasteries had a number of gentry patrons and the greatest houses had dozens, from whom they received gifts of all sizes and forms.

Some families gave remarkable amounts of land. The Haget family, besides founding Healaugh Park and Sinningthwaite, gave the manors of Thorpe, Dacre, Caldwell, and Welby (the last of which was in Leicestershire) to Fountains and made small gifts to St. Peter's and St. Mary's, York.[70] The Leathley family gave their manor of Stainton to Selby and made a host of other gifts of varying sizes to various religious foundations.[71] The Birkin family granted away the whole village of Halton; at least six carucates in various places, plus a large amount of land measured in bovates and acres; mills; meadows; a vivary; venison from their park;

67. For Walter's gift, see *EYC* 2:60. For other large gifts, see *EYC* 2:57, 156, 496–97; *EYC* 3:309; *EYC* 5:79, 121, 237, 307–8; *EYC* 7:238–39, 252; *EYC* 10:168; *Sallay Cartulary* 2:7; Cotton MSS., Claudius D.XI, 195v; *Meaux Chronicle*, 430.

68. Round, *Rotuli de Dominabus*, xxxiv; Lapsley, "Introduction to Boldon Book," 301.

69. *EYC* 12:55–62, 128–29. In total, these gifts consisted of one half bovate, twelve acres and five roods of arable, two pieces of land of unspecified size, fifteen acres of meadow, five tofts, pasture for two hundred sheep and other common pasture, two villeins and their families in Hessle in Yorkshire and five bovates, four acres and a villein family in Lincolnshire. John and Robert also made gifts to Guisborough, Watton and Meaux; *EYC* 12:63–64; *Yorkshire Deeds* 9:101–2; *Meaux Chronicle*, 227–28.

70. Hugh of Kirkstall "Narratio de Fundatione Fontanis," 123–24; *EYC* 1:402; Greenway, *Mowbray Charters*, 87–88, 116–17; *Fountains Cartulary* 1:203–4; *EYC* 1:192–93. The movement of property was not only in one direction, for St. Mary's leased three carucates to Geoffrey and Bertram Haget; *EYC* 1:495.

71. *EYC* 1:41–42; *EYC* 11:31, 142–43. The gift to Selby took place in King Stephen's reign. The Leathleys continued to be generous after the Angevin period. Isolde de Leathley, for instance, gave her marriage portion of five carucates in Stainburn to Fountains; *Fountains Cartulary* 2:667–68. For a comprehensive list of the many donations by the Leathley family in the twelfth and thirteenth centuries, see Baildon, "Family of Leathley," 3–36.

pasture land; and sites for smithies with the associated rights to dig for iron ore and gather charcoal for firewood. These gifts were divided among approximately a dozen religious houses.[72] The Hagets, Leathleys, and Birkins were all prosperous and unusually generous families. Nevertheless, one cannot help but be struck by the high level of generosity to monasteries shown by the gentry as a whole.

It would be naive, of course, to claim that donations to monasteries, or for that matter participation in crusades or entry into religious houses, were invariably motivated by religious beliefs alone. As stated earlier, scholars have found many secular motivations in what were purportedly religious acts and this was true for the gentry of Angevin Yorkshire as for other medieval donors and crusaders. Though there is no way to be certain, I strongly suspect that a desire for prestige, for "keeping up with the Hagets" as it were, probably played a role in many gentry donations. The pressure of lords to give land to favored foundations certainly played such a role, at least in the earlier part of the period.[73] Lordship and ties of patronage might also be a factor in crusade participation, as Simon Lloyd clearly demonstrated for the Crusade of the Lord Edward in the late thirteenth century.[74] For instance, the ill fated Robert Constable was steward to William de Mandeville and may have followed his lord's lead in taking a crusade vow; he in turn was followed by a squire.[75] Economic motives also played a role, especially in grants to monasteries. Some grants were simply sales or leases.[76] Others involved a mixture of economic and pious motives, as when Nigel de Stockeld gave Sallay one carucate which the monks were to hold at farm for seventeen years and in free alms thereafter.[77] The vast majority of gentry grants appear to be straightforward donations, but this raises the question of whether or not the claims and terms of charters can always be taken at face value. There is the possibility that sales could sometimes be carefully disguised as donations. For instance, one transfer, which appears to be a gift from the charter, is described as a sale in a later source.[78] There is little other evidence of disguised sales, but since the very point of such disguise is concealment, others may remain undetected and

72. *EYC* 3:357–72, 479–80; *EYC* 6:156; Cotton MSS, Vespasian E.XIX, 22; Atkinson, *Cartularium de Rievalle*, 250.

73. See chapter one, section three.

74. Lloyd, *English Society and the Crusades*, 118–25; see also 106–8.

75. Humberside Record Office, DDCC/141/68, 6.

76. For an example of each, see *EYC* 1:412, and *EYC* 11:154–56.

77. *EYC* 11:258.

78. *EYC* 6:216–17.

thus it is hard to say whether the case mentioned above is anomalous or merely one of many such cases.

It is ultimately impossible to evaluate the relative weight of religious and non-religious concerns in gentry support for monasteries and crusading. Simon Lloyd has pointed out, in regard to crusader motivation, that one can postulate many plausible motives but the evidence generally allows for inference rather than empirical proof or disproof.[79] The same could be said of motivation for joining or giving land to monasteries. A healthy skepticism about the pious claims of crusaders and donors is always in order. However, it is also important to listen to the voices and claims of contemporaries and to try to evaluate and understand them on their own terms. Pious claims need to be considered very seriously by historians in any discussion of motivation for religious acts. Historians should always be wary about measuring the actions and beliefs of medieval people too much by the standards of our modern, highly secular, society.

Whatever the motivation, support for the crusades and for monasteries by the gentry had an important impact on the world around them. On the larger scene, Yorkshire gentry and their counterparts from throughout Europe played a large role in European and Middle Eastern history by providing the main strength of crusading armies. The deeds of ordinary knights such as those recorded by Roger of Howden made the successes of the Crusades possible.

On a more local level, gentry support for religious houses had a profound influence on Yorkshire society in the Angevin period and thereafter because it so greatly strengthened the monastic revival. This is not to say that the gentry were the only ones involved. Magnates founded all of the most important Yorkshire monasteries, and by the end of the Angevin period families of free peasants were providing small gifts of land.[80] Nevertheless, during the Angevin period, the gentry provided the chief support for the monastic revival, adding new houses, especially nunneries, and allowing existing monasteries to grow far beyond the bases provided by initial baronial gifts. Joan Wardrop, in her study of Fountains abbey, has estimated that before 1300, knightly families were the source of sixty percent of the donations or sales to that monastery and provided nearly eighty percent of its land.[81] For other foundations of the mid- to late twelfth

79. Lloyd, *English Society and the Crusade*, 103.
80. One of the striking things about gift-giving to monasteries was the way it spread down the social ladder in the course of the twelfth and thirteenth centuries.
81. Wardrop, *Fountains Abbey*, 171; see also 133, 168–69.

centuries the figures would vary, but in almost all cases the gentry would have provided a very large proportion of the landed endowment, as well as a significant portion of the personnel.

These powerful new religious institutions in turn had an important influence on Yorkshire society as a whole, just as similar institutions throughout Europe influenced Western Christendom as a whole. These houses, strengthened in part by gentry piety, in turn provided new outlets for the exercise of that piety and new havens for the monastically inclined. The vast transfer of land to religious houses greatly reshaped landholding patterns in Yorkshire, just as the dissolution of the monasteries would radically reshape them years later.[82] Though the monks can no longer be seen as the sole pioneers of economic expansion, they certainly played an important role and may well have helped introduce new techniques, as some scholars have argued. As a result in large measure of gentry support, monasteries and nunneries were able to sink deep roots in Yorkshire and to become so fixed in local society that when Henry VIII sought to destroy them he was met by the violent Pilgrimage of Grace.

At the same time, generosity to monasteries could have grave and sometimes disastrous consequences for knightly families. When the Haget patrimony was divided among heiresses at the end of the twelfth century, the family had only four manors left, exactly the same number it had given to Fountains Abbey.[83] The Leathleys had to sell out late in the thirteenth century and generosity to religious houses, as well as to younger sons and daughters, certainly played a role in the collapse of this prosperous family.[84] Most families were more circumspect in their gift giving, but the period nevertheless saw an enormous transfer of resources from the gentry to the religious communities of men and women that had sprung up in Yorkshire since the Conquest. This, of course, had an obvious effect on the prosperity not only of individual families but of the gentry as a whole.

Why did one see such unusual generosity during the Angevin period? Neither the religious motives I have emphasized nor the non-religious motives other scholars have discussed suddenly emerged from nowhere in the twelfth century nor did they end in the 1220s and 1230s, during which

82. Smith, *Land and Politics*, 213–53.

83. Purvis, *Chartulary of Healaugh*, 1. The description of the shares of the heiresses also mentioned some unnamed lands; in one case this consisted of property in York; *EYC* 5:202–3. Against this must be measured other gifts by the Hagets. Unfortunately, the value of the various manors is unknown.

84. Baildon, "Family of Leathley," 24–26. For some other examples of feckless generosity, see Faull and Moorhouse, *West Yorkshire* 2:340; Wardrop, *Fountains Abbey*, 182–83.

period gentry generosity declined sharply.[85] A number of reasons explain the change in levels of generosity. First, the Cistercians and other new orders that expanded in the twelfth century were cheaper.[86] Most gentry could not afford the kind of gift that would make a great difference to the hugely endowed Benedictine monasteries of earlier periods, but to a struggling new house, a few bovates could be very important. Even after these houses became established, they continued to welcome and solicit such gifts, having developed management and economic policies suitable to administering them.

Moreover, the same factors that prompted gentry families to provide for younger children and followers would also have played a role. The new monastic orders arrived in Yorkshire at the end of a massive transfer of land to the gentry and in the middle of an economic boom. Gentry could afford to give land to monasteries without seriously endangering their economic positions or the social standing of their heirs. In such circumstances it made sense to respond to one's fears of damnation by giving land, an act that did represent real financial sacrifice, but did not entail financial ruin.

In this context, the larger opportunities for development in Yorkshire may have prompted greater generosity to the Church in that county than elsewhere. Other factors may have set Yorkshire apart as well. The unusually strong leadership of the new monastic movements in Yorkshire with figures such as Ailred of Rievaulx and Henry Murdac may have influenced the pious laity to unusual acts of generosity. The lack of great monasteries from the Anglo-Saxon period may have created a vacuum that gentry, seeing the relative lack of monasteries in Yorkshire, sought to help fill through greater than average generosity. However, gentry generosity to monasteries was common throughout England during the Angevin period and thus the difference, if any, was one of degree.

In any case, once the habit of generosity was formed there may have developed a feeling that not only was the giving of land to monasteries beneficial to salvation, but necessary. If this was so, the prospect of not doing so, or even of giving less than others, would have been frightening indeed, much more so than in a period in which the practice was not widespread. Thus, just as with gifts to younger sons and daughters, once the practice of giving to monasteries had started it was difficult to stop. However, as economic circumstances changed for the gentry, pious be-

85. J. E. Newman, "Greater and Lesser Landowners and Parochial Patronage: Yorkshire in the Thirteenth Century," 284–91.
86. Hill, *English Cistercian Monasteries*, 46.

lievers would have been faced with increasingly difficult choices. Not only piety, but rational self interest for those who feared hell would have prompted them to give land to monasteries regardless of the consequences to their heirs. Family feeling, on the other hand, would have dictated otherwise, and eventually this feeling and plain economic common sense would lead the gentry to scale down their generosity. Once this had happened, the wealthy could find other ways to salvation without feeling that not giving land would necessarily endanger their souls.[87] There might have been a time, however, in which fears of damnation would have struggled with fears of poverty, and the latter would not always have won. Thus, even members of the gentry who could not have afforded to may have given land. This, of course, brings us to the subject of the next chapter, the alleged crisis of the knightly class in the thirteenth century.

87. The growing wealth of the monks may also have played a role. Donors might see a great difference between giving to poor, struggling, deserving monks on the one hand and rich, powerful, and possibly complacent abbeys on the other.

6. Was There a Crisis of the Gentry?

In a 1975 article, Peter R. Coss, drawing upon suggestions by Rodney Hilton and Michael M. Postan, argued that the knightly class experienced a crisis in the thirteenth century. Coss pointed to the number of knights who became indebted from the late twelfth century on and were eventually forced to sell out, either to monasteries or nobles, or, as in the families Coss studied, to royal servants such as Sir Geoffrey de Langley. He argued that this was the result of the great inflationary period of 1180–1220. In his view, knightly families depended heavily on hereditary rents, the form of income most vulnerable to inflation, and lacked the large demesnes which allowed magnates to adjust successfully to new conditions. Many families therefore borrowed money in order to maintain standards of living, got in over their heads, and subsequently lost most if not all their lands.[1] It might be added that many parallels can be found for such difficulties among landlords in many areas on the Continent, though there the problems included the upper as well as the lower reaches of the aristocracy.[2]

Coss's arguments, however, have by no means won universal acceptance among historians of England. In 1977 J. E. Newman, concentrating on the ownership of advowsons in Yorkshire, showed that between c. 1215 and c. 1315 many advowsons passed from poor and middling knightly families to magnates and career officials, but this was not always because of sales, and Newman did not see as grave a crisis as Coss did.[3] Edmund King and K. J. Stringer, looking at groups of vassal or knightly families in the late twelfth and early thirteenth centuries, also argued against a general crisis, seeing instead the rise and fall of individual families.[4] Finally, in a systematic

1. P. R. Coss, "Sir Geoffrey de Langley and the Crisis of the Knightly Class in Thirteenth-Century England," 3–37. Hilton has made similar arguments about the effects of inflation; Hilton, *A Medieval Society*, 51–52. For the inflation, see P. D. A. Harvey, "The English Inflation of 1180–1220," 3–30.

2. Duby, *La société mâconnaise*, 487–512; Guy Devailly, *Le Berry du xᵉ siècle au milieu du xiiiᵉ*, 522–26; E. Warlop, *The Flemish Nobility Before 1300* 1:276–98; Parisse, *Noblesse et chevalerie*, 291–94.

3. Newman, "Greater and Lesser Landowners," 280–308.

4. King, "Large and Small Landowners," 26–50; Stringer, *Earl David*, 133–41.

study of the property of knightly families in Oxfordshire, David Carpenter has convincingly argued that there was a limited crisis at most, and that although individual families suffered a collapse of their fortunes, other families rose to take their place. In his view, the knightly class as a whole did not experience a crisis but adjusted successfully to the new economic circumstances.[5]

In a recent book, Coss has clarified his views by distinguishing between a "crisis of the knightly class" and a "decline of the knightly class." He does not dispute the findings of Carpenter and others but he nevertheless renews his argument that the knightly class faced a difficult adjustment to new economic circumstances that not all families made successfully. The class as a whole did not face a disastrous decline, but did face a period of sufficient difficulty to be termed a crisis.[6]

Ideally, this issue could be addressed with a quantitative study of the estates and incomes of Yorkshire gentry, at least for the Angevin period covered in this book. Unfortunately, the evidence necessary for such a study does not exist. Certainly inflation could affect gentry incomes in Angevin Yorkshire as is indicated by the single surviving survey of the estates of a Yorkshire gentry family from anywhere near the Angevin period, namely the survey of the estates of the Grimthorpe family found in the records of the 1218–19 eyre. In this survey, land held in demesne, in villeinage or for short term leases was valued at three, four, or five shillings per bovate, depending on the manor, and land leased to free tenants was only valued at approximately ten or sixteen pence per bovate, again depending on the manor.[7] However, as Carpenter has argued, even with demesnes as small as two hides (or carucates) gentry families would have sufficient demesne to adjust to and possibly counteract the effects of inflation; the Grimthorpes, who had large demesnes in two villages, remained prosperous through the thirteenth century and indeed struck it rich in the fourteenth by means of a marriage to the heiress of the Graystoke family.[8] Much depended on demesne sizes, and for the vast majority of Yorkshire gentry estates in the Angevin period, that is impossible to determine.

5. Carpenter, "Was There a Crisis?" 721–52.

6. Coss, *Lordship, Knighthood and Locality*, 19, 264–304.

7. *Yorkshire Eyre*, 326. The survey was made because the family heir was supposed to be in royal custody, but was not.

8. Carpenter, "Was There a Crisis?" 740–41; Clay and Greenway, *Early Yorkshire Families*, 38–39. The Grimthorpes had three carucates of demesne and seven bovates held by villeins in one village, and two carucates held by villeins and two and a half carucates which were probably leased out temporarily in another.

Certainly Yorkshire gentry had frequent resort to Jewish credit; more than fifteen owed on the accounts for Aaron of Lincoln in 1186 and fifty-eight Yorkshire landholders, the majority of them gentry, appear as Jewish debtors in payment schedules from late in John's reign.[9] However, most of the recorded debts were small. Without much fuller knowledge of the incomes of gentry and the full extent of gentry indebtedness, it is impossible to know how serious a threat Jewish debt was to the gentry as a group.

Certainly, indebtedness or general financial woes led at least some gentry to lease lands at unfavorable terms, to suffer forfeiture of lands to lenders, or to sell some or all their land.[10] A particularly plaintive note was sounded in a document in which Roger Bret, a cadet member of an important gentry family, sold thirty-six acres of assarted land to Fountains for twenty marks, twenty shillings, one plough of oxen, and one horse, so that "I can retain, for myself and my heirs, the remnant of our inheritance and not lose more or even all."[11] In another case, Adam de Cridling, heir of a prosperous gentry family, sold one manor to his uncle Malger Vavasour in the Angevin period, other land to Jordan and John de Ryther, and the rest of his land to the magnate, John de Lacy.[12] However, the question remains whether the surviving examples are isolated incidents, or representative of a widespread crisis for the gentry.

In contrast to the signs of economic difficulties are signs of prosperity, the most interesting being the purchase of land by members of the gentry. Malger Vavasour, who bought the manor of Halton from Adam de Cridling, was a member of the gentry, and he also bought twelve bovates in Elslack from four people in order to provide for one of his younger sons, and purchased other small parcels as well.[13] The knight Nigel de Plumpton

9. For those who owed money to Aaron of Lincoln, see *Pipe Roll 3 Richard I*, 17–23. The estimate of fifteen gentry is probably conservative, but includes some individuals such as Robert Daiville who held many lands in Yorkshire but whose debt is listed in the Lincolnshire section of Aaron's debts. The schedules of payment are in PRO, E401 1564. See Holt, *The Northerners*, 168–69 for a discussion of these schedules. For other evidence of Yorkshire gentry borrowing from Jewish money lenders, see *Rot. Litt. Claus.*, 33b, 58b; *Rot. Obl. & Fin.*, 122, 130; *Pipe Roll 1 John*, 53; *Pipe Roll 3 John*, 159, 160; *Pipe Roll 11 John*, 138; *Pipe Roll 13 John*, 49; *CRR* 1:389–91; *CRR* 5:309; *Yorkshire Eyre*, 148–49.

10. For examples, see *EYC* 3:287–88; *EYC* 5:147, 187–90; *EYC* 7:188; *EYC* 11:194–95; *Yorkshire Deeds* 6:23; Atkinson, *Cartularium de Whiteby* 2:387–88; York Minster Library, XVI.A.1:132–33, 160–66; *Fountains Cartulary* 1:23, 2:850–51; *Meaux Chronicle*, 306, 315, 318–19, 374–75, 367; *CRR* 5:309; *Yorkshire Eyre*, 148–49.

11. *EYC* 11:183–84; Roger was the younger son of the hereditary steward of the honor of Richmond.

12. *Sallay Cartulary* 2:60–61; *Fountains Cartulary* 1:123–25; *EYC* 3:387.

13. *EYC* 7:220–21; *Sallay Cartulary* 1:79, 2:60–63, 147; Dodsworth MSS 139:98v, 123r. It should be noted that Malger probably borrowed money to buy land since a document of his

bought a large piece of land from Walter de Stockeld and several other pieces of land from a variety of sellers and Roald son of Alan, Constable of Richmond, was buying many small parcels of land in the early part of the thirteenth century, many of them from his own tenants.[14] Several other gentry can be found buying land as well.[15] Again, however, it is impossible to tell if such examples are unusual or representative.

Unfortunately, the Yorkshire evidence for the Angevin period will not allow even the rough though convincing figures Carpenter was able to obtain for the number of rising, stable, and falling families in thirteenth-century Oxfordshire. All that remains for this study, as for other studies of gentry or knightly prosperity before the 1220s, is a mass of anecdotal evidence. For what it is worth, the impression drawn from this evidence is similar to Carpenter's picture of the rise and fall of individual families with no overall disaster for the gentry or knightly class. As Coss argues, however, this is not necessarily incompatible with a more restricted crisis prompted by the necessity of adjusting to new circumstances.

If the Yorkshire evidence for the Angevin period does not add much hard data for a discussion of the extent and effect of the economic problems faced by the gentry, it does add new perspectives to the debate by suggesting several new factors that need to be considered in any debate concerning gentry prosperity. First, there is the economic development by gentry landlords discussed in chapter three. Carpenter, in speaking of knightly adjustment to inflation, spoke in terms of concentrating on demesne farming.[16] However, for active gentry improvers in areas ripe for economic expansion, assarting, the building of mills, and the increasing of herds could also serve to offset the ravages of inflation. Even for gentry who were not active improvers, the general development and population growth would have added income by increasing the revenue from courts, mills, pannage, and other seigniorial sources of income. Even as inflation slowly

---

heir mentions debts related to Halton—it should not always be assumed that the gentry borrowed money simply to maintain a standard of living; *Sallay Cartulary* 1:81.

14. For Nigel, see *Yorkshire Deeds* 10:132–33; Add. MSS 32,113:15, 21, 29; *EYC* 7:137; *EYC* 11:272. For Roald, see *Yorkshire Deeds* 7:51; Egerton MSS 2827:8, 125, 155–56, 167, 190–92, 199–200, 211.

15. *EYC* 1:41, 210, 325; *EYC* 2:38, 525–26; *EYC* 5:128, 232, 253; *EYC* 8:155–56, 207; *EYC* 11:156, 298, 311–12; *EYC* 12:80–81; *Yorkshire Deeds* 2:5, 92; *Fountains Cartulary* 1:160, 323, 2:624–25, 643, 651, 667, 818; Atkinson, *Cartularium de Whiteby*, 67–68; Atkinson, *Cartularium de Rievalle*, 223; Brown, *Cartularium de Gyseburne* 2:34; Humberside Record Office, DDCC/101/1, DDCC/74/1; DDCC/135/2, 1; York Minster Library XVI.A.1:206–7; 2:47; Egerton MSS 2827:46r, 88; Dodsworth MSS 62:4v; *Pipe Roll 10 John*, 155.

16. Carpenter, "Was There a Crisis?" 740–45.

ate away at gentry incomes, growth slowly added to them. It is impossible to know either the extent to which inflation sapped gentry incomes or the extent to which economic improvements increased them, but clearly the one could to some degree counterbalance the other.

To economic development must be added paths to prosperity for the gentry which will not seem so new to scholars of this period. As argued in chapter one, baronial patronage declined drastically in the twelfth century. But it did not cease altogether and it is probably no accident that many of the gentry who purchased land in the Angevin period were honorial officials.[17] Royal patronage allowed a few existing gentry families to prosper as well, though there are no clear examples of new gentry families created in Yorkshire by royal favor in the Angevin period.[18] Marriage, as always, was another path to success. The FitzHughs of Ravensworth greatly expanded their income by the marriage of Ranulf son of Henry to Alice, the heiress of the wealthy knight, Adam de Staveley, and this marriage helped provide the family with enough wealth to enter the parliamentary nobility later in the thirteenth century.[19] Only a limited number of gentry families could prosper through service or marrying heiresses, but those families were in a strong position not just to adjust to inflation but to advance their fortunes.

Against the beneficial effects of economic development, patronage, and marriage to heiresses must be measured what may have been an even greater influence on the prosperity of gentry in the Angevin period, namely generosity to daughters, younger sons, and the Church. I have already shown just how generous the gentry could be in individual alienations. However, the study of a few families can show just how great the *cumulative* effects could be. The Constable fee on the honor of Richmond contained thirteen knights' fees and thirty-two holdings of at least one carucate. The fee was split as a result of conflicting claims in King Stephen's reign, but reunited under Roald son of Alan who already held half the fee, when the lord of the other half elected to remain in Normandy after 1204. A lawsuit not long thereafter reveals that of the thirty-two holdings only eight remained in Roald's hands; other litigation reveals that even these eight

17. See chapter one, note 54. Barbara English has estimated that Fulk de Oiry, an honorial official and a Lincolnshire knight with Yorkshire lands, paid out about £900 for land and privileges, and this figure comes from the surviving records alone; English, *Lords of Holderness*, 67–68.

18. I am excluding new lines introduced by marriage to heiresses of existing families. See chapter 7 for royal patronage of the gentry.

19. *Pipe Roll 13 John*, 29; George E. Cokayne, *The Complete Peerage of England, Scotland, Ireland, Great Britain and the United Kingdom* 5:416–33.

remaining holdings had many major free tenants or tenants by free alms on them.[20] Another Richmond tenant, Conan son of Elias, held two and one half of his five fees in Yorkshire and these two and one half fees consisted of five manors. Conan also held the manor of Hornby as a subtenancy. Early in the thirteenth century, when Conan made a gift of a second tithe to the hospital of St. Peter, York, he held only two of these six manors in his own hands.[21] The Hagets, who held one holding for a knight's fee from the Arches, one holding for one sixth of a knight's fee from the Bulmers, eight holdings from the Mowbrays for two fees and two holdings from the crown, had only four of the twelve estates in hand when the land was split among heiresses.[22]

All of these families held multiple fees and some of the dispersed estates may well have gone to provide for military tenants. Because of the need to give land to younger children, servants, and the Church, however, even the estates of gentry with only one or two fees were often split up as well, even if not to the same degree. For example, the Nevilles of Muston held six manors from the Gants for the service of two knights. When a claimant demanded this land in royal court between 1199 and 1201, he only mentioned four manors, suggesting that the other two were no longer held in demesne.[23] The Plumptons held a single knight's fee from the Percys and a total of nine holdings, some of them tenancies of other fees. A dower plea of 1212 reveals that only four of these were held in demesne.[24] All of these families had alienated substantial portions of their land. It should be emphasized, moreover, that most of the alienations were probably gifts. All of these families were prosperous and would not have been forced to sell off large portions of their estates to pay debts.

How common was this sort of large scale alienation? A late thirteenth-century survey, *Kirkby's Inquest*, traces the honorial hierarchy in Richmondshire in rich detail, showing tenants as many as four removes from the lords of Richmond, and reveals the cumulative impact of alienation by the vassals of that region. This survey reveals that the immediate tenants of the earls of Richmond had enfeoffed subtenants with approximately seventy-two percent of the nearly 860 carucates that they themselves had received from the earls. Of course, some of the immediate tenants were magnates in

20. *EYC* 5:82–83; *CRR* 5:147–48; *Rot. Obl. & Fin.*, 264, 289.

21. *EYC* 5:272, 284.

22. Greenway, *Mowbray Charters*, 262–63; *EYC* 1:401–2; *EYC* 2:113; Purvis, *Chartulary of Healaugh*, 1.

23. *EYC* 2:461–62; *CRR* 2:12.

24. *EYC* 11:266; *CRR* 6:363–64.

their own right or vassals with many fees, and they would have needed to provide lands to their own military followers, as well as to monasteries, daughters, and younger sons. However, with extremely rare exceptions, the tenants in the next rank of the honorial hierarchy, those who received land from the immediate tenants, would not have needed to provide for a military following. Nevertheless, they granted away approximately thirty-six percent of the land they received through further subinfeudation. In considering these sums, it must be remembered that they include grants made after the Angevin period and also any sales that were treated as subenfeoffments. On the other hand, they do not include many gifts made to monasteries in free alms.[25] Obviously, precise figures for the amount of land the gentry granted away to monasteries, younger sons, and daughters, will never be obtainable, but the amounts were clearly large.

Certain factors would have ameliorated the impact that such grants would have had on the fortunes of gentry families. Because the gentry tended, so far as can be determined, to marry people of similar wealth and status, marriage portions would bring lands into the family as well as out of it. For instance, Thomas de Etton Junior received a half carucate with his wife, which offset at least a fraction of the gifts his father, Thomas de Etton senior, had made to his siblings, as shown in chapter four.[26] Gentry who granted out land would have received any rents stipulated in the grant and so too would their heirs. As overlords, moreover, gentry grantors and their heirs received the profits of lordship, including feudal incidents such as wardship. They also reduced their own feudal burdens.

However, there were limits to these ameliorating factors. A woman's marriage portion was likely to be sufficient only to provide for one daughter or younger son, though many gentry couples had a number of children. Rent from grants to family members was usually symbolic in nature, as when Nigel de Plumpton granted a carucate and other lands to his son Peter for the payment of one pair of white gloves each Easter.[27] In a sample of one hundred donations by members of the gentry to religious houses taken from *Early Yorkshire Charters*, rent, excluding feudal dues, was demanded in only fourteen cases and in three of these cases the rent was merely passed on by the donor, who owed it to an overlord for the land.[28] In both secular and

25. Skaife, *Kirkby's Inquest*, 148–86.

26. Hall, *Etton*, 7.

27. *Yorkshire Deeds* 10:134.

28. In addition, payments for forensic service were levied in four of the grants. Each of the hundred gifts was from a different family or from a different lineage within an extended family. Otherwise they were chosen as randomly as possible. The sample is as follows: *EYC* 1,

religious grants, feudal dues such as scutage were similarly passed on by the gentry to their overlords, for the feudal burden imposed in the grants was almost always proportional to the amount of land granted.[29] As for feudal incidents such as marriage and wardship, these obviously did not apply to grants to monasteries, and in the case of secular grants the occasional profits from feudal incidents could not replace the permanent income lost through grants. Despite the ameliorating factors described above, the grants to religious houses, daughters, and younger sons represented a tremendous transfer of resources and income away from gentry families and particularly from the main branches of these families.

In many cases, the troubles faced by gentry families may have been due more to alienation of land than to inflation. The case of the Leathleys has been described in chapter five. It is probably no coincidence that the Ettons, who saw so much land flow to younger children, faced severe economic difficulties in John's reign.[30] Another family, the Thorntons, received five carucates in Thornton from the abbot of St. Mary's in the middle of the twelfth century in return for quitclaiming other lands; they then parceled this land out among themselves and ended up selling much of it back to the abbey in the thirteenth century.[31] Even when the alienation of land did not lead to selling out, it could lead to a severe decline in the fortunes of a family. For instance, the Willerby family, once among the gentry, fell into obscurity as a result of generosity to the Church or to family members.[32]

The Yorkshire evidence, then, shows that a variety of factors affected gentry incomes. Obviously the relative weight of these factors would vary

nos. 50, 54, 58, 394, 519, 537, 588, 612, 616, 639; *EYC* 2, nos. 702, 708, 725, 727, 739, 772, 788, 901, 917, 989, 995, 1040, 1055, 1062, 1065, 1075, 1084, 1175, 1210, 1228; *EYC* 3, nos. 1346, 1370, 1371, 1404, 1532, 1545, 1551, 1553, 1579, 1592, 1631, 1633, 1645, 1655, 1662, 1716, 1732, 1785, 1846, 1867; *EYC* 4, no. 92; *EYC* 5, nos. 131, 134, 145, 149, 177, 191, 251, 273, 279, 293, 327, 338, 353, 368, 377; *EYC* 6, nos. 59, 90, 128; *EYC* 7, nos. 63, 111, 131, 142, 151; *EYC* 8, nos. 102, 136, 154; *EYC* 9, nos. 68, 78, 83, 90, 105, 168; *EYC* 10, nos. 43, 57, 82, 111; *EYC* 11, nos. 102, 146, 166, 175, 189, 198, 216; *EYC* 12, nos. 22, 46, 54, 65, 80, 88.

29. Theoretically, of course, a vassal could parcel out portions of his estate at a much higher rate of knight service and pocket the difference, as did the magnate Roger de Mowbray on one occasion; Greenway, *Mowbray Charters*, 230. In practice, however, the gentry almost invariably based feudal service in their grants on a rate commensurate with the size of their fees; if a gentry landholder had a fee of ten carucates and granted two away, the charter would specify that the land be held "for the service of two carucates where ten carucates make a knight's fee."

30. For family debts, see *Pipe Roll 1 John*, 53 and PRO, E401 1564; for leases and sales to pay off debts, see *Meaux Chronicle*, 318–19, 374–75. See also Holt, *The Northerners*, 169–70, for a discussion of the Etton family and their problems.

31. York Minster Library XVI.A.1:160–66.

32. *EYC* 2:497.

from family to family. Opportunities for economic development depended on geographic location and other variables, and those families with greater access to such opportunities had better chances of avoiding economic difficulties. The degree to which families were affected by inflation would depend on how much land their ancestors had leased out and on what terms. As for the effects of generosity, larger families or pious ones would be likely to alienate more land than smaller or less pious ones. Thus any crisis that occurred might have been very selective in nature: nonexistent for some, mildly difficult for others, overpowering, perhaps, for a few.

The Yorkshire evidence also shows that the situation for the gentry was both less dangerous and more dangerous than hitherto suspected: less dangerous because of economic development, but more dangerous because of the habits of generosity built up as a result of the great flow of lands from tenants-in-chief to their vassals and sustained by the possibility of economic development. However, it must be pointed out that generosity was a different sort of danger than inflation. Individual gentry could not control inflation. They could control their own giving, and though there is no sign that they did so during the Angevin period, they probably did so not long afterwards. Newman's work shows that few Yorkshire gentry gave advowsons to monasteries after c. 1230 and it is almost certain that this reflects a general decline in gentry giving to religious houses.[33] Even earlier, some gentry may have begun trying to counteract the effects of the generosity of their forbears to monasteries, for Joan Wardrop argues that from c. 1190 Fountains began to face litigation from the descendants of donors who wanted land back.[34] At some point before the late Middle Ages there was also a shift in the way parents provided for daughters and younger sons designed to protect the integrity of family estates. Fathers began giving money rather than land for marriage portions and began trying whenever possible to provide for their younger sons without diminishing their patrimony.[35] It would be interesting to learn whether this shift also took place in the thirteenth century. If so, if would explain why the cumulative effects of generosity did not sink more gentry families.

Even before this shift, gentry families could avoid the dangers of massive debt even if their incomes were reduced by inflation and alienation. An heir could react to a diminution of income by reducing expenditure,

33. Newman, "Greater and Lesser Landowners," 284–91.
34. Wardrop, *Fountains Abbey*, 122.
35. Wright, *The Derbyshire Gentry*, 46–50; Carpenter, "Fifteenth-Century English Gentry," 51–52; Jefferies, "Medieval Use," 66; Payling, *Political Society*, 70–73.

scaling down his household and eschewing luxuries, and thus avert financial collapse. As both Carpenter and Coss have suggested, cost-cutting measures may have played a role in the rapid decline in the number of landowners who assumed knighthood in the decades after the Angevin period.[36] The avoidance of knighthood is likely to have been representative of wider sacrifices. Chapter three has shown the economic savvy of many gentry, with their eagerness to take advantage of economic opportunities, and it is likely that most would have seen the pitfalls of borrowing too heavily simply to maintain expenditure in the face of a drop in income.

However, it is unlikely that most gentry viewed with equanimity the difficult circumstances brought by the declining generosity of magnates, the cumulative effects of several generations of generosity, and the decline of income due to inflation. Few people relish downward mobility, and economizing had its own subtle dangers. A scaling down of one's household meant a smaller number of supporters in a feud. It also meant a decline of prestige, which was painful in its own right, but which might also harm a gentry landlord in the quest for patronage and local standing, factors that would be useful in increasing one's fortune. At the same time, as suggested in earlier chapters, scaling down one's gifts might be psychologically and socially very difficult. How could one disappoint the expectations of family members or risk one's soul by refusing gifts to the Church? As Carpenter has noted, the thirteenth century writer, Walter of Henley, emphasized personal failings when he described how some people fell into poverty.[37] Undoubtedly mistakes and foolish choices often caused disaster, but in the circumstances described above it would have been much easier to miscalculate and to make disastrous economic choices. Equally, members of the gentry would be more likely to make choices harmful to the long-term prosperity of their family with full awareness of the consequences. It this is true, it was a more dangerous time than usual for the prosperity of gentry lineages. Moreover, even those who made economically intelligent decisions may have felt great inner tensions in doing so. This may not have been a time of overwhelming crisis for the gentry, but neither was it a time of "business as usual," for the gentry had to make many difficult adjustments and may have had to begin making them even before the onset of inflation.

It is perhaps in the context of difficult adjustments, fears of failure, and psychological tensions that the widespread concern about Jewish debt must

36. Carpenter, "Was there a Crisis?" 739; Coss, *Lordship, Knighthood and Locality*, 303.
37. Carpenter, "Was There a Crisis?" 746; Dorothy Oschinsky, *Walter of Henley and other Treatises on Estate Management and Accounting*, 308–11.

be placed. Contemporaries were constantly preoccupied with indebtedness to Jews through the latter half of the Angevin period and beyond. As Sally Harvey points out, as early as 1181, in the Assize of Arms, the royal government expressed concern about the knightly arms that were in the hands of Jews, clearly as a result of indebtedness.[38] More specifically, the accounts of two chroniclers relating to the massacre at York in 1190 refer explicitly to widespread indebtedness and financial distress among the upper classes of Yorkshire. The *Meaux Chronicle* stated that many of the nobles and the middling sort lost their patrimonies and possessions through the usury of the Jews and fell into great poverty. William of Newburgh made a similar statement about the leaders of the attack, stating that they were indebted for great sums, that their estates had been taken as pledges, and that they themselves were in great poverty.[39] In 1213, during a brief period in which John was trying to conciliate the North, royal commissioners were sent to Yorkshire and Lincolnshire to investigate grievances, and among their tasks was to learn about the lands held in pledge by Jewish money lenders.[40] Concern about the effects of Jewish money lending appears in the documents of the Magna Carta revolt and played a large role in political discourse until the expulsion of the Jews.

If only a few feckless or unusually unfortunate landlords were caught up in crisis, the preoccupation with indebtedness to Jews is puzzling, even when one factors in the growing anti-Semitism of the central Middle Ages. If, however, many gentry were facing the need for adjustment and the difficult decisions and tensions involved, the preoccupation becomes more understandable. Even if only a small number of families actually suffered disaster as a result of excessive debt, in times of uncertainty many more families might fear that possibility, even if they only owed small sums to Jewish lenders, as many Yorkshire gentry did, or no money at all.

In sum, I would agree with Coss that there was a crisis, beginning in the late twelfth century, though I would argue that the crisis had more causes than inflation alone. This was a time in which knights and other members of the gentry faced serious threats to their economic position and to traditional forms of behavior, notably their generosity with grants of land.[41] I also accept Carpenter's view that the knightly class, or in this case,

---

38. Harvey, "The Knight and the Knight's Fee," 41; Stubbs, *Select Charters*, 183.
39. *Meaux Chronicle*, 244; William of Newburgh, *Historia Rerum Anglicanum* 1:313.
40. *Rot. Litt. Pat.*, 97a.
41. The economic circumstances of Yorkshire gentry, it is true, may have been unusual in certain respects. Knights' fees were larger than in many areas and economic development and generosity may also have been greater. Nevertheless, this was a matter of degree rather than an absolute difference.

the gentry, passed through the period of crisis relatively unscathed. However, in my view the crisis was limited not because the problems were minimal but because the gentry were in a strong position to adjust to them. Moreover, I suspect that because of the tensions created by difficulties of adjustment, the crisis had a serious impact not just on the gentry but indirectly, through the actions of the gentry, on others as well.

The most obvious example of this indirect impact is the attack on the Jews of York in 1190. The York pogrom must not only be seen within the context of gentry proclivities towards violence, but also in the context of widespread economic difficulties, not just for the leaders of the pogrom but for the gentry as a whole.[42] As has so often been the case in Jewish history, wealthy Jewish money lenders who sometimes profited from the difficulties of debtors and who were victims of absurd but widespread calumnies, could serve as scapegoats for complex economic problems and provide convenient targets for the outlet of tensions and hostilities created by those problems. If Jewish communities formed one focus for gentry hostility, however, the royal government may have formed another, and not just because it protected Jewish lenders. Even as gentry landholders faced the multiple problems of inflation, decreasing patronage, and the effects of generosity, they faced more and more economic pressure from the royal government. In the next chapter I will discuss this pressure and how it led to widespread gentry participation in the Magna Carta revolt.

42. The economic difficulties may have played a more general role in the disputes and violence discussed in chapter two, though no measurement of the impact of such difficulties is possible, and in any case medieval aristocracies usually showed violent proclivities even in prosperous times. Eleanor Searle, however, has been able to show a link between the problems of inflation and violence by gentry against peasants in Sussex in this period; Searle, *Lordship and Community*, 162–65.

7. The Gentry, Royal Government, and Magna Carta

The creation of Magna Carta has long been seen as one of the most important events in English history. Magna Carta was the result of many trends, ideals, and circumstances, but this fundamentally important document must be seen at least partially within the context of the changes described in this book. The Magna Carta revolt was in large measure the reaction of provincial elites, including the gentry, to the perceived injustices of an increasingly strong royal government. The decline of the honor and the increasing independence of the gentry from honorial ties opened the way for the growth of local influence by the royal government, particularly on the gentry. This in turn gave all levels of elite society a direct interest in the conduct of royal government.[1] The financial burdens imposed by the crown also grew, but at the same time, the economic troubles experienced by the gentry made them less able to bear, and therefore increasingly hostile to, these burdens.

As a result of their hostility to and grievances against the royal government, large numbers of gentry supported the rebel magnates, giving them the backing they needed to challenge the king. The gentry had not yet achieved an independent political voice through the county court or other means. Nevertheless, the concerns and interests of the gentry helped shape Magna Carta in important ways, because the baronial leaders and negotiators needed to address those gentry concerns and interests to win and retain gentry support.

In order to explain gentry participation in the Magna Carta revolt it is necessary to explore relations between the gentry and the crown throughout the Angevin period. This will be seen first from the point of view of the crown, since the Angevin kings played so large a role in shaping and altering these relationships over time. It will then be discussed from the point of view of the gentry, in order to explain their attitudes toward royal government at the time of the Magna Carta revolt.

1. See Wales, "The Knight," 106–7, for a similar point.

The most important fact, from either point of view, is that ties were growing between the crown and the gentry and that royal government was having an increasingly large impact on the lower rungs of the landowning elite. One of the most striking and best known features of this period is the extraordinary expansion of royal influence, which was partially a reconstruction of royal authority lost during Stephen's reign, but which soon went beyond reconstruction to the creation of new institutions and policies. The increase of royal influence in the judicial arena has already been discussed in relation to the Yorkshire gentry, but royal power increased in other areas as well. A sense of this expansion can be gained simply from looking at the published editions of the pipe rolls, the size of which increases from the thin volumes of Henry II's early years to the fat tomes of John's reign.

The Norman Kings had never completely abandoned direct ties with rear vassals. The famous Salisbury oath shows William the Conqueror's awareness of and concern for the direct allegiance of rear vassals. Nevertheless, in the Norman period, the strength of the honorial system placed a certain distance between kings and the majority of the gentry as connections with rear vassals were largely channeled and mediated through tenants-in-chief. Honorial courts limited the direct authority of royal courts over that group, though they did not eliminate it. Tenants served in the feudal host not as royal subjects but as members of honorial contingents. As long as honors remained strong, the direct influence of kings on a local level was limited. However, honors also simplified royal government, for the attention of the crown could be concentrated on the relatively small number of tenants-in-chief who held large honors. By controlling, coopting, or influencing the magnates, kings could indirectly do the same for the lower echelons of the feudal hierarchy. By gaining baronial support, kings could also get the support of the vassals of the barons.[2]

As honors disintegrated, kings were less and less able to rule simply by dealing with the tenants-in-chief, though of course the relations between king and magnates were always a focal point of medieval English politics. The generosity of the tenants-in-chief to their vassals had made the gentry a wealthy and powerful group and the changes described in chapter one made it increasingly independent. Kings could not afford to ignore the potential support this group could provide, but were less and less able to

2. It must be noted that this picture of the Norman period derives in large measure from traditional historiography and in particular from Stenton's work, *The First Century of English Feudalism.* Future scholarship may modify the picture, but my own impression is that honors were quite strong in the Norman period.

tap this support via the traditional honorial hierarchy. An example of this problem is the decay of the feudal host, discussed in chapter one.

The decline of the honorial or feudal system is generally seen as a factor which strengthened royal government, and in many respects this is quite true.[3] However, this system had been established in England by the first Norman king and its decay caused problems, such as the decline of the feudal host, as well as opportunities for the royal government. The increased use of mercenaries, of course, could offset the decline of the feudal host, but in a larger sense, for the royal government to be as effective as possible, it had to be able to influence honorial vassals and to tap their resources. Since it could no longer do so via the leading tenants-in-chief, it had to do so directly.

The Angevin kings built up their ties with the gentry through a variety of means. The most traditional route was to exploit as many direct tenurial ties as possible. A few gentry families held one or more manors directly from the crown and though such families often held the bulk of their land from a baron, the king could still easily exploit the direct tenurial link.[4] Direct ties could also exist because honors had escheated to the crown or were temporarily in royal custody because the heirs were underage or in the case of the ecclesiastical honors, a vacancy had occurred. Most honors passed into royal hands at one time or another and some honors stayed in royal hands for years on end.[5] The fact that the most important gentry often held from several honors increased their chances of having direct if temporary tenurial ties with the king, at least upon occasion, and this made the use of this traditional route surprisingly effective in the case of the gentry that mattered most.

The reliefs, wardships, and marriages that the crown gained through direct tenurial ties with the gentry enriched the royal coffers and also broadened the network of royal patronage. In John's reign, if not earlier, however, these ties were most extensively exploited in times of war. The royal government used direct tenurial ties, including those held through escheat, wardship or vacancy, to personally summon as many landholders

3. Indeed, in Coss's view, it was such a great opportunity for the royal government that it presented a grave if ultimately unrealized threat to baronial power; "Bastard Feudalism Revised," 41–45, 50–52.

4. Robert de Percy of Bolton Percy, for instance, held most of his estates from his Percy relatives but held one manor from the king.

5. For instance, the honor of Tickhill was in royal hands for most of the Angevin period and the honor of Richmond was held by the crown for long periods of time. The disputes between Archbishop Geoffrey and his half-brothers, Richard I and John, meant that the archbishopric was in royal custody for large portions of their reigns.

as possible to war. When summoned in this manner, vassals could not avoid going to fight simply by paying scutage but had to attend in person or pay a personal fine larger than scutage, in the same way magnates sometimes paid to avoid personal attendance in a feudal host.[6] The best illustrations of this come from the Irish expedition of 1210. This expedition almost certainly saw reduced quotas, for most magnates seem to have brought or sent small groups of knights.[7] However, a number of prominent Yorkshire knights were present in Ireland, and they were clearly there independent of a baronial contingent since they had to borrow money for themselves from the royal government, whereas members of baronial contingents seem to have charged loans to their lord's account.[8] Others had to pay personal fines to avoid service.[9] At a time when honorial contingents were shrinking in size, kings could use direct tenurial ties to reach down and force many honorial vassals, and particularly the most important ones, to perform personal service in the feudal host, or to pay enough to hire sufficient replacements.[10]

There were, however, severe limits to this tenurial method of creating ties with the gentry. Only a small if important percentage of the gentry could be reached through such direct tenurial ties, for most honors remained in the hands of barons. Moreover, most of these ties were temporary, for they ended when escheats were granted anew or heirs in wardship became adults. On one occasion, the king tried to make temporary ties

6. See *Rot. Litt. Claus.*, 143, for a personal summons to Jordan Foliot, a knight with interests in Yorkshire. Robert Walensis, who held chiefly of the honor of Pontefract but held one holding from the king, appears on a roll of summonses for the 1214 expedition to Poitou; J. C. Holt, ed., "Roll of Summonses for the Expedition to Poitou, 1214," in *Pipe Roll 17 John*, 101. See *Rot. Litt. Claus.*, 116b; *Pipe Roll 8 John*, 209–10; *Pipe Roll 13 John*, 4, 31–32, for knights who had actually participated in expeditions and received quittance of the scutage they owed the crown. See *Rot. Obl. & Fin.*, 158, 161, 166, 173; *Pipe Roll 4 John*, 58; *Pipe Roll 5 John*, 214; *Pipe Roll 7 John*, 61, 233–34; *Pipe Roll 12 John*, 219, for knights who paid to avoid expeditions.

7. The size of contingents was frequently mentioned when loans were recorded and generally the magnates had less than ten knights; Hardy, *Rotuli de Liberate*, 177ff.

8. These included Robert de Percy of Bolton Percy, who held one manor of the crown, Ranulf son of Robert de Middleham, Hugh Malebisse, Adam de Novo Mercato, and Adam de Staveley, all of whom held of honors that were in the king's hand. Many other Yorkshire knights borrowed money during the expedition as well and were probably there through direct tenurial ties with the crown; Hardy, *Rotuli de Liberate*, 180, 182–84, 187, 189, 198, 201, 203, 205, 207, 212, 214–15, 219, 221–23.

9. Roald, Constable of Richmond and Thomas de Burgh, whose holdings of the honor of Richmond brought them temporary direct tenurial ties to the king, had to pay £65, 1 mark, and £34 respectively to avoid the Irish expedition; *Pipe Roll 13 John*, 55.

10. It might be noted that this would in turn undermine contingents, for many of the gentry summoned in this manner would have held of more than one honor and a prior summons by the crown would make it more difficult for their other lords to extract service from them.

more permanent; when King John granted the honor of Richmond to Earl Ranulf of Chester, he retained all the fees outside Richmondshire and the fees of two important vassals within Richmondshire in his own hand. This proviso provided him with direct ties to all the leading vassals of the honor.[11] However, this was an isolated case, and not representative of any conscious policy, but was the sort of ad hoc arrangement that was just as typical of Angevin royal government as the systematic and sweeping changes that are so often studied. In the absence of any conscious policy, direct tenurial ties under the traditional honorial system would only be a partial solution to the problem of how to influence and tap the talents and resources of the gentry.

Another solution was to bring members of the gentry into royal government as local officials. Chapter two described the activities of some members of the gentry as local bailiffs and undersheriffs.[12] Others served as typical multi-purpose Angevin administrators, though on a smaller scale than the most important royal servants. A single example will suffice to illustrate this practice. The first Yorkshire knight to enter the royal administration in this capacity was William Vavasour, an important tenant of the Percys. During the last few years of Henry II's reign, William served as a justice in a series of judicial and forest eyres in northern and eastern England. William was also one of a group in charge of tallaging the royal demesnes in several counties. He served as one of the custodians of the Archbishopric of York during a vacancy and as the sole custodian of the lands of William Paynel after Paynel's death. William was an extremely active royal servant, but his activity was cut short by his death soon after Richard I took the throne.[13] Other royal servants drawn from the local gentry included Richard and Hugh Malebisse, Robert de Percy of Bolton Percy, who performed many tasks besides acting as sheriff for a short time, Henry son of Hervey, Geoffrey Haget, and William de Cornborough.[14]

---

11. *Rot. Litt. Pat.*, 51a.

12. See chapter two.

13. *Pipe Roll 29 Henry II*, 59; *Pipe Roll 30 Henry II*, 39; *Pipe Roll 31 Henry II*, 11, 78, 96; *Pipe Roll 32 Henry II*, 6, 17, 27, 35, 65, 204; *Pipe Roll 33 Henry II*, 17, 20, 56, 75, 88, 91, 96, 97, 184, 185; *Pipe Roll 34 Henry II*, 6, 9, 52, 72, 87, 89, 90, 99, 100, 191, 196; *Pipe Roll 1 Richard I*, 9, 139.

14. For the activities of these men, see *Pipe Roll 1 Richard I*, 3; *Pipe Roll 3 Richard I*, 74–75; *Pipe Roll 6 Richard I*, 163; *Pipe Roll 7 Richard I*, 30; *Pipe Roll 9 Richard I*, 181; *Pipe Roll 10 Richard I*, 28; *Pipe Roll 1 John*, 39, 121, 212; *Pipe Roll 2 John*, 15, 34, 91, 102, 117; *Pipe Roll 3 John*, 143, 145; *Pipe Roll 4 John*, 49, 162; *Pipe Roll 6 John*, 188, 194; *Pipe Roll 7 John*, 43; *Pipe Roll 8 John*, 23, 160, 193, 208; *Pipe Roll 9 John*, 79; *Pipe Roll 10 John*, 142; *Pipe Roll 12 John*, 149; *Pipe Roll 13 John*, 47, 86; *Pipe Roll 16 John*, 84; *Rot. Obl. & Fin.*, 334; *Rot. Litt. Pat.*, 17a, 30a, 83–84, 97a; *Rot. Litt. Claus.*, 104b, 114–15, 135; *Rot. Chart.*, 99a; Hardy, *Rotuli de Liberate*, 134, 212, 234–36; Brown, *Pedes*

Two important points can be gleaned from a study of these individuals. First, the Angevin kings were willing to reach down to the level of subvassal to recruit royal servants, disregarding such traditional bonds as the tie of the Vavasours to the Percys and the Malebisse family to the Mowbrays. Kings simply ignored the honorial hierarchy in attracting followers.[15] A second point is the importance of personal contact between king and subject. William de Cornborough, who acted as custodian of Galtres forest during part of John's reign, may have received his introduction to the royal house when he picked up and returned a valuable belt that Richard I had lost in a skirmish on the Third Crusade.[16] Hugh Malebisse became a member of the royal *familia* and this was undoubtedly a key to his standing in local royal government.[17] The powerful Richmondshire landholder Henry son of Hervey, perhaps seeing Hugh's success, placed his younger son John in the royal household, where John became a royal valet.[18] Medieval governments depended fundamentally, and to a degree which is sometimes forgotten, on "old boy" networks.

The second point, however, brings up the real limitation of the informal, non-institutional ties with the gentry. Kings could have personal contact of even the most casual sort with only a limited number of people, and their attention always had to remain focused on the magnates. Moreover, the king was generally far removed from Yorkshire, and the periodic visits of the king to the North could only partially alleviate this.[19] In addition, personal interaction and active service, for the king as for lesser lords, often brought expectations of reward. Royal service did bring rewards for the royal servants drawn from the Yorkshire gentry, but the royal government had severe limitations on the rewards it could shell out when it came to people of less than primary political importance or usefulness. Personal interaction *could* provide the king with some useful contacts and servants, but the numbers involved were very small, and thus the more

---

Finium Ebor., xxi; Roger of Howden, *Chronica* 4:91, 163–64; PRO, C47 11/1/1; C47 11/1/11; Holt, *The Northerners*, 161; Crook, *General Eyre*, 59, 64, 68.

15. Indeed, Richard Fitz Nigel stressed that this was the king's prerogative; *Dialogus de Scaccario*, 84.

16. Roger of Howden, *Chronica* 3:133.

17. Hugh's proffer of a large sum for the king's "goodwill" after he had fallen into disfavor is a strong if somewhat artificial indication of the importance of the personal relationship between king and subject, and one found in a number of instances; *Rot. Obl. & Fin.*, 334.

18. *Rot. Obl. & Fin.*, 504, 525.

19. One can, however, follow Henry son of Hervey as he accompanied the king on one northern tour, serving as host at his chief manor of Ravensworth, negotiating business and acquiring privileges. *Rot. Chart.*, 86b, 88b, 89a, 101b.

informal ties, like direct tenurial ties, were entirely inadequate for either influencing or tapping the resources and abilities of the gentry as a whole.

The real successes of the Angevin kings in influencing the gentry and tapping their resources came in three areas: the utilization of the gentry, and especially knights, for many routine tasks of royal government in local areas; the creation of new, impersonal, institutions and legislation which allowed kings to have an impact on the gentry; and the extraction of large sums of money from that group.

The judicial reforms of the Angevin period created the greatest success in the first two areas and also played a role in the third. Chapter two has shown how great an impact royal justice had on the gentry. As a result of new legislation, new writs, eyres, and increased activity at Westminster, land litigation and even criminal cases involving the gentry were much more likely to come under royal jurisdiction. The holding of land, and to a lesser degree violent coercion, were at the center of gentry power, and this meant that the royal courts touched gentry life in areas of fundamental importance. Gentry who had never even seen the king might be affected by the actions of his justices. Moreover, it was the gentry who did most of the routine judicial work for the king, under the supervision of his justices. To a large degree the gentry kept the system of royal justice running in the localities. In terms of influencing not only the gentry but also all groups above the level of serf, and in terms of tapping gentry resources, the Angevin legal reforms were a remarkable triumph.

The utilization of gentry for government purposes can also be seen in areas outside the judicial system. When the royal government introduced innovations such as Richard I's new land tax of 1198, or the demand that all over the age of fifteen should swear an oath to keep the peace, royal directives called for the administrative participation of knights.[20] Knights were also chosen to participate in the administration of the forest, and the same juries of knights that reported on crimes to the justices in eyre also reported on royal wardships, on encroachments against royal rights, and on other matters of interest to the crown.[21] Knights were often selected for

20. For the tax, see Roger of Howden, *Chronica* 4:46–47. The *Book of Fees* contains a list of knights and free men who were present at the assessment of three Yorkshire sergeantcies in that year; *Book of Fees* 1:4. For the oaths, see Roger of Howden, *Chronica* 3:300; C. R. Cheney, *Hubert Walter*, 93; Charles R. Young, *Hubert Walter, Lord of Canterbury and Lord of England*, 119.

21. For the work of knights in the forest, see Roger of Howden, *Chronica* 2:246, 4:64; Charles R. Young, *The Royal Forests of Medieval England*, 49. For their reports on royal rights and so on, see Roger of Howden, *Chronica* 3:262–67. For the background to this practice, see van Caenegem, *Royal Writs*, 61–68.

very specific tasks as well. For instance, on one occasion twelve knights were appointed to assign twenty marks rent in the manor of Pocklington to the Count of Aumale.[22]

Not all attempts by the royal government to tap the service of the gentry were successful. Henry II's effort in 1181 to supplement the feudal host, probably already in decline, with a public burden of military service graded by wealth in the assize of arms never had much success.[23] This, however, was an exception. Just as the knights served as the cogs and wheels in the administration of royal justice, so too they supported all other aspects of local royal administration.[24] The use of local figures for the purposes of royal government was a practice that dated back at least to the Carolingian style government of the late Anglo-Saxon kings, if not before, but the ability of the Angevin kings to adapt this for the new and increasing tasks of their government allowed them to have a direct and growing influence on local areas at the same time as their indirect influence through the honors was decreasing. As A. L. Poole wrote, "Already by the end of the twelfth century knights were training themselves in the arts of local government which in the following centuries they were so largely to control.[25]

The royal government also had great success in extracting money from the gentry. By doing so, it tapped into gentry wealth, which was collectively enormous even after such factors as alienation and inflation are taken into account. Money had the advantage that it could be translated into influence wherever and whenever the king felt that it was needed; money, in the twelfth century as in the twentieth, was the lifeblood of government. One of the reasons for the many successes of the Angevin kings was their extraordinary ability to bring money into the royal coffers from all classes of society, including the upper classes and more specifically the gentry.

The royal government drew money from gentry purses in a variety of manners, some traditional, some innovative, and most of them influencing groups other than the gentry as well. As wealthy landowners, the gentry paid taxes to local wapentake bailiffs and sheriffs, which taxes helped support these royal officials and contributed to the county farm.[26] They also paid the Danegeld early in Henry II's reign, and new taxes based on

22. *Rot. Litt. Claus.*, 182b.

23. Stubbs, *Select Charters*, 183–84; Powicke, *Military Obligation*, 54–56.

24. For some overviews of the various activities of knights in this period and slightly later on behalf of the royal government, see Lapsley, "Buzones," 177–93, 545–67; Poole, *Obligations of Society*, 53–56; Treharne, "Knights in the Period of Reform," 3–4.

25. Poole, *Obligations of Society*, 56.

26. See Gale, *Registrum Honoris de Richmond*, 21–23, for the payments from several Richmondshire wapentakes in 1184.

carucage or movables later.[27] The royal government got most of the scutage paid by subtenants and profited from feudal incidents such as marriage and wardship where those with temporary or permanent direct tenurial links with the crown were concerned.[28] Indirectly, the payments by Jewish communities funneled gentry money into royal coffers, for much of the money would have come from loans to the gentry. Amercements levied against the gentry through forest law and the royal courts brought in healthy sums of money. Various members of the gentry also proffered and paid handsome sums of money for everything from judicial writs to favorable hearing in legal cases, and from good marriages to royal help in debt collection.

The collective sums the royal government drew through this bewildering variety of means were huge. The amounts of a few shillings, a mark or two, five or ten pounds, that gentry generally had to pay for proffers, amercements or other reasons may not seem much but collectively they added up to large sums of money for the royal government. Moreover, individual sums could sometimes be much more impressive, as a sampling of feudal incidents, proffers, and amercements will show. One wealthy knight, Hugh de Verly, proffered five hundred marks that his son be in the king's protection as a royal clerk; another, Alan de Wilton, proffered £100 for a package of miscellaneous rights and privileges.[29] In 1211, John Malebisse, son of Richard Malebisse, was assigned a relief of three hundred marks to have his father's lands.[30] Malger Vavasour was amerced three hundred marks, plus three palfreys, for neither participating in the Irish expedition nor paying the king for the privilege of staying home; William de Cornborough was levied a sum of one thousand marks for the goodwill of the king, probably in relation to his failure to do a proper job as forester of Galtres forest.[31] It should be emphasized that these are only a handful of the many large individual sums of £100 or more owed and generally paid by the gentry to the crown.[32]

27. For the danegeld, see J. A. Green, "The Last Century of Danegeld," 241–58. For other discussions of taxation under the Angevins, see Painter, *English Feudal Barony*, 79; Sydney Knox Mitchell, *Studies in Taxation under John and Henry III*.

28. For the most up-to-date discussion of feudal levies, see Keefe, *Feudal Assessments*, throughout.

29. *Pipe Roll 28 Henry II*, 46; *Pipe Roll 6 John*, 189.

30. *Pipe Roll 12 John*, 160.

31. *Pipe Roll 12 John*, 216; *Pipe Roll 11 John*, 139.

32. For examples other than those discussed above and below, see *Pipe Roll 22 Henry II*, 102, 112–18; *Pipe Roll 33 Henry II*, 78; *Pipe Roll 25 Henry II*, 23; *Pipe Roll 26 Henry II*, 73; *Pipe Roll 28 Henry II*, 45–46; *Pipe Roll 31 Henry II*, 72; *Pipe Roll 6 Richard I*, 161, 163; *Pipe Roll 8 Richard I*,

These amounts are even more impressive when one realizes that individuals or families could make a series of such payments. The Novo Mercato family, during Henry II's reign, provided the exchequer 1,010 marks as a result of two custodies, one relief and one amercement.[33] Early in Richard's reign, Alan son of Roald racked up an account of 270 marks with the exchequer for the right to keep his office as constable of Richmond and for certain debts he had owed Aaron of Lincoln. He paid this off within seven years. Over an eleven year period during John's reign his son Roald accounted for debts totaling nearly one thousand marks for keeping his office as constable, for having lands and privileges, and for offending the king by refusing the pay the Thirteenth of 1207. During the same period, he paid off almost all of this. In the four exchequer accounts from 1209 to 1212, Robert Vavasour was assessed 565 marks for various amercements and proffers and paid 372½. His brother, Malger, was assessed 510 marks and three palfreys and paid 312 marks.[34] If gentry wealth as a whole provided a gold mine for the royal government, the wealth of certain families presented particularly rich veins in that mine.

Moreover, the amount of money the royal government drew from the gentry, as from all other groups, rose steadily during the Angevin period. New revenues were raised in a variety of ways. First, traditional taxes were increased. For instance, scutages were much more frequent and tended to be at a higher rate in the reigns of Richard and John than that of Henry II. The wapentake and county levies also appear to have been raised.[35] Second, as royal government expanded, more and more people were brought into its financial net. The pipe rolls grew larger and larger because more and more people were making proffers, suffering amercements or paying money in other ways, and a large percentage of those people were members of the gentry. Third, the kings and their advisors developed new forms of

---

171–72; *Pipe Roll 2 John*, 110; *Pipe Roll 3 John*, 160; *Pipe Roll 5 John*, 213; *Pipe Roll 6 John*, 188–189; *Pipe Roll 8 John*, 219; *Pipe Roll 9 John*, 169; *Pipe Roll 10 John*, 51; *Pipe Roll 12 John*, 40–41; *Pipe Roll 13 John*, 29, 33, 34; *Pipe Roll 14 John*, 37, 38; *Pipe Roll 16 John*, 93; *Rot. Obl. & Fin.*, 9, 111, 334; 383, 169. These sums include a few payments by magnates for custody and marriage of gentry since a large part of the money would have come out of the gentry estates.

33. The entire debt was paid off before Henry II's death. The sum includes the purchase of the wardship of two Novo Mercato heirs by close relatives, for undoubtedly the cost would have been paid from the family estates. For the original sums owed, see *Pipe Roll 7 Henry II*, 37; *Pipe Roll 16 Henry II*, 41; *Pipe Roll 18 Henry II*, 63; *Pipe Roll 26 Henry II*, 72. Records of payment come from throughout Henry II's pipe rolls.

34. These figures are drawn from throughout the pipe rolls of Richard and John's reigns. In each of these cases, the sums cited exclude payments to avoid personal attendance in the royal host, scutage, and any other form of regular taxation.

35. *Rot. Litt. Pat.*, 97a.

revenue by creating new taxes, such as the taxes on movables, or by offering new services, such as royal help in the collection of debts. Few if any members of the gentry appear directly in the early pipe rolls of Henry II's reign, though of course they were paying taxes. By John's reign, dozens appear in every roll, a symptom of the degree to which the royal government could now pull money from that group. The pipe roll of John's fourteenth year, one of the peak years of royal financial pressure, records that over seven hundred pounds were paid into the royal coffers from Yorkshire either by gentry, from gentry lands held in royal custody, or for custody of gentry heirs. More than sixty named members of the gentry were involved in these payments.[36]

William I successfully conquered all of England and then he and his sons gave most of it away to their followers, retaining only a small percentage of land as royal demesne. As long as the honorial system remained strong, however, they could call on the resources of the rest of the country through summoning the support of their tenants-in-chief. As subinfeudation caused the continuing diffusion of landed power, however, and as the honorial system weakened, the kings had to reach beyond, and in some ways around, their magnates to rule their country and tap its resources. By exploiting direct tenurial or personal ties with some of the gentry, by drawing more gentry into the orbit of royal government, and above all by extracting money from the gentry, the Angevin government succeeded in doing so. Because of this success, the royal government not only survived the decay of the honorial system, once one of its major props, but emerged stronger than ever before. Thus from the royal point of view, the relations between the crown and the gentry were on the whole very satisfactory. From the gentry point of view, however, the situation was mixed.

The few gentry who became active royal servants naturally benefitted handsomely from their link to the crown, both in licit and illicit ways.[37] For instance, Hugh Malebisse, member of a cadet line of that family, gained four manors through marriage with a Yorkshire and Cambridgeshire heiress and Hugh almost certainly owed this marriage to royal patronage.[38]

36. *Pipe Roll 14 John*, 5, 16–18, 26–40. The sum of seven hundred pounds does not include scutage payments passed on to the royal government by tenants-in-chief or anonymous payments for amercements on villages or regions—the gentry share of such payments is impossible to calculate.

37. Among the illicit sources of gain were Richard Malebisse's sale of wood from the royal forest in his custody for his own profit and William Vavasour's acquisition of half the village of Bolton, almost certainly made through abuse of his position as a royal justice. PRO, C47 11/1/11; *Sallay Cartulary* 1:68.

38. The heiress held of the honor of Richmond, controlled by the crown at the time of the marriage. See Brown, *Pedes Finium Ebor.*, 86–87, for a fine over dower resulting from this

The royal government, of course, provided special privileges and material rewards only to very active royal servants, but the vast majority of gentry who performed such routine tasks as participating in the grand assize or assessing taxes without any hope of material reward nevertheless gained intangible rewards such as power, influence, and authority. These intangible rewards have been discussed in chapter two with respect specifically to judicial tasks, but the same factors apply for most other tasks as well.[39] In a sense, the gentry got a fraction of the royal government's authority and the opportunity to use or misuse that authority in return for their efforts on its behalf.

On a broader scale, the growing strength of the royal government brought many benefits to the gentry. Although royal legal reforms were not the sole cause of the growing independence of vassals, they certainly strengthened it by increasing tenurial security. Strong royal government also prevented the sort of anarchy present in Stephen's reign which, though providing opportunities to the aggressive, on the whole could not have been very conducive to the prosperity of a landed class. In general, royal government protected the status quo, in which the gentry had a strong stake, and provided at least partial protection from more powerful members of the elite.

This, however, is only one side of the coin. For every positive aspect noted above, there was a negative. The number of local gentry who benefitted from the royal patronage network was extremely limited and most of the benefits of that network, many of them drawn from the marriages or wardships of local gentry, went to outsiders. The routine tasks of royal government did take time and effort and even the best proffers were generally costly. If the royal government provided the gentry some protection, tenurial or otherwise, from magnates, it also to a certain degree limited the ability of the gentry to oppress those weaker than they, which may seem praiseworthy to modern historians, but may not have been nearly so welcome to many members of the Angevin gentry.

It was in the financial arena, however, that the relationship between crown and gentry shifted from a balance of positives and negatives to a

---

marriage which describes Hugh's holdings. See H. G. Richardson, ed., "The Liberate Roll of the Second Year of King John," in the *Memoranda Roll 1 John*, for some other possible rewards to Hugh. See *Pipe Roll 2 John*, 110–11; *Pipe Roll 4 John*, 64–65; *Rot. Obl. & Fin.*, 55, 68; *Rot. Chart.*, 42b, 51b, 88b; *Pipe Roll 10 John*, 155; *Rot. Litt. Pat.*, 41a, for other rewards and privileges which royal officials from the ranks of the Yorkshire gentry were able to purchase from the crown as a result of their service.

39. See chapter two.

largely negative situation from the gentry point of view. It is in the context of fiscal policies and burdens that the widespread participation of the gentry in the Magna Carta revolt must be seen. One of the great strengths of Holt's *The Northerners* is that Holt was able to link the demands of the Magna Carta rebels with specific policies and actions of the royal government and to show how the substantial and growing demands of that government sparked a backlash. Much of Holt's material, of course, relates to the baronial leaders, but a surprising amount relates to the gentry, including the Yorkshire gentry.[40] This is no accident. As elite landholders, members of the gentry shared many of the same grievances and faced many of the same burdens as magnates. They also had grievances of their own. A review of gentry grievances and burdens will place gentry participation in the Magna Carta revolt in a proper perspective.

The majority of gentry would not have paid the huge sums described earlier in the cases of a few families, but rather a multitude of small sums. Most would have faced wapentake and county levies on a yearly basis and scutage payments relatively frequently. Most could expect to get tangled up in a lawsuit or breach of royal law at some point and could expect to face at least minor amercements, payments for writs, or proffers for judicial privileges. Later in the Angevin period they would face occasional new taxes such as the Saladin tithe, the Fourth levied to pay King Richard's ransom, the Seventh of 1203, and the Thirteenth of 1207. Individually, none of these payments would have been particularly heavy, at least in most cases, but collectively they may well have been very burdensome.

Unfortunately it is very difficult to be precise about royal burdens on gentry families, because individual payments for scutage and taxes are not recorded in the pipe rolls and because information about family incomes does not survive for this period. However, in the assize of arms, Henry II decreed that anyone with an income of sixteen marks should have the equipment of a knight, and this may give some idea of at least the lower range of gentry incomes.[41] For families in this lower income range payments of a few shillings for a tax, a couple of pounds for a scutage, a mark or two for an amercement, and a fourth, seventh, or thirteenth of one's

40. Holt, *The Northerners*, especially 143–93. See pages 161–63 for Yorkshire gentry and the royal forest, 171 for pressure on two members of the Yorkshire gentry to pay royal debts, and 179, 190 for reliefs affecting the Yorkshire gentry that were exorbitant or might have provoked resentment.

41. Stubbs, *Select Charters*, 183–84. In *inquisitions post mortem* of Henry III's reign, several Yorkshire gentry families are recorded as having incomes ranging from £16 to just over £120; *Yorkshire Inquisitions* 1:8, 104, 116–18.

movable property could add up to a sizable chunk of income even when spread over several years.

Moreover, for most families the amount of money paid was rising at the very time when they were facing a less favorable economic climate and difficult choices between the economic well-being of their lineage, their desire to support daughters, younger sons and followers, and their hope of assuring their salvation through generosity to the Church.[42] From the royal point of view, the new taxes and increased scutages were perfectly reasonable responses to the growing costs of war that resulted from inflation and the growing threat from the Capetians, responses that were even more reasonable in light of the economic growth of the country. From the gentry point of view, however, the growing burden of taxes and other payments was yet one more threat to traditional patterns of generosity and family prosperity. Thus, even those who escaped the excesses of Angevin government might nonetheless feel strong resentment against the government over average financial exactions because of their own financial situation.[43]

A substantial minority of the gentry, moreover, were faced with the sort of huge payments discussed earlier in the chapter. Those so afflicted were usually among the wealthier gentry, but even for the richest of the gentry, payments of £100 or more, even if spread over a number of years, must have been extraordinarily burdensome. The occasional proffer would pay for itself over time, but most charges, including some proffers, represented a complete loss financially. At the very least, members of the gentry owing such large sums would have to cut their expenditures severely over a period of years, which would require a lower standard of living and might threaten the prestige and power that wealth and large households represented.

Many gentry, moreover, must have been forced to borrow money or lease or sell land, which could threaten the long term prosperity of the family. It is not surprising to find William de Novo Mercato, who paid the crown 140 marks for his nephew's custody and 120 marks for license to concord, owing money to Aaron of Lincoln.[44] Holt has shown how royal

42. The burden of some traditional taxes would have been lessened by inflation, of course, but inflation was also affecting the gentry's ability to pay.

43. Keefe argues that taxation was not especially severe during Henry II's reign and suggests that traditional ideas about the heaviness of Angevin financial exactions should be reconsidered. I think he is right that regular taxation at least was not crippling, but this ignores extraordinary charges and also the financial difficulties of many; Keefe, *Feudal Assessments*, 116–40.

44. *Pipe Roll 3 Richard I*, 22.

financial pressure forced Thomas de Etton, a member of the Yorkshire gentry, to lease and grant land in return for cash.[45] Similarly, the Goodmanham family lost several of its estates for more than a generation, and perhaps one permanently, because one of its members needed to borrow money to pay a large debt to the crown.[46] The economic changes of the period made finances tricky enough for gentry families without the added danger of accumulating an enormous debt with the royal government and being forced to borrow, lease, or sell. These transactions, which cut into the long-term prosperity of families, however, were not the worst that could happen to a debtor to the crown. William de Cornborough couldn't possibly hope to pay the one thousand marks demanded from him for his shortcomings as a royal forester, and he ended up in prison, presumably for debt, where he died.[47]

William de Cornborough's case was an isolated one, and most of the gentry families who paid large sums avoided disaster.[48] Nevertheless, the fact remains that many gentry families, including a large percentage of the wealthiest ones, must have suffered severe inconveniences and difficulties as a result of royal financial policy, and this would not have created strong ties of affection to the Angevin kings or their advisors. Since the number of large payments tended to increase as time went on, the concomitant resentment would increase as well.

It was not only the amount of money the crown gathered which could breed resentment among the gentry but also the way the money was gathered. There are a number of methods of royal revenue collection which were designed to offend sensibilities. The resentment against the forest laws, theoretically designed to protect the king's hunting but in practice largely transformed into a source of revenue (especially in the North, where kings were likely to hunt only very occasionally), is very well known. Those gentry who lived within the forest undoubtedly shared the resentment. The resentment against Jewish moneylenders is also well known, and part of that resentment was bound to spill over to the royal government, which

45. *Meaux Chronicle*, 375; Holt, *The Northerners*, 168–70.

46. *EYC* 2:421–22. In one document William son of Peter conceded two villages, one of them Goodmanham itself; the other village was returned in a later agreement, but the return of Goodmanham was not mentioned, although part of that same agreement concerned a grant of a marriage portion in Goodmanham by William son of Peter. It is likely that some relevant documents are missing.

47. *Pipe Roll 11 John*, 139; *Yorkshire Eyre*, 151.

48. The Constables of Richmond were an exception, but their fall came because of later actions and mistakes, though these earlier payments may have had a role.

protected and profited from the moneylenders; William of Newburgh, in his account of the York pogrom, described the Jews at one point as the royal usurers (*regiis foeneratoribus*).[49] Gentry like William de Novo Mercato who borrowed money to pay royal debts suffered a double squeeze, paying the royal government the original sum and then paying interest on the money they had borrowed to pay this sum, and this would only increase the resentment.

A source of resentment particular to the gentry was the sudden growth of burdens that occured when the crown gained direct tenurial ties with them through accidents of escheat or vacancy. As a result of such ties, gentry families might find heiresses or minor heirs in the hands of unscrupulous royal favorites or might be forced to pay huge sums to keep the wardship in the hands of a relative. In war, they were probably more likely to be summoned, which involved not only time and danger but great expense.[50] Whereas their peers might simply pay scutage to avoid participating in an expedition, those with direct tenurial ties often had to pay a larger, sometimes much larger, sum. These people could well feel that they were treated unfairly.[51]

When honors passed to the crown, moreover, gentry were often forced to pay the crown so that they could keep lands or offices which they had acquired through service to a baron. For instance, the hereditary family of constables of Richmond paid both Richard and John for their constableship, which had been gained from the earls of Richmond, and Robert de Percy had to pay the king for confirmation of the manor of Osmotherley when the bishopric of Durham passed to the king by a vacancy. When William de Stuteville died, the honor of Knaresborough which he had received passed back to the crown and a number of followers who had received land on the honor had to pay the crown to keep their land.[52] From

49. William of Newburgh, *Historia Rerum Anglicanum* 1:313.

50. Adam de Novo Mercato borrowed nineteen marks on his own account during the Irish campaign, in addition to money for the contingent of his stepfather Henry du Puiset which Adam and his brother were leading. Robert de Percy, Hugh Malebisse, and Ranulf son of Robert borrowed twenty-one and one half, fifteen and one half, and sixteen marks respectively in Ireland. This would presumably have been in addition to whatever money they raised or borrowed before the expedition and to the costs of their equipment. Hardy, *Rotuli de Liberate*, 180, 184, 187, 189, 200, 203, 205, 207, 210, 212, 214, 221–23, 229. For other prests, some of them equally large, see *Pipe Roll 3 John*, 160–61; *Pipe Roll 3 Henry III*, 204.

51. Holt, *Magna Carta*, 218.

52. *Pipe Roll 8 John*, 218–19; *Rot. Obl. & Fin.*, 332. John demanded an enormous relief from William's heir, Nicholas, who had to grant the king Knaresborough and Boroughbridge as guarantees for his payment. Since Nicholas was never able to pay the relief, the Stutevilles lost these lands permanently, though they tried to recover them during the Magna Carta

the king's point of view there was probably justification for at least some of these payments. The crown may not have felt that the constableship of Richmond was in fact hereditary and the gift of Osmotherley, coming from the illegitimate son of the Bishop, may have been of doubtful validity. Even with this justification, gentry must have resented paying the crown for lands and offices they had earned through baronial patronage, especially when the prospects of royal patronage were denied to most of them.

In addition to these general sources of resentment, there were a number of individual cases that indicated bad faith or a disregard of custom on the part of the kings and that must also have provoked a great deal of anger. An early instance and perhaps the most sweeping one came in the aftermath of the 1173–74 revolt, when the king ignored his suspension of the forest laws during the revolt and collected huge sums of money through a forest eyre. Heavy amercements of ten to sixty marks were common and there were a number of amercements of up to one hundred pounds levied against gentry as well as against magnates; payment was demanded promptly, to judge by the speed with which most amercements were paid. Not all of these amercements would have related to the period of the revolt itself, but the king's breaking of his promise must have been galling; it brought protests even from Richard de Lucy, the justiciar.[53]

More specific cases affecting Yorkshire gentry may also be cited. Holt has described how the men of Ainsty Wapentake purchased the disafforestation of their wapentake in 1190 and twice paid King John for confirmation of that disafforestation but nevertheless were heavily amerced in the forest eyre of 1212. Undoubtedly the "men" of Ainsty included the gentry who held land there.[54] When the honor of Knaresborough passed back into royal hands, one of the new tenants enfeoffed by William de Stuteville, Adam de Staveley, immediately proffered three palfreys in return for confirmation of his tenancy. Despite this confirmation, he had to pay twenty marks two years later when all of William de Stuteville's followers had to pay for their new lands.[55] On two occasions, kings took large sums of money (one hundred and two hundred marks respectively) as a result of

revolt. *EYC* 9:13–14, 122; *Rot. Obl. & Fin.*, 305; H. G. Richardson, "The Morrow of the Great Charter," 442–43.

53. *Pipe Roll 22 Henry II*, 108–18; *Pipe Roll 23 Henry II*, 73–77; *Pipe Roll 24 Henry II*, 67–69; Benedict of Peterborough, *Gesta Regis* 1:99; Young, *Royal Forests*, 24; Keefe, *Feudal Assessments*, 127–28.

54. Holt, *The Northerners*, 160; *Pipe Roll 2 Richard I*, 67; *Rot. Obl. & Fin.*, 54, 434; *Pipe Roll 14 John*, 39.

55. *Pipe Roll 6 John*, 188; *Pipe Roll 8 John*, 218–19; *Rot. Obl. & Fin.*, 207, 332.

marriages, even though the marriages were arranged by the families and there was no question of an heiress in wardship. It is significant that in the second case the payment was made so that the marriage would take place "with the goodwill of the king."[56] In both cases, the king simply moved in and took his cut from a profitable marriage. Finally, the huge amercements occasionally demanded from gentry must sometimes have been seen as unjustly exorbitant. The death in prison of William de Cornborough, a former crusader, as a result of such a debt would only have compounded the sense of injustice.

In sum, the gentry had many reasons to be unhappy with the royal government. Royal financial policies, though very successful in the short term, were bound to cause trouble in the long run, and that trouble would come from gentry as well as magnates. Because of the economic circumstances described in the previous chapter, even the gentry families least affected by the royal government were likely to resent the financial burden. Many of the most important, moreover, suffered much heavier burdens, burdens that could threaten their long-term prosperity. Others had suffered burdens they would consider unfair, whatever their weight, and all would know of incidents that might be considered unjust. Finally, the anxiety that could be caused in others by the heavy payments demanded of some by the royal government in a difficult and even dangerous economic period may have caused as much resentment as the financial burdens themselves.

To what degree could or did the gentry combat the perceived injustices of the royal government through an organized and politicized county community of the sort found in later periods? To what degree did such a county community exist? Certainly many of the prerequisites for a county community could be found in the late Angevin period. Counties and hundreds, or in Yorkshire, wapentakes, which could form the foci for local political communities, had existed since Anglo-Saxon times.[57] Moreover, by the Angevin period, if not earlier, the gentry had forged many horizontal ties among themselves that cut across honors and even across regions within the county.[58] This may be seen from the description of one complex of marriage ties between some of the leading gentry families of the county in the Angevin period. The Percys of Kildale, a cadet branch of the Percys

56. *Pipe Roll 26 Henry II*, 73.

57. Indeed, J. R. Maddicott states that county communities predated the Conquest; "Magna Carta and the Local Community 1215–1259," 25.

58. C. J. Wales, using evidence of marriage patterns, pledging and witness lists, argues that knights began creating such horizontal networks with little reference to honors as feudal ties declined. Wales, "The Knight," xxxiii–xxxv, 89–91, 93–94, 213–60, 283–85.

who held knights' fees of the Brus honor, had marriage ties to the Nevilles of Muston, who held chiefly of the Gants; the Ettons, tenants of the Stutevilles; the Flamvilles, tenants of the Mowbrays; and the Staveleys, tenants of the Mowbrays, the honor of Skipton, and the king. These families had marriage ties in turn to the FitzHughs, tenants of Richmond; the Conyers, tenants of the Bishop of Durham; and the Birkins, tenants of the Lacys. The families involved lived across the length and breadth of Yorkshire.[59] Similar networks cutting across honorial and regional lines may be seen in the lists of pledges that members of the gentry gathered to guarantee payment of proffers or other sums owed the royal government.[60] Thus there existed the raw material for a united, politically active community, possibly at the county level or perhaps at some more local level, for Yorkshire, after all, was a county unique for its size.

There is some evidence that such communities had begun to emerge by the end of the Angevin period. Maddicott and Holt have both discussed the early actions of local communities in buying communal privileges such as the right to elect the sheriff of a county or to disafforest a part of the royal forest.[61] In Yorkshire, this phenomenon is represented by the collective actions of the men of Ainsty wapentake and of those between the Ouse and Derwent either to gain disafforestation of their regions or to gain confirmation of privileges within the forest.[62] Even the language later associated with local community and particularly with the county community was already present. In reference to a custom particular to Yorkshire, Roald son of Alan in one document spoke of the county as the *patria*.[63] Elsewhere one encounters such phrases as "the knights of the shire" (*milites de comitatu*) which are also suggestive of a sense of county community.[64]

59. Clay and Greenway, *Early Yorkshire Families*, 25–26, 30–31, 72, 90; *EYC* 2:90–91, 93, 463; *EYC* 9:192; *EYC* 11:9.

60. The best example of this comes from a list of pledges for £100 owed by William Gramary in 1201. William lived in the West Riding and was primarily a tenant of the honor of Pontefract. His pledges included nine gentry landholders almost all of whom held of various other honors and some of whom lived outside the West Riding; *Rot. Obl. & Fin.*, 138.

61. Maddicott, "Magna Carta and the Local Community," 27–37; Holt, *Magna Carta*, 51–60.

62. *Pipe Roll 2 Richard I*, 67; *Rot. Obl. & Fin.*, 54, 434; *Pipe Roll 12 John*, 216.

63. This was in one of a series of nearly identical documents confirming customary grain renders to the Hospital of St. Leonards. Roald's confirmation used the term *patria* where most of the other documents said Yorkshire; Cotton MSS Nero D.III, 49, 59–61. For a discussion of this custom, see Kapelle, *Norman Conquest of the North*, 72–74. Coss, it should be noted, cautions against investing *patria* "with some technical meaning like county community." Coss, *Lordship, Knighthood, and Locality*, 10.

64. *Yorkshire Eyre*, 176. This instance, however, may refer specifically to the knights of the county court.

However, aside from the examples described above, there is very little evidence of a county or other local community resisting the demands of the royal government or playing an effective political role. Perhaps this is simply a matter of inadequate sources, but I suspect that local communities, at least in Yorkshire, had not yet attained a sufficient level of political development to have much impact. Local political communities emerged because of the decline of the honorial system and the growing royal influence in the counties, but in John's reign those developments were probably too recent for strong political communities to have emerged.

Instead of being channeled through a county community, gentry resistance to the crown centered around unrest and revolt. Gentry resistance to the royal government can be seen even in the protests and conspiracies that led up to the actual Magna Carta revolt.[65] One of the most prominent figures in the resistance to the Thirteenth levied in 1207 was Roald, constable of Richmond. He was disseised of Richmond castle for his resistance and was forced to proffer two hundred marks and four palfreys to recover seisin.[66]

Other instances of gentry resistance before the revolt are more shadowy. Holt has suggested that Adam de Novo Mercato was suspected of involvement in Eustace de Vescy and Robert fitz Walter's conspiracy of 1212, for the king held hostages from his family in 1213.[67] Given the financial beating his family had taken in Henry II's reign, his opposition to royal government would not be surprising. I argue in appendix four that the charter of grants and privileges that Peter de Brus granted to the knights and tenants of the wapentake of Langbargh, which he had purchased from the king, should be seen in light of its witness list, which was made up neither of Brus retainers nor of Langbargh landowners but of strong opponents of the king, not only as a working document but as a manifesto of good government designed to implicitly attack John's rule. Seven of the witnesses were members of the gentry, and if my hypothesis about the charter is correct, they were already in active though perhaps not openly defiant opposition to royal policies in the period 1207–1209, when the charter was issued.[68]

The extraordinary demand of one thousand marks from William de Cornborough for his bad custody of Galtres forest also raises interesting

65. See Holt, *The Northerners*, 79ff, 205–8, for some of the unrest leading up to the revolt.
66. *Rot. Obl. & Fin.*, 372; *Rot. Litt. Pat.*, 72b.
67. *Rot. Litt. Pat.*, 105; Holt, *The Northerners*, 83.
68. For the agreement, see Brown, *Cartularium de Gyseburne* 1:92–94.

possibilities. William's predecessor, Richard Malebisse, had robbed the king blind, selling the king's wood and appropriating an enormous number of oak trees for his own building projects. He suffered an amercement of only £100. In contrast, William's only crime seems to have been in allowing others to exploit the wood at will. Perhaps William's refusal to guard the forest resulted not from laxity but from open defiance of forest law or policies. Perhaps William was tacitly going along with the defiance of others. In either case, the punishment may have had political overtones. John may not simply have been disciplining a lazy official but making an example for potential opponents. This would explain why the amercement was so large. If this hypothesis is correct, it would put William's death in prison in an even more incendiary light and make him not just a victim but a martyr.[69]

As for the revolt itself, the evidence of gentry participation is extensive and unequivocal. Two important tenants of the honor of Richmond, Ranulf son of Robert de Middleham and Conan son of Elias, joined the barons who met at Stamford at Easter, 1215. Ranulf was excommunicated by name later that year for his participation in the rebellion and he appeared with a group of magnates with whom John was negotiating in 1216.[70] Another Richmond tenant, Roald son of Alan, the man amerced for opposition to the Thirteenth, held Richmond castle against the king, and in John's 1216 chevauchée through the north several other members of the Richmondshire gentry were captured when Richmond castle was successfully besieged.[71] Fighting was hot around the king's stronghold of Knaresborough, with Brian de Lisle's royalist troops dispossessing rebellious local landowners and local gentry raiding in retaliation even after peace had been concluded.[72] As early as July 23, 1215, John wrote to the barons, knights, and free tenants of Yorkshire ordering them to return the lands, tenements, and castles they had seized and to make restitution for the chattels they had taken, thus showing the participation of the gentry, as well as barons, in the early stages of the revolt.[73]

69. For Malebisse, see *Pipe Roll 6 John*, 188; PRO, C47 11/1/1. For Cornborough, see *Pipe Roll 11 John*, 139; PRO, C47 11/1/11; *Yorkshire Eyre*, 151.

70. Matthew Paris, *Chronica Majora* 2:585, 643; *Rot. Litt. Pat.*, 180a.

71. *Rot. Litt. Pat.*, 163b; *Rot. Obl. & Fin.*, 569, 603.

72. *Rot. Litt. Claus.*, 245b, 249b, 285b, 326a. It is not clear that all the lands granted in the close rolls to Brian de Lisle and his followers around Knaresborough were actually held by them, but the mention of specific manors near Knaresborough in some grants does suggest that the lands were seized.

73. *Rot. Litt. Pat.*, 150.

The most impressive evidence for widespread gentry participation, however, comes from the close rolls of the summer and autumn of 1217 which record the names of hundreds of rebels who had made their peace with the royal government and who received writs of seisin to sheriffs and local officials.[74] Nearly two hundred of these rebels were from Yorkshire or owned land there. A handful of these were magnates, and others may have been prosperous peasants, but the greatest number were gentry. The scope of gentry participation can be seen from a comparison of the lists of rebels with those individuals appearing as knights in royal judicial records. Of the nearly two hundred rebels, forty-six were described as knights in royal judicial records between 1190 and 1230. Approximately twenty more men and women can be identified as close relatives of such knights. Many more came from prosperous families that may have been of knightly status and certainly can be counted among the gentry.[75]

The large amount of gentry participation in the revolt from Yorkshire comes as no surprise. Most magnates in Yorkshire were rebels and personal ties of lordship, whether honorial or extra-honorial, would have prompted many gentry to rebel, while the absence of large numbers of active royalist magnates would have removed any potential damper on rebellion. A far more important explanation of gentry participation, however, were the grievances and burdens described earlier; indeed, in many cases one can correlate the participation of individual members of the gentry to specific grievances. It is clearly no accident that a Walter de Cornborough, almost certainly a relative of William, took up arms against King John.[76] The participation of Roald son of Alan and of Robert Vavasour, despite the fact that the latter's father had been an active royal servant, can be seen to result from the vast sums they had to pay the royal government.[77] Adam de Staveley, who had to pay to marry his own daughter to the member of another Yorkshire family and who was charged twenty marks to retain his lands on the honor of Knaresborough though he had already received a confirmation, would have needed little urging to make his attacks on the lands of Brian de Lisle, the royal official who took over custody of Knaresborough after William de Stuteville's death.[78] Of the nearly two hundred

---

74. *Rot. Litt. Claus.*, 244, 245, 250, 254–55, 301, 311, 314, 318–41, 373–76.
75. It is difficult to be more precise, given the problems of identifying individuals and differentiating between members of the various social ranks.
76. *Rot. Litt. Claus.*, 374b.
77. *Rot. Litt. Claus.*, 338a, 376a.
78. *Rot. Litt. Claus.*, 326.

rebels associated with Yorkshire in the close rolls, thirty-four, most of them magnates or gentry, were recorded as owing money to the king in the pipe roll of John's fourteenth year alone.[79] In the Magna Carta revolt, the royal government reaped what it had sown.

What affect did gentry participation in the revolt have? Without widespread gentry support in Yorkshire and elsewhere it is unlikely that the rebels would have had enough power or military strength to force John to the bargaining table or to persuade Henry III's regents that a modified form of Magna Carta was a necessity. At the most basic level, gentry support allowed the rebel barons to achieve their important if incomplete successes in reforming and limiting royal government.

To what degree did gentry influence go beyond military support to a shaping of rebel demands and thus to an influence on Magna Carta itself? J. R. Maddicott has argued that the gentry did not emerge as a significant force in English politics until the baronial revolt of the middle of the thirteenth century. In one sense, I think Maddicott is right about this; in 1215, the gentry had no independent voice or agenda of the sort that they began to have in the later rebellion.[80]

However, the absence of an independent gentry voice does not mean that the gentry had no influence on Magna Carta; instead, their influence was channeled through the demands of the barons. In chapter one I described the close association between service and reward among the elites of Angevin England. The baronial leaders of the revolt clearly rewarded the support of their Welsh, Scottish, and London allies by gaining concessions for them in Magna Carta. So too they rewarded their gentry supporters and allies by gaining concessions for them. The fact that gentry and magnates shared many grievances made this easier, but nevertheless the need of the rebel leaders to win and retain gentry support shaped the charter in fundamental ways.

The first way gentry participation influenced the charter was probably by contributing to its very existence. When only a few leading barons had to be satisfied, personal negotiation and private concessions could bring peace. When grievances and opposition were widespread, however, uniform concessions had to be made. A charter would allow large numbers of personal grievances to be boiled down to a set of rights and privileges. The participation of hundreds of gentry from around England who were not

79. *Pipe Roll 14 John*, 16–18, 26–40.
80. Maddicott, "Magna Carta and the Local Community," 25–65.

simply following their lords but had their own grievances made a charter imperative in 1215. The creation of such a charter is what set the revolt against King John apart from earlier revolts and caused the rebellion to have such a long term impact.

The influence of the gentry, moveover, can also be seen in several specific clauses. Many of the Magna Carta demands, of course, were common to both gentry and barons, but some were directed primarily to the former. The demand that knights could not be forced to offer money for castle guard rather than performing it (clause twenty-nine) was clearly of more interest to gentry than to magnates. Clause forty-three, which stated that the king could demand no more from the tenants of an escheated honor than a baron could demand, was designed to protect those who had been feeling the heavy hand of the crown because of temporary but direct tenurial ties. Clause fifteen of Magna Carta, which limited the occasions on which a lord could take an aid, actually limited the rights of barons in favor of tenants. More striking still, clause sixty applied the terms of the charter to the way all lords, not just kings, treated their vassals, clearly an important concession to the interests of the gentry.[81] The appointment of twelve knights, mandated by clause forty-eight of Magna Carta, to enquire into and eliminate evil customs connected with forests and local officials, as well as the demand in clause eighteen that local knights take part in the hearing of petty assizes, shows that the barons recognized that knights had a crucial role in government, a role that they should be allowed to exercise in the interests of reform. Thus, the negotiators with the king saw that specific gentry interests were met, just as they incorporated the interests of the Scottish, Welsh, and urban allies.[82]

However, the most important influence of gentry support in shaping Magna Carta came in the extension of many rights and privileges to all free men, an aspect of the charter that has been commented upon more than any other. In chapter four, I argued that a major reason that Angevin legal reforms provided protection so far down the social and economic ladder

81. The king may have had a role in negotiating this clause in order to weaken or get back at the barons, but it was the gentry who benefitted most from the clause and most likely it was they who bargained for it.

82. Holt, *Magna Carta*, appendix 4, 322, 323, 324, 328; *The Northerners*, 35. Maddicott argues that concessions to local communities, and therefore to the gentry, were limited in 1215 and even more so in 1225; "Magna Carta and the Local Community," 28. This may well be right, but the precedent for gentry involvement and influence in politics had been set and this precedent lay behind the growing activism of gentry that Maddicott describes for the reign of Henry III.

and that the dividing line came only with servility was because of gentry inheritance patterns. Members of the gentry would have relatives who were peasants at least in economic terms and would know that some of their own descendants could end up in the same category. Therefore, they had an interest in protecting the legal standing of free peasants. The same pattern could work in the Magna Carta revolt. Rebel barons needed gentry support and the gentry might in turn rely on less powerful relatives and followers. The negotiators had to gain concessions for the gentry in order to retain their support and the gentry in turn had to gain concessions for their followers and allies. Indirectly, the fact that so many ties of kinship existed between various levels of free tenants tended to erase distinctions between those ranks, and this made it hard to find a good cut-off point between the level of baron and the level of serf.[83] Magna Carta may have been based partly on social ideals and norms, and these may have included beliefs about the rights of the free and the unfree. In the end, however, the document was a result of negotiation in the midst of warfare and political strife, and it was the importance of the gentry in the struggle that guaranteed the extension of rights and privileges so far down the social and economic scale.

Without seeing this aspect of Magna Carta as the fountainhead of English democracy, one can nevertheless note its importance and in general the impact of the gentry on Magna Carta. The decline of the honorial system, the growth of royal government, the growing involvement of gentry in royal government on a local level, and the increasing tax burden all brought the gentry into the political arena. The political involvement of the gentry would evolve greatly in the decades following the Magna Carta revolt and of course the development of Parliament and of the House of Commons in the later Middle Ages gave gentry an even greater say in royal government.[84] Even before these developments, however, they were already helping to reshape royal government at the end of the Angevin period.

83. The concept of knighthood could have formed a break, but it was still too fluid to do so well.

84. See Maddicott, "Magna Carta and the Local Community," 25–65, for gentry involvement in politics in the decades after Magna Carta.

Conclusion

Periodically throughout this work I have had occasion to point out the similarities between the gentry of Angevin Yorkshire and their successors in later periods. In many respects, the degree of continuity with later periods is striking. The reader familiar with the gentry in the later Middle Ages or even of the Early Modern period may get a sense of déjà vu from this book, for the Yorkshire gentry, particularly by the end of the Angevin period, resembled their successors of later centuries in a remarkable number of ways. The bloody feuds and violent proclivities of later medieval gentry were nothing new, nor were their judicial activities. Improving landlords, those characters beloved of historians, could be found during the Angevin period as well as in the agricultural revolution. The ties of gentry with magnates were marked by the same fluidity that characterized bastard feudalism and subsequent patronage systems. Nuclear families, family closeness, a sense of lineage, and lay religiosity, all characteristics of later gentry society, can also be found in the late twelfth and early thirteenth centuries. If gentry participation in and influence on royal government was only in a fledgling state, nevertheless it had already begun.

There were, of course, also pronounced differences between the behavior and situation of gentry in the Angevin periods and later. The unusual generosity of Angevin gentry in handing out land is perhaps the most obvious contrast in behavior. The growth of Parliament and particularly the inclusion of knights of the shire in the House of Commons greatly altered the possibility and manner of gentry influence on royal government and helped shape local political communities. The growing categorization of elites into firm ranks such as baron, knight, squire, and gentleman may have affected gentry self-awareness, though I think one needs to be wary of making too much of such classification.[1] Nevertheless, the similarities are very striking. In many respects, the Pastons would have

1. As I suggested in the introduction, more work on knighthood and its meaning in the twelfth century needs to be done. Such work might shed light on the impact of changing systems of rank and of increasingly formal stratification.

felt very much at home in Angevin Yorkshire. Historians tend to focus on change, but it is worthwhile sometimes to point out continuity; what did not change can sometimes be as important as what did change. After the completion of the Norman Conquest, change in elite society tended to be gradual rather than abrupt in nature and for that reason great stability in some areas of elite life could coexist alongside radical change in other areas. The gentry of the Angevin period can therefore fruitfully be compared to their successors of later periods.

Nevertheless, this book is primarily about change, or rather about a series of changes in which the gentry were intimately involved. Indeed, some of the similarities described above came about only as the result of changes in the Angevin period. The close relationship between the gentry and the royal government had its roots in the growth of royal government and the gentry response to that growth during the reigns of Henry II and his sons. The declining flow of lands from magnates to gentry may have forced the gentry to become improving landlords during the Angevin period, if they were not so already.

More important, the changes described in this book reshaped local society in fundamentally important ways. The transformation of the honor and the growth of new avenues of patronage among the elite; the economic development of gentry estates; the shift of land to cadet lines and followers; the blossoming of monastic life in Yorkshire; and the growing influence of royal government on the gentry and of the gentry on royal government, all had a strong impact on local society as well as on the gentry. By the end of the Angevin period, the structure of landholding and the organization of elite power had been transformed in Yorkshire, and undoubtedly in England as a whole, with consequences that would be felt for centuries to come.

The historian must be wary of telescoping too much change into his or her period of study. Many of the changes discussed in this book had their roots in the Norman period. For instance, the transformation of the honor clearly began before 1154. This and other changes would continue well after 1216. The political activities of the gentry, to cite one example, had only their barest beginnings in the Magna Carta revolt. Nevertheless, the amount of change that occurred within the Angevin period itself was both profound and of lasting consequence.

The historian must also be wary of attributing exaggerated importance to the event, thing, or people he or she is studying. Other actors, from peasants to kings, played important roles in the transformations discussed in this book. Nevertheless, the role of the gentry was clearly important and often at the heart of these changes. By sheer inactivity as well as the more active breaking of close ties they helped transform the honor. By shifting their activities from honorial courts to royal ones they strengthened the latter, and through their service made it possible for these courts to function. They were at least as active as any other group in promoting economic development. By their generosity, they caused the monasteries to flourish and brought the further diffusion of land and resources down the social scale. Their military strength helped make the Crusades and the Magna Carta revolt possible.

The gentry brought change through the accumulation over time of individual decisions and actions. Some actions were dramatic, even heroic, such as the valiant rescue by several Yorkshire knights of a war engine at the siege of Acre. Most were very ordinary and mundane activities, such as assarting another few acres, giving a little land to the church or a younger son, or deciding not to join the retinue of a feudal superior. No individual member of the gentry had great influence, at least on a national scale, and no individual decision had very great impact. It was as a group that the Yorkshire gentry had influence and it was through the accumulation of actions and decisions that that influence was exerted both in and out of Yorkshire. That individuals and individual actions were relatively unimportant should not disguise the profound collective importance of the Yorkshire gentry in changing their world. Reacting to events around them as well as to their own desires, the Yorkshire gentry and their peers throughout the country reshaped their society in ways that would influence England long after the death of King John. The importance of the gentry in later periods has long been recognized. As it turns out, this importance was nothing new.

Appendix One: The Mowbray and Percy Honors

I. Categorization of individuals and families on the Mowbray honor.

Category A: those established on the honor before 1129 and receiving no additional reward: Tison, Riparia, Luvel, Walter son of Asketil, St.Martin, Gainsborough, Wappenbury, Wiseg, Griselee, Arden, Queniborough, Rampan, Takel, Simon son of Simon (Kyme?), Rames, d'Aubigny Brito, Moreville, Montfort, Moles, Cundy, Perces, Roger son of Geoffrey, Ralph son of Aldelin, Prince, Dapifer, Herbert son of Richard, Croxley, Gramary, Bulmer.

Category B: those established on the honor before 1129 and receiving subsequent reward: Flamville,[1] Daiville, Stuteville, Haget, Malebisse, Wyville,[2] Camville.[3]

Category C: those established on honor between 1129 and 1166: Vescy, Lancaster, Coleville, Vere, Buscy, Beler, Carlton, Graindorge, Warin son of Warin, Buher, Cramville.[4]

Category D: those established after 1166: Bellun, Belvoir, Billinghay, Montpincon.[5]

1. Roger de Flamville received the heiress to the Arches fee, presumably through Roger de Mowbray's help. The Arches inheritance eventually passed to the Brus family through the earlier marriage of the heiress to Adam de Brus, but even the temporary tenure of this large fee was an important reward which strengthened the economic and social position of the Flamvilles. For the marriage and Roger's probable role, see Greenway, *Mowbray Charters*, xxxix.
2. For gifts to the Haget, Wyville, and Malebisse families, see Greenway, *Mowbray Charters*, 46, 232–33, 255.
3. Greenway, *Mowbray Charters*, 225. This gift was to a cadet member of the Camville line. Except for the Stutevilles, who were magnates in their own right and rivals of the Mowbrays, the Camvilles were the least active attestors in category B. Almost all the attestations from this category came from the other five families.
4. Walter Buher received a subenfeoffment which Roger held of the honor of Richmond and the Cramvilles received another subenfeoffment held of the archbishopric of York; Greenway, *Mowbray Charters*, lxi, n. 8, 126, 230.
5. For the gifts to or fees of these families, see Greenway, *Mowbray Charters*, 220–22, 224–25, 242–43. In addition to land, two of the Belvoirs married two of the four heiresses to the Tison fee, almost certainly through Roger's help; Greenway, *Mowbray Charters*, xxxix.

There were a couple of other vassals and families whose position cannot easily be categorized. The Meinilhermers attested a number of Roger's early charters and may well have held an old fee. Since they had disappeared by 1166, however, no record of their status survives. Similarly, it is unclear what the status was of Geoffrey de Haia, who exchanged lands with Roger de Mowbray. Because of these uncertainties, I have not included their attestations in the tables concerning the Mowbray retinues. However, their attestations would not have affected the patterns shown in those tables in any significant manner.[6]

II. Frequency of attestation by family to Roger de Mowbray's charters. Those tenants who were magnates or tenants-in-chief in their own right are marked as (m).

Zero attestations:
   A: Tison, Walter son of Asketil, Gainsborough, Wiseg, Griselee, Rames, Moles, Roger son of Perces, Roger Prince, Robert Dapifer, Bulmer (m)
   C: Lancaster, Vere (m), Graindorge
One to five:
   A: Wappenbury, Takel, Simon son of Simon, Montfort, d'Aubigny Brito
   B: Stuteville (m), Camville
   C: Cramville, Vescy (m)
Six to fifteen:
   A: Rampan, Ralph son of Aldelin, Arches, Arden, Roger son of Geoffrey, Queniborough, Croxley, Gramary, St. Martin
   D: Billinghay
Sixteen to twenty-five:
   A: Luvel, Herbert son of Richard, Moreville
   B: Haget
   C: Buher, Warin son of Simon
Twenty-six to thirty-five:
   A: Riparia
   B: Wyville
   C: Coleville, Carlton
Thirty-six to fifty:
   A: Cundy

6. For the Meinilhermers and de Haia, see Greenway, *Mowbray Charters*, 233–34, 255.

    B: Flamville
    D: Bellun, Montpincon
Fifty-one to one hundred:
    B: Malebisse
    C: Buscy
    D: Belvoir
One hundred or more:
    B: Daiville
    C: Beler

III. Description of frequent Percy attestors and their tenurial position.

Eleven individuals attest five or more of the twenty-six witness lists connected to charters of William II de Percy (this includes one charter incorporating four lists). Only one of these, Robert de Percy of Bolton Percy, came from a family of old tenants and received no known reward from William. Gilbert de Arches and Ralph and Jollan de Hallay came from families which held both old and new fees, and I suspect that the Gilbert son of Fulk who is recorded as holding one half new fee in 1166 should be identified as a recently deceased member of the family which provided stewards for the Percys and held three old fees. Marmaduke Darel was another member of a family holding an old fee. He was a younger son but founded the Darels of Sessay and it may have been he who received Sessay from the Percys, probably from William II de Percy. Baldwin de Bramhope received one new fee and fractions of others from William. Three more, Orm son of Godfrey, William son of Godfrey, and Walter de Benton or de Denton held minor interests in the honor, but it is impossible to know the date at which they or their families received this interest. Of the eleventh frequent attestor, William son of Ernald, nothing more is known.

Appendix Two: Gentry Families With Property in York

FAMILY	REFERENCE
Basset	*Percy Cartulary*, 30–31.
Beningbrough	*EYC* 1:192.
Birdsall	*Chartulary of Helaugh*, 158–59.
Birkin[1]	*Fountains Cartulary* 2:272.
Boniface	Egerton MSS, 2827:136.
Bulmer (cadet)	*EYC* 1:202.
Constable of Richmond	*EYC* 1:207–8, 211.
Cruer[2]	Cotton MSS Claudius D.XI, 202.
Daiville	*Early Yorkshire Families*, 108.
Darel	*EYC* 1:240, 259.
Follifoot	*EYC* 1:193–94.
Frisemareis	*EYC* 1:328.
Haget	*EYC* 1:192–94.
Huddleston	*EYC* 1:180.
Lardiner	*EYC* 1:182, 197.
Lascelles of Kirby Wiske	Egerton MSS, 2827:136.
Malebisse	*Mowbray Charters*, 239–40; *Fountains Cartulary* 1:274–75.
Malesoures	*EYC* 1:405–7.
Mauleverer of Allerton[3]	Cotton MSS Nero D.III, 87–88.
Morers	*EYC* 1:188.
Musters	*EYC* 1:210.

1. The reference is to a charter from after the Angevin period but it contains a specific mention of the land of John de Birkin.
2. I have not been able to date this charter exactly, but it was a grant by Richard Cruer and the name Richard tended to appear among the earlier generations of the family living in the Angevin period.
3. In addition, Matilda Mauleverer, whom I have not been able to identify with either branch of the Mauleverer family, held land in Micklegate; *EYC* 1:177–78.

Percy of Bolton Percy	*EYC* 1:252.
Puher	*Mowbray Charters*, 244.
Rouellé heirs	*EYC* 1:203–4, 253.
Tison heirs	*Mowbray Charters*, 193.
Verly	*EYC* 1:218.
Warrum/Basset	*EYC* 1:228, 232–35.

Appendix Three: History and a Miraculous Rise from the Dead

Any miracle story, especially one involving a person rising from the dead, is bound to raise the doubts of the historian by its very nature, and thus it is necessary to justify the use of the miracle story concerning Jordan son of Essulf in chapter four. This miracle story is preserved in two written versions by the Canterbury monks, Benedict and William, and in stained glass at Canterbury.[1] Some event must have lain behind the account. Jordan was a well attested figure, the ancestor of the Thornhills of Thornhill, and the hagiographers knew too much about him for the story to have been a simple fabrication of the sort that the writers of the lives and miracles of saints sometimes concocted. The hagiographers knew, for instance, that he was one of the close followers of the Earl Warenne, and indeed at one point Jordan was the Earl's constable of Wakefield.[2] Moreover, the story must have been recorded within a couple of decades and quite possibly within a few years of whatever happened.[3] How, then, does one approach this story of a boy's revival from death, if one has little faith in miracles? Does one assume that William fell into some sort of a coma from which he recovered and that the hagiographers were faithfully retelling a story told to them by Jordan when he made the pilgrimage? Or does one assume that the monks took the story of a less dramatic recovery and exaggerated it in order to enhance Becket's reputation, in which case one must accept the possibility that some of the vivid details in the story may also have come from the imagination of the monks and been used to improve the story? There is no way to be certain. Even if one does not trust the details, however, the story can be useful, for in the intellectual climate of the late twelfth century, miracles had at least to seem plausible. Even if a hagiographer indulged in

1. Robertson and Sheppard, *Materials* 1:160–62, 2:229–34. See Clay, "The Family of Thornhill," 289–90, for a summary.

2. *EYC* 8:114.

3. Benedict died in 1193, a little more than two decades after Becket's death. Frank Barlow, *Thomas Becket*, 4.

invention, he had to give the appearance of truth, which would involve making incidental aspects of the story, such as family relationships, seem as realistic as possible. Thus, at best this story gives us a very real and detailed picture of one of the families studied in this work. At worst it reveals the assumptions about gentry family life of contemporary fabricators who at the very least would have known more about gentry families than any modern historian can and who were very interested in verisimilitude. The truth probably lies in between. However, since our interest lies not in the specific family but in family life in general, realistic fiction can be nearly as useful as fact. Thus, I take the story as a useful source for family history, even if the specific events warrant doubt.

Appendix Four: The Langbargh Charter and Political Dissent

In this appendix, I wish to advance a hypothesis that would indicate the resistance by magnates and gentry to King John's government was more organized and had a stronger theoretical basis, well before the Magna Carta revolt, than has hitherto been suspected. This hypothesis is that Peter de Brus's charter of liberties to Langbargh wapentake, which was issued between 1207 and 1209, was not simply a working document, though it was certainly that, but also contained implicit criticism of royal government.[1]

In this charter, Peter agreed to certain limitations in the exercise of his authority in return for a guarantee that the knights and free tenants of the wapentake would make up any shortfall in the difference between Peter's income from the wapentake court and the rent of forty marks charged by the king. Peter agreed that people would not be impleaded except by what were traditional means, that anyone amerced would be amerced according to his wealth and according to his offense, that the wapentake officials would swear to maintain the liberties in the charter, that they would be replaced if they failed to do so, and that their number would be limited. J. C. Holt has discussed the charter in detail and pointed out the similarities of many of its ideas with ideas and assumptions in Magna Carta. He has also pointed out the number of future rebels in the witness list.[2] He does not, however, argue that any criticism of the government was intended but simply suggests that both the Langbargh charter and Magna Carta reflect similar ideals and beliefs.

My hypothesis is based on the witness list, and not only upon who the witnesses were, but also on who they were not. There were ten attesters, three magnates and seven knights. The attesters were Roger de Lacy; Robert de Ros; Eustace de Vescy; Robert Walensis (identified, as under-sheriffs often were, as sheriff of Yorkshire); Walter de Fauconberg; Roald,

---

1. For the charter, see Brown, *Cartularium de Gyseburn* 1:92–94.
2. Holt, *Magna Carta*, 58–59. See also M. J. Vine, "Two Yorkshire Rebels: Peter de Brus and Richard de Percy," 73.

constable of Richmond; Brian son of Alan; John de Birkin; William son of Ralph; and Walter de Bovington. One might expect that such a charter would be attested chiefly by Peter's followers, as most baronial charters were, or by some of the prominent landholders of Langbargh wapentake who would benefit from the charter. None of the attesters, however, was a tenant or follower of Peter and none held the bulk of his lands in Langbargh wapentake. Indeed, most held no land there at all. Instead, the attesters were prominent Yorkshire magnates and knights.

This may indicate no more than that the charter was issued at a county court, but it seems distinctly odd that no one witnessing the document had much direct interest in it and I suspect the significance is deeper. Here it is useful to return to the political sentiments of the witnesses. Eustace de Vescy and Robert de Ros were among the most important rebels at the end of John's reign, as was Peter de Brus, grantor of the charter. Among the knightly attesters, Roald, constable of Richmond, resisted the Thirteenth, and he, John de Birkin, and Brian son of Alan were all rebels. Walter de Fauconberg was not listed among the rebels and Walter de Bovington was dead by the time of the revolt, but the heirs of both participated. William son of Ralph's stance cannot be determined, but the fact that he was relieved of the custody of a castle in 1214 suggests that John did not consider him politically reliable.[3]

In contrast, Roger de Lacy was noted for his close ties to King John and for his heroic defence of Château Gaillard. However, Roger was not an unquestioning supporter of the king. He was one of the magnates who swore allegiance to John in 1199 only on certain conditions. Moreover, when he received the shrievalty of Yorkshire, he resisted the payment of anything above the traditional farm.[4] This resistance may have been based on greed, but it may also have been based on principle, which raises in turn the possibility that the amercement of one thousand marks placed, after Roger's death, on Robert Walensis, who was Roger's undersheriff and another witness to the Langbargh charter, and the amercements levied on Roger's other shrieval deputies, may not have been for corruption, but for an unwillingness to enforce King John's policy fully. Roger de Lacy was too important a follower to chastise, especially after his defense of Château

---

3. *Rot. Litt. Pat.*, 113. William was murdered around the time of the revolt, so the fact that he does not appear among the lists of those who made peace with the royal government after the revolt is probably not significant. It is interesting that his heirs were in the custody of the prominent rebel, Robert de Ros, before the 1218–19 eyre, although the family held of the crown. *Yorkshire Eyre*, 324, 326.

4. Roger of Howden, *Chronica* 4:88; Holt, *The Northerners*, 154, 219–20.

Gaillard, but after his death the king could make an example of Robert in the same way that he made an example of William de Cornborough, as I have suggested in chapter seven. Thus, Roger may have been loyal to the king but strongly opposed to his policies.[5] It is notable that Roger's son John was another of the baronial leaders of the rebellion and was involved in conspiracies against King John as early as 1209, around the time of the Langbargh charter.[6]

In short, the witness list to the Langbargh charter was dominated by opponents to royal policy, future rebels, and men with rebel connections. Even for so rebellious a county as Yorkshire, the combined record of opposition of Peter de Brus and the witnesses is impressive. This raises the possibility that the charter was in fact a kind of manifesto about good government, stressing customary procedure, the accountability of officials, and the cooperation of local landowners. "This," Peter de Brus and the attesters may have been proclaiming to the world at large, "is the way government should really be run."

Such a charter would have been an ideal vehicle for protest and criticism by those not yet willing or able to attempt open rebellion. On the surface, the document contains not a hint of sedition or protest, and it would therefore have been difficult for John or his ministers to make an issue out of it, yet the implicit contrast to King John's rule and to Angevin rule in general would have been clear to everyone. It would also have formed a means through which some of the ideals of opponents to royal government could be openly publicized.

Ultimately this hypothesis is unprovable, for the evidence can only be circumstantial. If the hypothesis is true, however, it would shed some new light on the background to the Magna Carta revolt, suggesting that opposition was not only extensive earlier in John's reign, but perhaps more fully organized and articulated than the scanty evidence for unrest would by and large suggest. If so, it is notable that many members of the gentry were involved.

5. An interesting parallel was the future Lincolnshire rebel, Thomas de Moulton, who was supported in his bid for the shrievalty of his county by a large number of gentry. As a local candidate, Thomas would have been reluctant to run roughshod over his neighbors and he soon fell behind in the extra payments over the Lincolnshire farm the king demanded as part of the bargain for giving him the office. Thomas, like Robert Walensis and William de Cornborough, was amerced one thousand marks. Like William, he was placed in prison. *Pipe Roll 13 John*, 33–34; Holt, *The Northerners*, 155–56, 182–83.

6. Philip Augustus wrote a letter to John de Lacy concerning this plot; Sidney Painter, *The Reign of King John*, 253–56.

Bibliography

MANUSCRIPT SOURCES

PUBLIC RECORD OFFICE

C47 11/1/1; C47 11/1/10; C47 11/1/11; C47 11/1/35. Documents concerning the administration and bounds of Yorkshire forests.
E32 235. Forest regards.
E401 1564. Schedule of payments for Jewish debts.

BRITISH LIBRARY

Add. MSS, 32,113. Book of Evidences of Edward Plumpton.
Cotton MSS, Claudius B. III. Cartulary of St. Peter's, York.
Cotton MSS, Claudius D. XI. Cartulary of Malton Priory.
Cotton MSS, Nero C. XII. Cartulary of Burton Lazar.
Cotton MSS, Nero D. III. Cartulary of St. Leonard's Hospital, York.
Cotton MSS, Vespasian E. XIX. Cartulary of Nostell Priory.
Cotton MSS, Vit. C. VI. Cartulary of Meaux Abbey.
Egerton MSS, 2823. Cartulary of Byland Abbey.
Egerton MSS, 2827. Cartulary of St. Agatha's Abbey, Easby.
Harley MSS, 236. Cartulary of St. Mary's Abbey, York.
Lansdowne MSS, 402. Cartulary of the Archbishop of York.
Lansdowne MSS, 424. Cartulary of Meaux Abbey.
Harley Charter 83 G 53.
Cotton Charter V. 13.

BODLEIAN LIBRARY, OXFORD

Bodleian MS Rolls Yorks. 21. Roll containing charters of the Hebden family.
Dodsworth MSS, 8, 45, 62, 64, 68, 70, 91, 92, 94, 100, 108, 117, 118, 125, 126, 127, 128, 129, 135, 139, 143, 148, 155.
Dugdale MSS, 13.
Fairfax MSS, 9. Cartulary of Warter Priory.
Rawlinson MSS, B455. Cartulary of St. Leonard's and St. Peter's Hospital, York.

HUMBERSIDE RECORD OFFICE

DDCC/135/2: DDCC/135/51: DDCC/141/68. From originals in the Chichester-Constable papers on deposit in the County Archive Office, Beverley.

SHAKESPEARE BIRTHPLACE TRUST RECORD OFFICE

DR10. Gregory-Hood collection.

YORK MINSTER LIBRARY

L 2/1. Registrum Magnum Album.
XVI.A.1. Cartulary of St. Mary's, York.
XVI.A.2. Cartulary of St. Mary's, York.
Hailstone Collection.

JOHN RYLANDS UNIVERSITY LIBRARY OF MANCHESTER

Latin MSS, 251. Cartulary of the Wilstrop family.

PRINTED SOURCES

Abrahams, Israel, Henry P. Stokes, and Herbert Loewe, eds. *Starrs and Jewish Charters Preserved in the British Museum*. 3 vols. Cambridge: Cambridge University Press, 1930–32.
Appleby, John T., ed. *The Chronicle of Richard of Devizes of the Time of King Richard the First*. London: Thomas Nelson, 1963.
Atkinson, John C., ed. *Cartularium Abbathiae de Whiteby*. Surtees Society, nos. 69, 72. Durham, 1879–81.
———, ed. *Cartularium Abbathiae de Rievalle*. Surtees Society, no. 83. Durham, 1889.
Austen, David, ed. *Boldon Book*. Chichester: Phillimore, 1982.
[Benedict of Peterborough]. *Gesta Regis Henrici Secundi Benedicti Abbatis*. Ed. William Stubbs. 2 vols. Rolls Series. London, 1867. Reprint: Kraus, 1965.
Birks, Peter and Grant McLean, eds. *Justinian's Institutes*. Ithaca, NY: Cornell University Press, 1987.
Bond, Edward A., ed. *Chronica Monasterii de Melsa*. Vol. 1. Rolls Series. London, 1866. Reprint: Kraus, 1967. (Abb. *Meaux Chronicle*).
Book of Fees. 3 vols. London: HMSO, 1920–31.
Brown, William, ed. *Cartularium prioratus de Gyseburne*. 2 vols. Surtees Society, nos. 86 & 89. Durham, 1889–94.

———, ed. "Pedes Finium Ebor., Tempore Ricardi Primi." *YAJ* 11 (1891): 174–88.
———, ed. *Yorkshire Inquisitions of the Reigns of Henry III and Edward I.* YAS Record Series, no. 12. Worksop, 1891. (Abb. *Yorkshire Inquisitions*).
———, ed. *Pedes Finium Ebor. Regnante Johanne.* Surtees Society, no. 94. Durham, 1897.
Brownbill, John, ed. *The Coucher Book of Furness Abbey.* Vol. 2, part 2. Chetham Society, n.s., 76. Manchester, 1916.
Calendar of Charter Rolls. Vol. 2. London: HMSO, 1906.
Calendar of Inquisitions Miscellaneous. Vol. 1. London: HMSO, 1916.
Calendar of Inquisitions Post Mortem. Vols. 1 & 2. London: HMSO, 1904–6.
Clark, E. K., ed. "Fundacio Abbathie de Kyrkestall." In *Miscellanea,* 169–208. Thoresby Society, no. 4, 1895.
Clay, Charles, ed. *York Minster Fasti.* 2 vols. YAS Record Series, nos. 123–24. Wakefield, 1958–59.
———. "Yorkshire Final Concords of the Reign of Henry II." *YAJ* 40 (1959): 78–89.
Cole, Henry, ed. *Documents Illustrative of English History in the Thirteenth and Fourteenth Centuries Selected from the Records of the Department of the Queen's Remembrancer of the Exchequer.* London: Record Commission, 1844.
Curia Regis Rolls. 16 vols. London: HMSO, 1922–79. (Abb. *CRR*).
Daniel, Walter. *The Life of Ailred of Rievaulx.* Ed. F. M. Powicke. London: Thomas Nelson, 1951. Reprint: Clarendon Press, 1978.
Duckett, George F., ed., "Charters of the Priory of Swine in Holderness." *YAJ* 6 (1881): 113–24.
Dugdale, William, ed. *Monasticon Anglicanum.* Vol. 5. 2nd ed. London: T. G. March, 1849.
Early Yorkshire Charters. 13 vols. Vols. 1–3 ed. William Farrer, Edinburgh, 1914–16. Index to vols. 1–3 ed. Charles Clay and E. M. Clay, Wakefield, 1942. Vols. 4–12 ed. Sir Charles Clay, Wakefield, 1935–65. YAS Record Series, extra series. (Abb. *EYC*).
Fantosme, Jordan. *Jordan Fantosme's Chronicle.* Ed. R. C. Johnston. Oxford: Clarendon Press, 1981.
Farmer, Hugh. "The Vision of Orm." *Analecta Bollandiana* 75 (1957): 79–82.
Faull, Margaret L. and Marie Stimson, eds. *Domesday Book, Yorkshire.* Chichester: Phillimore, 1986.
Foreville, Raymonde and Gillian Keir, eds. *The Book of St Gilbert.* Oxford: Clarendon Press, 1987.
Fowler, J. T., ed. *Memorials of the Church of SS Peter and Wilfrid, Ripon,* vols. 1 & 4. Surtees Society, nos. 74 & 115. Durham, 1882–1908.
———, ed. *The Coucher Book of Selby.* 2 vols. YAS Record Series, nos. 10 & 13. Durham, 1891–93.
———, ed. "Selebeiensis Monasterii Historia." In *The Coucher Book of Selby.* YAS Record Series, no. 10. Durham, 1891.
Gale, Roger, ed. *Registrum Honoris de Richmond.* London: R. Gosling, 1722.
Gerald of Wales. *Expugnatio Hibernica: The Conquest of Ireland.* Ed. A. B. Scott and F. X. Martin. Dublin: Royal Irish Academy, 1978.

———. *De Principis Insructione Liber*. Ed. George F. Warner. In *Giraldi Cambrensis Opera*, vol. 8. Rolls Series. London, 1891. Reprint: Kraus, 1964.

———. *Itinerarium Kambriae*. Ed. James F. Dimock. In *Giraldi Cambrensis Opera*, vol. 6. Rolls Series. London, 1868. Reprint: Kraus, 1964.

———. *The Journey Through Wales*. Trans. Lewis Thorpe. Harmondsorth: Penguin, 1978.

Greenway, D. E., ed. *Charters of the Honour of Mowbray, 1107–1191*. British Academy, Records of Social and Economic History, n.s., 1. London: Oxford University Press, 1972.

Grosjean, Paul, ed. *Vitae S. Roberti Knaresburgensis*. In *Analecta Bollandiana 57* (1939): 364–400.

Guibert of Nogent. *Gesta Dei per Francos*. In *Recueil des historiens des Croisades: Historiens Occidentaux*, vol. 4. Paris: l'Academie des inscriptions et belles lettres, 1879. Reprint, 1969.

Hall, G. D. G., ed. *The Treatise on the Laws and Customs of the Realm of England Commonly Called Glanvill*. London: Thomas Nelson, 1965.

Hall, Hubert, ed. *The Red Book of the Exchequer*. Rolls Series. London, 1896. Reprint: Kraus, 1965.

Hardy, Thomas D., ed. *Rotuli Litterarum Clausarum in Turri Londinensi Asservati*. Vols. 1–2. London: Record Commission, 1833–44. (Abb. *Rot. Litt. Claus.*).

———, ed. *Rotuli de Oblatis et Finibus in Turri Londinensi Asservati, Tempore Regis Johannis*. London: Record Commission, 1835. (Abb. *Rot. Obl. & Fin.*).

———, ed. *Rotuli Litterarum Patentium in Turri Londinensi Asservati*. Vol. 1, part 1. London: Record Commission, 1835. (Abb. *Rot. Litt Pat.*).

———, ed. *Rotuli Chartarum*. Vol. 1, part 1. London: Record Commission, 1837. (Abb. *Rot. Chart.*).

———, ed. *Rotuli de Liberate ac de Misis et Praestitis Regnante Johanne*. London: Record Commission, 1844.

Henry of Bracton. *On the Laws and Customs of England*. Ed. George Woodbine. Rev. and trans. Samuel E. Thorne. 4 vols. Cambridge, MA: Harvard University Press, 1968–77.

———. *Bracton's Note book*. Ed. F. W. Maitland. 3 vols. London: C. J. Clay, 1887.

Holmes, Richard, ed. *The Chartulary of St. John of Pontefract*. YAS Record Series, nos. 25 & 30. Wakefield, 1899–1902.

Holt, J. C., ed. "Praestita Roll 14–18 John," "Roll of Summonses, 1214," and "Scutage Rolls." In *Pipe Roll 17 John*, ed. R. Allen Brown. Pipe Roll Society, n.s., 37. London, 1961.

Hugh of Kirkstall. "Narratio de Fundatione Fontanis Monasterii in Comitatu Eboracensi." In *Memorials of the Abbey of St. Mary of Fountains*, vol. 1, ed. John R. Walbran. Surtees Society, no. 42. Durham, 1863.

Jocelin of Brakelond. *The Chronicle of Jocelin of Brakelond*. Ed. H. E. Butler. London: Thomas Nelson, 1949. Reprint, 1951.

Jocelin of Furness. *Vita S. Waltheni*. In *Acta Sanctorum*, no. 35, *Augusti Tomus Primus*. Paris: Victorem Palme, 1867.

Lancaster, William T., ed. *Abstracts of the Charters and Other Documents Contained in the Chartulary of the Cistercian Abbey of Fountains.* 2 vols. Leeds: J. Whitehead and Son, 1915–18. (Abb. *Fountains Cartulary*).

———, ed. *Abstracts of the Charters and Other Documents Contained in the Chartulary of the Priory of Bridlington.* Leeds: J. Whitehead and Son, 1915.

Lancaster, William T. and W. Paley Baildon, eds. *The Coucher Book of the Cistercian Abbey of Kirkstall.* Thoresby Society, no. 8. Leeds, 1904.

Lawrence of Durham. *Dialogi Laurentii Monachi ac Prioris.* Ed. James Raine. Surtees Society, no. 70. Durham, 1880.

Leclercq, J. and H. Rochais. *S. Bernardi Opera,* vol. 7. Rome: Editiones Cisterciensis, 1974.

Lees, Beatrice A., ed. *Records of the Templars in England in the Twelfth Century.* British Academy, Records of the Social and Economic History of England and Wales, no. 9. London: Oxford University Press, 1935.

Liber Vita Ecclesiae Dunelmensis. Surtees Society, no. 136. Facsimile edition. Durham, 1923.

Littledale, Ralph Pudsay, ed. *The Pudsay Deeds.* YAS Record Series, no. 56. Wakefield, 1916.

McNulty, Joseph, ed. *The Chartulary of the Cistercian Abbey of St. Mary of Sallay in Craven.* 2 vols. YAS Record Series, nos. 87 & 90. Wakefield, 1933–34. (Abb. *Sallay Cartulary*).

Map, Walter. *De Nugis Curialium: Courtiers' Trifles.* Ed. and trans. M. R. James. Revised by C. N. L. Brooke and R. A. B. Mynors. Oxford: Clarendon Press, 1983.

Martin, M. T., ed. *The Percy Cartulary.* Surtees Society, no. 117. Durham, 1911.

Meyer, Paul, ed. *L'Histoire de Guillaume le Maréchal.* 3 vols. Paris: Société de l'Histoire de France, 1891–1901.

Oschinsky, Dorothy. *Walter of Henley and other Treatises on Estate Management and Accounting.* Oxford: Clarendon Press, 1971.

Palgrave, Francis, ed. *Rotuli Curiae Regis.* 2 vols. London: Record Commission, 1835. (Abb. *RCR*).

Paris, Matthew. *Chronica Majora.* Ed. Henry R. Luard. 6 vols. Rolls Series. London, 1872–82. Reprint: Kraus, 1964.

Parker, John, ed. *Feet of Fines for the County of York, From 1218 to 1231.* YAS Record Series, no. 62. Wakefield, 1921.

Patent Rolls of the Reign of Henry III, A.D. 1216–1225. London: HMSO, 1901.

Pipe Roll 31 Henry I. Ed. Joseph Hunter. London: HMSO, 1929. Facsimile of 1833 edition.

Pipe Roll 2–3-4 Henry II. Ed. Joseph Hunter. London: HMSO, 1930. Facsimile of 1844 edition.

Pipe Rolls 5 Henry II to 3 Henry III. Pipe Roll Society 1 to n.s. 42. London, 1884–1976.

Purvis, J. S., ed. *The Chartulary of the Augustinian Priory of St. John the Evangelist of the Park of Healaugh.* YAS Record Series, no. 92. Wakefield, 1936.

Raine, James, ed. *Vita Sancti Willelmi Auctore Anonymo* and *Miraculi quaedam Sancti Willelmi.* In *The Historians of the Church of York* 2:270–91, 531–43. Rolls Series. London, 1886. Reprint: Kraus, 1965.

Reginald of Durham. *Libellus de Admirandis Beati Cuthberti Virtutibus*. Surtees Society, no. 1. London, 1835.

Report on the Historical Manuscripts of the late Reginald Rawdon Hastings, Esquire. Historical Manuscripts Commission. Vol. 1. London, 1928.

Richard fitz Nigel. *Dialogus de Scaccario. The Course of the Exchequer*. Ed. and trans. Charles Johnson, with corrections by F. E. L. Carter and D. E. Greenway. Oxford: Clarendon Press, 1983.

Richard, Prior of Hexham. *The Chronicle of Richard, Prior of Hexham*. In *Chronicles of the Reigns of Stephen, Henry II, and Richard I* 3:139–78, ed. Richard Howlett. Rolls Series. London, 1886. Reprint: Kraus, 1964.

Richardson, H. G., ed. "Fragment of the Originalia Roll of 7 Richard I," and "The Liberate Roll of the Second Year of King John." In *Memoranda Roll 1 John*. Pipe Roll Society n.s., 21. London, 1943.

Riley-Smith, Louise and Jonathan. *The Crusades: Idea and Reality, 1095–1274*. London, 1981.

Robertson, J. C. and J. B. Sheppard, eds. *Materials for the History of Thomas Becket, Archbishop of Canterbury*. 7 vols. Rolls Series. London, 1875–85. Reprint, Kraus, 1965.

Roger of Howden. *Chronica Magistri Rogeri de Hoveden*. 4 vols. Ed. William Stubbs. Rolls Series. London, 1868–71. Reprint, Kraus, 1964.

"A Roll of the King's Court in the Reign of King Richard I." In *Feet of Fines of the Tenth Year of the Reign of King Richard I*. Pipe Roll Society, vol. 24. London, 1900.

Rolls of the King's Court in the Reign of King Richard the First A.D. 1194–1195. Pipe Roll Society, vol. 14. London, 1891.

Round, J. H., ed. *Rotuli de Dominabus et Pueris et Puellis de XII Comitatibus*. Pipe Roll Society, vol. 35. London, 1913.

Searle, Eleanor, ed. *The Chronicle of Battle Abbey*. Oxford: Clarendon Press, 1980.

Skaife, Robert H., ed. *The Survey of the County of York, taken by John de Kirkeby, Commonly Called Kirkby's Inquest*. Surtees Society, no. 49. Durham, 1867.

Stapleton, Thomas, ed. *Plumpton Correspondence*. Camden Society, no. 4. London, 1839.

The Statutes of the Realm. Vol. 1. London: Record Commission, 1810.

Stenton, Doris, M., ed. *Rolls of the Justices in Eyre Being the Rolls of Pleas and Assizes for Yorkshire in 3 Henry III*. Selden Society, no. 56. London, 1937. (Abb. *Yorkshre Eyre*).

———, ed. *Pleas Before the King or His Justices, 1198–1212*. 4 vols. Selden Society, nos. 67–8, 83–84. London, 1948–49, 1966–67. (Abb. *Pleas*).

Stenton, Frank M., ed. *Transcripts of Charters Relating to the Gilbertine Houses of Sixle, Ormsby, Catley, Bullington and Alvingham*. Lincoln Record Society, no. 18. Horncastle, 1922.

———. *Documents Illustrative of the Social and Economic History of the Danelaw*. The British Academy, Records of the Social and Economic History of England and Wales, no. 5. London: Oxford University Press, 1920.

Stubbs, William, ed. *Select Charters and Other Illustrations of English Constitutional History*. 9th edition. Revised H.W.C. Davis. Oxford: Clarendon Press, 1913.

Walker, J. T., ed. *Abstracts of the Chartularies of the Priory of Monkbretton*. YAS Record Series, no. 66. Wakefield, 1924.

Walter of Guisborough. *The Chronicle of Walter of Guisborough*. Ed. H. Rothwell. Camden Society, 3rd series, 89. London, 1957.

William of Newburgh. *Historia Rerum Anglicanum*. Ed. Richard Howlett. 2 vols. Vols. 1 & 2 in *Chronicles of the Reigns of Stephen, Henry II and Richard I*. Rolls Series. London, 1884–85. Reprint: Kraus, 1964.

Yorkshire Deeds. 10 vols. Ed. William Brown (1–3), C. T. Clay (4–8), M. J. Hebditch (9), M. J. Stanley Price (10). YAS Record Series, 39, 50, 63, 65, 69, 76, 83, 102, 111, 120. Leeds, Wakefield, and York, 1907–55.

SECONDARY WORKS

Abbott, Mary. "The Gant Family in England, 1066–1191." Ph.D. diss., Cambridge, 1973.

Alexander, James W. *Ranulf of Chester, a Relic of the Conquest*. Athens: University of Georgia Press, 1983.

Allerston, P. "English Village Development: Findings From the Pickering District of North Yorkshire." *Transactions of the Institute of British Geographers* 51 (1970): 95–109.

Altschul, Michael. *A Baronial Family in Medieval England: The Clares, 1217–1314*. Baltimore: Johns Hopkins University Press, 1965.

Arnold, Benjamin. *German Knighthood, 1050–1300*. Oxford: Clarendon Press, 1985.

Astill, G. G. "Social Advancement through Seigniorial Service: The Case of Simon Pakeman." *Transactions of the Leicestershire Archaeological Society* 54 (1978–80): 14–25.

Baildon, W. Paley. "The Family of Leathley or Lelay." Thoresby Society, no. 11, *Miscellanea*, 2–36. Leeds, 1904.

Bailey, Mark. *A Marginal Economy? East Anglian Breckland in the Later Middle Ages*. Cambridge: Cambridge University Press, 1989.

Baker, Alan R. H. and Robin A. Butlin, eds. *Studies of Field Systems in the British Isles*. Cambridge: Cambridge University Press, 1973.

Baker, Derek, ed. *Religious Motivation: Biographical and Sociological Problems for the Church Historian*. Oxford: Published for the Ecclesiastical History Society by Basil Blackwell, 1978.

———. "The Foundation of Fountains Abbey." *Northern History* 4 (1969): 29–43.

———. "The Desert in the North." *Northern History* 5 (1970): 1–11.

Barber, M. C. "The Social Context of the Templars." *TRHS* 5th series, 34 (1984): 27–46.

Barlow, Frank. *Thomas Becket*. Berkeley: University of California Press, 1986.

Barnes, Guy D. *Kirkstall Abbey, 1147–1539: An Historical Study*. Thoresby Society, no. 58. Leeds, 1984.

Barrow, G. W. S. "Northern English Society in the Early Middle Ages." *Northern History* 4 (1969): 1–28.

Bean, J. M. W. *The Estates of the Percy Family, 1416–1537*. London: Oxford University Press, 1958.

———. *The Decline of English Feudalism, 1215–1540*. Manchester: Manchester University Press, 1968.

———. *From Lord to Patron: Lordship in Late Medieval England*. Philadelphia: University of Pennsylvania Press, 1989.

Beech, G. T. *A Rural Society in Medieval France: the Gâtine of Poitou in the Eleventh and Twelfth Centuries*. Baltimore: Johns Hopkins University Press, 1964.

Beeler, John. *Warfare in England: 1066–1189*. Ithaca, NY: Cornell University Press, 1966.

Bellamy, J. *Crime and Public Order in England in the Later Middle Ages*. London: Routledge and Kegan Paul, 1973.

Bennett, M. J. *Community, Class and Careerism: Cheshire and Lancashire Society in the Age of Sir Gawain and the Green Knight*. Cambridge: Cambridge University Press, 1983.

Bishop, T. A. M. "The Distribution of Manorial Demesne in the Vale of Yorkshire." *EHR* 49 (1934): 386–406.

———. "Assarting and the Growth of the Open Fields." *Economic History Review* 6 (1935–36): 13–29.

———. "The Norman Settlement of Yorkshire." In *Studies in Medieval History Presented to Maurice Powicke*, ed. R. W. Hunt, W. A. Pantin, and R. W. Southern, 1–14. Oxford: Clarendon Press, 1948.

Bonenfant, P. and G. Despy. "La noblesse en Brabant aux xiie et xiiie siècles." *Moyen Âge* 64 (1958): 27–66.

Bouchard, Constance. "The Structure of a Twelfth-Century French Family: The Lords of Seignelay." *Viator* 10 (1979): 39–56.

Brand, P. A. "The Control of Mortmain Alienation in England, 1200–1300." In *Legal Records and the Historian*, ed. J. H. Baker, 29–40. London: Royal Historical Society, 1978.

———. "The Origins of the English Legal Profession. *Law and History Review* 5 (1987): 31–50.

Brett, Martin. *The English Church Under Henry I*. Oxford: Clarendon Press, 1975.

Bridbury, A. R. "The Farming Out of Manors." *Economic History Review* 2nd ser., 31 (1978): 503–20.

Britnell, R. H. "Production for the Market on a Small Fourteenth Century Estate." *Economic History Review* 2nd ser., 19 (1966): 380–87.

Brown, Elizabeth A. R. "The Tyranny of a Construct: Feudalism and Historians of Medieval Europe." *American Historical Review* 79 (1974): 1063–88.

Brown, R. Allen. "The Status of the Norman Knight." In *War and Government in the Middle Ages: Essays in Honor of J. O. Prestwich*, ed. John Gillingham and J. C. Holt, 21–30. Cambridge: Boydell Press; Totowa, NJ: Barnes and Noble, 1984.

Burrows, Toby. "The Geography of Monastic Property in Medieval England: A Case Study of Nostell and Bridlington Priories." *YAJ* 57 (1985): 79–86.

Burton, Janet E. *The Yorkshire Nunneries in the Twelfth and Thirteenth Centuries*. Borthwick Papers, no. 56. York: University of York, Borthwick Institute, 1979.

———. "Monasteries and Parish Churches in Eleventh- and Twelfth-Century York-shire." *Northern History* 23 (1987): 39–50.

Cantor, Leonard, ed. *The English Medieval Landscape*. London: Croom Helm; Philadelphia: University of Pennsylvania Press, 1982.

Carpenter, Christine. "The Beauchamp Affinity: A Study of Bastard Feudalism at Work." *EHR* 95 (1980): 514–32.

———. "The Fifteenth-Century English Gentry and Their Estates." In *Gentry and Lesser Nobility in Late Medieval Europe*, ed. Michael Jones, 33–60. New York: St. Martin's Press, 1986.

Carpenter, David A. "Was There a Crisis of the Knightly Class in the Thirteenth Century? The Oxfordshire Evidence." *EHR* 95 (1980): 721–52.

———. *The Minority of Henry III*. Berkeley: University of California Press, 1990.

Chandler, Victoria. "Politics and Piety: Influences on Charitable Donations During the Anglo-Norman Period." *Revue Bénédictine* 90 (1980): 63–71.

Chédeville, A. *Chartres et ses campagnes, xie-xiiie siècles*. Paris: Klincksieck, 1973.

Cheney, C. R. *Hubert Walter*. London: Thomas Nelson, 1967.

Chew, Helena M. *The English Ecclesiastical Tenants-in-Chief and Knight Service*. London: Oxford University Press, 1932.

Clanchy, Michael T. *From Memory to Written Record: England, 1066–1307*. London: Edward Arnold; Cambridge, MA: Harvard University Press, 1979.

———. *England and Its Rulers, 1066–1272: Foreign Lordship and National Identity*. Oxford: Clarendon Press; Totowa, NJ: Barnes and Noble, 1983.

Clay, Charles. "Notes on the Early Generations of the Family of Horbury." *YAJ* 26 (1922): 334–45.

———. "The Family of Eland." *YAJ* 27 (1924): 225–48.

———. "The Family of Wridlesford of Woodlesford." Thoresby Society, no. 26, *Miscellanea*, 243–52. Leeds, 1924.

———. "The Family of Lacy of Cromwellbottom and Leventhorpe." Thoresby Society, no. 28, *Miscellanea* 28, 468–90. Leeds, 1928.

———. "The Family of Thornhill." *YAJ* 29 (1929): 286–321.

———. "Notes on the Origin of the FitzAlans of Bedale." *YAJ* 30 (1931): 281–90.

———. "A Holderness Charter of William Count of Aumale." *YAJ* 39 (1957): 339–42.

———. "Notes on the Early Generations of the Family of Constable of Halsham." *YAJ* 40 (1960): 197–204.

———. "The Family of Longvillers." *YAJ* 42 (1967): 41–51.

———. "The Family of Meaux: I Meaux of Bewick and II Meaux of Owthorne." *YAJ* 43 (1971): 99–111.

———. *Notes on the Family of Clere*. Wakefield: privately printed, 1975.

Clay, Charles and Diana E. Greenway. *Early Yorkshire Families*. YAS Record Series, no. 135. Wakefield, 1973.

Cokayne, George E. *The Complete Peerage of England, Scotland, Ireland, Great Britain and the United Kingdom*, 2nd ed., rev. Vicary Gibbs and H. A. Doubleday, vol. 5. London: St. Catherine's Press, 1926.

Constable, Giles. "Aelred of Rievaulx and the Nun of Watton: An Episode in the

Early History of the Gilbertine Order." In *Medieval Women*, ed. Derek Baker, 205–26. Oxford: Published for the Ecclesiastical History Society by Basil Blackwell, 1978; reprint, 1984.

Corner, David. "The *Gesta Regis Henrici Secundi* and *Chronica* of Roger, Parson of Howden." *BIHR* 56 (1983): 126–44.

Coss, Peter R. "Sir Geoffrey de Langley and the Crisis of the Knightly Class in Thirteenth-Century England." *Past and Present* 68 (1975): 3–37.

———. "Knighthood and the Early Thirteenth-Century County Court." In *Thirteenth Century England* 2, Proceedings of the Newcastle Upon Tyne Conference, ed. Peter R. Coss and Simon D. Lloyd, 45–57. Woodbridge, Suffolk, 1988.

———. "Bastard Feudalism Revised." *Past and Present* 125 (1989): 27–64.

———. *Lordship, Knighthood and Locality: A Study in English Society, c. 1180–c. 1280.* Cambridge: Cambridge University Press, 1991.

Critchley, J. S. "Summonses to Military Service Early in the Reign of Henry III." *EHR* 86 (1971): 79–95.

Crook, David. *Records of the General Eyre.* London: HMSO, 1982.

Crouch, David. *The Beaumont Twins: The Roots and Branches of Power in the Twelfth Century.* Cambridge Studies in Medieval Life and Thought, 4th ser., no. 1. Cambridge: Cambridge University Press, 1986.

———. *William Marshal: Court, Career and Chivalry in the Angevin Empire, 1147–1219.* London: Longman, 1990.

Crouch, David, David A. Carpenter, and Peter R. Coss. "Debate: Bastard Feudalism Revised." *Past and Present* 131 (1991): 165–203.

Darby, H. C. and I. S. Maxwell, eds. *The Domesday Geography of Northern England.* Cambridge: Cambridge University Press, 1962.

Davies, R. G. and J. H. Denton. *The English Parliament in the Middle Ages.* Philadelphia: University of Pennsylvania Press, 1981

Davies, R. R. *Lordship and Society in the March of Wales, 1282–1400.* Oxford: Clarendon Press, 1978.

DeAragon, RaGena C. "In Pursuit of Aristocratic Women: A Key to Success in Norman England." *Albion* 14 (1982): 258–67.

Denholm-Young, Noel. "Feudal Society in the Thirteenth Century: The Knights." *History* 29 (1944): 107–19.

———. *The Country Gentry in the Fourteenth Century with Special Reference to Heraldic Coats of Arms.* Oxford: Clarendon Press, 1969.

Devailly, Guy. *Le Berry du xe siècle au milieu du xiiie.* Paris: Mouton, 1973.

Dobson, R. B. *The Jews of Medieval York and the Massacre of March 1190.* Borthwick Papers, no. 45. York: St. Anthony's Press, 1974.

Dodgshon, Robert A. "The Landholding Foundations of the Open-Field System." *Past and Present* 67 (1975): 3–29.

———. *The Origin of British Field Systems: An Interpretation.* London: Academic Press, 1980.

Donkin, R. A. "Settlement and Depopulation on Cistercian Estates During the Twelfth and Thirteenth Centuries, Especially in Yorkshire." *BIHR* 33 (1960): 141–65.

————. *The Cistercians: Studies in the Geography of Medieval England and Wales*. Toronto: Pontifical Institute of Mediaeval Studies, 1978.

Douie, D. L. *Archbishop Geoffrey Plantagenet and the Chapter of York*. St. Anthony's Hall Publications, no. 18. York: St. Anthony's Press, 1960.

Du Boulay, F. R. H. *The Lordship of Canterbury: An Essay on Medieval Society*. London: Thomas Nelson; New York: Barnes and Noble, 1966.

Duby, Georges. *La société aux xie et xiie siècles dans la région mâconnaise*. Paris, 1953. Reprint, S.E.V.P.E.N., 1971.

————. *Rural Economy and Country Life in the Medieval West*. Trans. Cynthia Postan. Columbia: University of South Carolina, 1968. Reprint, 1976.

————. "Au XIIe siècle: les 'jeunes' dans la société aristocratique dans France du nord-ouest." *Annales. Économie, société, civilisation* (1964): 835–46.

————. *The Chivalrous Society*. Trans. Cynthia Postan. Berkeley: University of California Press, 1977. Reprint, 1980.

————. *Medieval Marriage: Two Models from Twelfth-Century France*. Trans. Elborg Forster. Baltimore: Johns Hopkins University Press, 1978.

————. *William Marshal: The Flower of Chivalry*. Trans. Richard Howard. New York: Pantheon Books, 1985.

Dyer, Christopher. "A Small Landowner in the Fifteenth Century." *Midlands History* 1 (1971): 1–14.

————. *Lords and Peasants in a Changing Society: The Estates of the Bishopric of Worcester, 680–1540*. Cambridge: Cambridge University Press, 1980.

English, Barbara. "Additional Records of the Yorkshire Eyre of 1218–1219." *YAJ* 48 (1976): 95–96.

————. *The Lords of Holderness, 1086–1260: A Study in Feudal Society*. Oxford: Oxford University Press, 1979.

Evans, G. R. *The Mind of St. Bernard of Clairvaux*. Oxford: Clarendon Press, 1983.

Farmer, D. L. "Some Price Fluctuations in Angevin England." *Economic History Review* 2nd ser., 9 (1956–57): 34–43.

————. "Some Grain Price Movements in Thirteenth-Century England." *Economic History Review* 2nd ser., 10 (1958): 207–20.

————. "Some Livestock Price Movements in Thirteenth-Century England." *Economic History Review* 2nd ser., 22 (1969): 1–16.

Faull, Margaret L. and S. A. Moorhouse, eds. *West Yorkshire: An Archaeological Survey to A.D. 1500*. West Yorkshire Metropolitan County Council. 3 vols. Wakefield, 1981.

Fleming, Donald. "*Milites* as Attestors to Charters in England." *Albion* 22 (1990): 185–98.

————. "Landholding and *Milites* in Domesday Book: A Revision." In *Anglo-Norman Studies* 13, ed. Marjorie Chibnall, 83–98. Woodbridge, Suffolk; Rochester NY: Boydell Press, 1991.

Finn, R. Welldon. *The Making and Limitations of the Yorkshire Domesday*. Borthwick Papers, no. 41. York: St. Anthony's Press, 1972.

Flori, Jean. *L'Essor de la chevalerie, XIe-XIIe siècles*. Geneva: Droz, 1986.

Flower, Cyril. *Introduction to the Curia Regis Rolls, 1199–1230*. Selden Society, no. 62. London, 1944.

Foss, Edward. *The Judges of England*. Vols. 1–2. London, 1848. Reprint, New York: AMS Press, 1966.

Freed, John B. "Nobles, Ministerials and Knights in the Archdiocese of Salzburg." *Speculum* 62 (1987): 572–611.

———. "The Origins of the European Nobility: The Problem of the Ministerials." *Viator* 7 (1976): 211–41.

Gransden, Antonia. *Historical Writing in England c. 550 to c. 1307*. Ithaca, NY: Cornell University Press, 1974.

Green, Judith A. "The Last Century of Danegeld." *EHR* 96 (1981): 241–58.

Hall, T. Walter. *Etton: An East Yorkshire Village*. Sheffield: J. W. Northend, 1932.

Hallam, H. E. *Settlement and Society: A Study of the Early Agrarian History of South Lincolnshire*. Cambridge: Cambridge University Press, 1965.

———. *Rural England, 1066–1348*. Glasgow: Fontana, 1981.

Harper-Bill, C. "The Piety of the Anglo-Norman Knightly Class." *Proceedings of the Battle Conference on Anglo-Norman Studies* 2, ed. R. Allen Brown, 63–77. Woodbridge, Suffolk: Boydell Press, 1979.

Harvey, Barbara. *Westminster Abbey and Its Estates in the Middle Ages*. Oxford: Clarendon Press, 1977.

Harvey, Mary. "Regular Field and Tenurial Arrangements in Holderness, Yorkshire." *Journal of Historical Geography* 6 (1980): 3–16.

———. "Irregular Villages in Holderness, Yorkshire: Some Thoughts on Their Origin." *YAJ* 54 (1982): 63–71.

———. "Open Field Structure and Land Holding Arrangements in Eastern Yorkshire." *Transactions of the Institute of British Geographers* n.s.,9 (1984): 60–74.

———. "Regular Open-Field Systems on the Yorkshire Wolds." *Landscape History* 4 (1982): 29–39.

———. "Planned Field Systems in Eastern Yorkshire: Some Thoughts on Their Origin." *Agricultural History Review* 31 (1983): 91–103.

Harvey, P. D. A. "The English Inflation of 1180–1220." *Past and Present* 61 (1973): 3–30. Reprinted in Hilton, ed., *Peasants, Knights and Heretics*, 57–84.

———. "The Pipe Rolls and the Adoption of Demesne Farming in England." *Economic History Review* 2nd ser., 27 (1974): 345–59.

Harvey, Sally. "The Knight and the Knight's Fee in England." *Past and Present* 49 (1970): 3–43. Reprinted in Hilton, ed., *Peasants, Knights and Heretics*, 133–73.

Herlihy, David. *Medieval Households*. Cambridge, MA: Harvard University Press, 1985.

Hey, David. *A Regional History of England: Yorkshire from A.D. 1000*. London and New York: Longman, 1986.

Hill, Bennett D. *English Cistercian Monasteries and Their Patrons in the Twelfth Century*. Urbana: University of Illinois Press, 1968.

Hilton, R. H. "Freedom and Villeinage in England." *Past and Present* 31 (1965): 3–19. Reprinted in *Peasants, Knights and Heretics*, 174–91.

———. *A Medieval Society: The West Midlands at the End of the Thirteenth Century*. Cambridge: Cambridge University Press, 1967.

———, ed. *Peasants, Knights and Heretics: Studies in Medieval English Social History*. Cambridge: Cambridge University Press, 1976. Reprint, 1981.

Hollister, C. Warren. *Monarchy, Magnates, and Institutions in the Anglo-Norman World*. London and Roncevert, WV: Hambledon Press, 1986.

Holmes, G. A. *The Estates of the Higher Nobility in Fourteenth-Century England*. Cambridge: Cambridge University Press, 1957.

Holt, James C. *The Northerners: A Study in the Reign of King John*. Oxford: Clarendon Press, 1961.

———. *Magna Carta*. Cambridge: Cambridge University Press, 1965.

———. "Politics and Property in Early Medieval England." *Past and Present* 57 (1972): 3–52.

———. "Feudal Society and the Family in Early Medieval England: I. The Revolution of 1066." *TRHS* 5th series, 32 (1982): 193–212.

———. "Feudal Society and the Family in Early Medieval England: II. Notions of Patrimony." *TRHS* 5th series, 33 (1983): 193–220.

———. "Feudal Society and the Family in Early Medieval England: III. Patronage and Politics." *TRHS* 5th series, 34 (1984): 1–25.

———. "Feudal Society and the Family in Early Medieval England: IV. The Heiress and the Alien." *TRHS* 5th series, 35 (1985): 1–28.

———. *What's in a Name? Family Nomenclature and the Norman Conquest*. The Stenton Lecture for 1981. Reading: University of Reading, 1982.

———. "The *casus regis*: The Law and Politics of Succession in the Plantagenet Dominions 1185–1247." In *Law in Mediaeval Life and Thought*, ed. Edward B. King and Susan J. Ridyard. Sewanee, TN: University of the South, Sewanee Mediaeval Colloquium, 1990.

Hudson, John. "Life-Grants and the Development of Inheritance in Anglo-Norman England." In *Anglo-Norman Studies* 12, ed. Marjorie Chibnall, 67–80. Woodbridge, Suffolk; Rochester NY: Boydell Press, 1990.

Hyams, Paul R. *King, Lords, and Peasants in Medieval England: The Common Law of Villeinage in the Twelfth and Thirteenth Centuries*. Oxford: Clarendon Press, 1980.

———. "Warranty and Good Lordship in Twelfth-Century England." *Law and History Review* 5 (1987): 437–503.

Hyams, Paul R. and Paul A. Brand. "Debate: Seigneurial Control of Women's Marriage." *Past and Present* 99 (1983): 123–33.

Jefferies, Peggy. "The Medieval Use as Family Law and Custom: The Berkshire Gentry in the Fourteenth and Fifteenth Centuries." *Southern History* 1 (1979): 45–69.

Jeulin, P. "Un grand 'honneur' Anglais: Aperçus sur le 'comté' de Richmond." *Annales de Bretagne* 42 (1935): 265–302.

Jones, Andrew. "Land Measurement in England, 1150–1350." *Agricultural History Review* 27 (1979): 10–18.

Jones, Michael, ed. *Gentry and Lesser Nobility in Late Medieval Europe*. New York: St Martins Press, 1986.

Kapelle, William E. *The Norman Conquest of the North: The Region and Its Transformation, 1000–1135*. Chapel Hill: University of North Carolina Press, 1979.

Kaye, J. M. "The Eland Murders 1350–1351: A Study of the Legend of the Eland Feud." *YAJ* 51 (1979): 61–79.

Kealey, Edward J. *Harvesting the Air: Windmill Pioneers in Twelfth-Century England.* Berkeley: University of California Press, 1987.

Keefe, Thomas K. *Feudal Assessments and the Political Community Under Henry II and His Sons.* Berkeley: University of California Press, 1983.

Kershaw, Ian. *Bolton Priory: The Economy of a Northern Monastery, 1286–1385.* London: Oxford University Press, 1973.

King, Edmund. "The Peterborough 'Descriptio Militum' (Henry I)." *EHR* 84 (1969): 84–101.

———. "Large and Small Landowners in Thirteenth-Century England." *Past and Present* 47 (1970): 26–50.

———. *Peterborough Abbey, 1086–1310: A Study in the Land Market.* Cambridge: Cambridge University Press, 1973.

Knowles, David. *The Monastic Order in England: A History of Its Development from the Times of St. Dunstan to the Fourth Lateran Council, 943–1216.* 2nd. ed. Cambridge: Cambridge University Press, 1963. Reprint, 1966.

Knowles, David and R. Neville Hadcock. *Medieval Religious Houses: England and Wales.* New York: St. Martin's Press, 1971.

Kosminsky, E. A. *Studies in the Agrarian History of England in the Thirteenth Century.* Oxford: Basil Blackwell, 1956.

Lally, J. E. "Secular Patronage at the Court of King Henry II." *BIHR* 49 (1976): 159–84.

Lapsley, G. "Buzones." *EHR* 47 (1932): 177–93, 545–67.

———. "Introduction to the Boldon Book." In *The Victoria History of the County of Durham*, ed. William Page, 1:259–326. 1905. Reprint, London: Published for the University of London Institute of Historical Research by Dawsons, 1968.

Lennard, Reginald V. *Rural England, 1086–1135: A Study of Social and Agrarian Conditions.* Oxford: Clarendon Press, 1959.

Le Patourel, John. "The Norman Conquest of Yorkshire." *Northern History* 6 (1971): 1–21.

Lloyd, Simon D. *English Society and the Crusade, 1216–1307.* Oxford: Clarendon Press; New York: Oxford University Press, 1988.

Lythe, S. G. E. "The Organization of Drainage and Embankment in Medieval Holderness." *YAJ* 34 (1939): 282–95.

MacKenzie, H. "The Anti-Foreign Movement in England, 1231–1232." In *Anniversary Essays in Medieval History by Students of Charles Homer Haskins*, ed. C. H. Taylor, 183–203. Boston: Houghton Mifflin, 1929.

Maddicott, J. R. "The County Community and the Making of Public Opinion in Fourteenth-Century England." *TRHS* 5th series, 28 (1978): 27–43.

———. "Magna Carta and the Local Community 1215–1259." *Past and Present* 102 (1984): 25–65.

Maitland, Frederic W. *The Collected Papers of Frederic William Maitland*, vol. 1. Ed. H. A. L. Fisher. Cambridge: Cambridge University Press, 1911. Reprint Buffalo, NY: W. S. Hein, 1981.

Major, K. "Conan Son of Ellis, an Early Inhabitant of Holbeach." *Architectural and Archaeological Associated Societies Reports* 42 (1934): 1–28.

Mason, Emma. "Timeo barones et donas ferentes." In Baker, ed., *Religious Motivation*, 61–75.

May, Teresa. "The Cobham Family in the Administration of England, 1200–1400." *Archaeologia Cantiana* 82 (1967): 1–31.

———. "Estates of the Cobham Family in the Later Thirteenth Century." *Archaeologia Cantiana* 84 (1969): 211–29.

McDonnell, John. *Inland Fisheries in Medieval York, 1066–1300.* Borthwick Papers, no. 60. York: University of York, Borthwick Institute of Historical Research, 1981.

———. "Medieval Assarting Hamlets in Bilsdale, North-East Yorkshire." *Northern History* 22 (1986): 269–79.

McFarlane, K. B. "Bastard Feudalism." *BIHR* 20 (1945): 161–80.

McLane, Bernard. "A Case Study of Violence and Litigation in the Early Fourteenth Century: The Disputes of Robert Godsfield of Sutton-Le-Marsh." *Nottingham Mediaeval Studies* 28 (1984): 22–44.

Meisel, Janet. *Barons of the Welsh Frontier: The Corbet, Pantulf and Fitz Warin Families, 1066–1272.* Lincoln: University of Nebraska Press, 1980.

Michelmore, D. J. H. "The Reconstruction of the Early Tenurial and Territorial Divisions of the Landscape of Northern England." *Landscape History* 1 (1979): 1–9.

Miller, Edward. "The State and Landed Interests in Thirteenth Century France and England." *TRHS* 5th series, 2 (1952): 109–29.

———. "England in the Twelfth and Thirteenth Centuries: An Economic Contrast?" *Economic History Review* 2nd ser., 24 (1971): 1–14.

———. "Farming in Northern England During the Twelfth and Thirteenth Centuries." *Northern History* 11 (1976): 1–16.

Milsom, S. F. C. *The Legal Framework of English Feudalism.* Cambridge Studies in Legal History. Cambridge: Cambridge University Press, 1976.

Mitchell, Sydney Knox. *Studies in Taxation Under John and Henry III.* New Haven, CT: Yale University Press, 1914.

Morris, Colin. "Equestris Ordo: Chivalry as a Vocation in the Twelfth Century." In Baker, ed., *Religious Motivation,* 87–96.

Mortimer, Richard. "Religious and Secular Motives for Some English Monastic Foundations." In Baker, ed., *Religious Motivation,* 77–85.

———. "The Beginnings of the Honour of Clare." In *Anglo-Norman Studies* 3, ed. R. Allen Brown, 119–41. Woodbridge, Suffolk; Wolfeboro, NH: Boydell Press, 1980.

———. "The Family of Rannulf de Glanvill." *BIHR* 54 (1981): 1–16.

———. "Land and Service: the Tenants of the Honour of Clare." In *Anglo-Norman Studies* 8, ed. R. Allen Brown, 177–97. Woodbridge, Suffolk; Wolfeboro, NH: Boydell Press, 1985.

Newman, Charlotte A. "Family and Royal Favor in Henry I's England." *Albion* 14 (1982): 293–306.

———. *The Anglo-Norman Nobility in the Reign of Henry I: The Second Generation.* Philadelphia: University of Pennsylvania Press, 1989.

Newman, J. E. "Greater and Lesser Landowners and Parochial Patronage: Yorkshire in the Thirteenth Century." *EHR* 92 (1977): 280–308.

Nichol, David. *Thurstan, Archbishop of York (1114–1140).* York: Stonegate Press, 1964.

Owen, Dorothy M. *Church and Society in Medieval Lincolnshire.* Vol. 5 of *History of Lincolnshire.* Ed. Joan Thirsk. Lincoln: Lincoln Local History Society, 1971.

Painter, Sidney. *French Chivalry: Chivalric Ideas and Practices in Mediaeval France*. Baltimore: Johns Hopkins University Press, 1940. Reprint, Ithaca, NY: Cornell University Press, 1980.

―――. *Studies in the History of the English Feudal Barony*. Studies in Historical and Political Sciences ser. 61, no. 3. Baltimore: Johns Hopkins University Press, 1943.

―――. *The Reign of King John*. Baltimore: Johns Hopkins University Press, 1949.

―――. "The Family and the Feudal System in Twelfth-Century England." *Speculum* 35 (1960): 1–16. Reprinted in Painter, *Feudalism and Liberty*, ed. Fred A. Cazel. Baltimore: Johns Hopkins University Press, 1961.

Palmer, Robert C. "The Feudal Framework of English Law." *Michigan Law Review* 79 (1981): 1130–64.

―――. *The County Courts of Medieval England, 1150–1350*. Princeton, NJ: Princeton University Press, 1982.

―――. "The Origins of Property in England." *Law and History Review* 3 (1985): 1–50.

―――. "The Economic and Cultural Impact of the Origins of Property, 1180–1220." *Law and History Review* 3 (1985): 375–96.

Parisse, Michel. *Noblesse et chevalerie en Lorraine Médiévale: les familles nobles du XIᵉ au XIIIᵉ siècle*. Nancy: Université de Nancy II, 1982.

Payling, Simon. *Political Society in Lancastrian England: The Greater Gentry of Nottinghamshire*. Oxford: Clarendon Press; New York: Oxford University Press, 1991.

Platts, Graham. *Land and People in Medieval Lincolnshire*. Vol. 4 of *History of Lincolnshire*. Ed. Joan Thirsk. Lincoln: Lincoln Local History Society, 1985.

Pollard, A. J. "Richard Clervaux of Croft: A North Riding Squire in the Fifteenth Century. *YAJ* 50 (1978): 151–69.

―――. "The Burghs of Brough Hall, c. 1270–1574." *North Yorkshire County Record Office Journal* 6 (1978): 5–33.

―――. "The Richmondshire Community of Gentry During the Wars of the Roses." In Ross, ed., *Patronage, Pedigree and Power in Later Medieval England*.

Pollock, Frederick and Frederic W. Maitland. *The History of English Law Before the Time of Edward I*. 2 vols. 2nd ed. Rev. S. F. C. Milsom. Cambridge: Cambridge University Press, 1968.

Poole, Austin L. *Obligations of Society in the Twelfth and Thirteenth Centuries*. Oxford: Clarendon Press, 1946.

Postan, Michael M. "The Chronology of Labour Services." *TRHS* 4th Ser., 20 (1937): 169–93. Reprinted in Postan, *Essays on Medieval Agriculture and General Problems of the Medieval Economy*, 89–106. Cambridge: Cambridge University Press, 1973.

―――. *The Famulus: The Estate Labourer in the Twelfth and the Thirteenth Centuries*. London and New York: Published for the Economic History Society by Cambridge University Press, 1954.

―――. *The Cambridge Economic History of Europe*, vol. 2. Cambridge: Cambridge University Press, 1966.

―――. "A Note on the Farming Out of Manors." *Economic History Review* 2nd ser., 31 (1978): 521–25.

Powicke, Michael. "Distraint of Knighthood and Military Obligation Under Henry III." *Speculum* 25 (1950): 457–70.

———. *Military Obligation in Medieval England: A Study in Liberty and Duty.* Oxford: Clarendon Press, 1962.

Powley, Edward B. *The House of de la Pomerai.* Liverpool: University Press of Liverpool, 1944.

Quick, J. "The Number and Distribution of Knights in Thirteenth Century England: The Evidence of the Grand Assize Lists." In *Thirteenth Century England,* ed. Peter R. Coss and Simon D. Lloyd, 114–23. Proceedings of the Newcastle upon Tyne Conference, 1985. Woodbridge, Suffolk: Wolfeboro, NH: Boydell Press, 1986.

Raban, Sandra. *The Estates of Thorney and Crowland: A Study in Mediaeval Monastic Land Tenure.* Cambridge: University of Cambridge, 1977.

Raftis, J. Ambrose. *The Estates of Ramsey Abbey: A Study in Economic Growth and Organization.* Toronto: Pontifical Institute of Mediaeval Studies, 1957.

Richardson, Henry G. "The Morrow of the Great Charter." *Bulletin of the John Rylands Society* 28 (1944): 422–43.

Richardson, Henry G. and G. O. Sayles. *The Governance of Mediaeval England from the Conquest to Magna Carta.* Edinburgh: Edinburgh University Press, 1963.

Richmond, Colin. *John Hopton: A Fifteenth-Century Suffolk Gentleman.* Cambridge: Cambridge University Press, 1981.

———. "The Pastons Revisited: Marriage and the Family in Fifteenth-Century England." *BIHR* 58 (1985): 25–36.

Riley-Smith, Louise and Jonathan. *The Crusades: Idea and Reality, 1095–1274.* London: Edward Arnold, 1981.

Robinson, I. S. "Gregory VII and the Soldiers of Christ." *History* 58 (1973): 169–92.

Ross, Charles D., ed. *Patronage, Pedigree and Power in Later Medieval England.* Gloucester: A. Sutton; Totowa NJ: Rowman and Littlefield, 1979.

Rowney, Ian. "Arbitration in Gentry Disputes of the Later Middle Ages." *History* 67 (1982): 367–76.

———. "The Hastings Affinity in Staffordshire and the Honour of Tutbury." *BIHR* 57 (1984): 35–45.

Sanders, Ivor John. *Feudal Military Service in England: A Study of the Constitutional and Military Powers of the Barons in Medieval England.* London: Oxford University Press, 1956.

———. *English Baronies: A Study of Their Origin and Descent, 1086–1327.* Oxford: Clarendon Press, 1960.

Saul, Nigel. "The Religious Sympathies of the Gentry in Gloucestershire, 1200–1500." *Transactions of the Bristol and Gloucestershire Archaeological Society* 98 (1980): 99–112.

———. *Knights and Esquires: The Gloucestershire Gentry in the Fourteenth Century.* Oxford: Clarendon Press, 1981.

———. *Scenes from Provincial Life: Knightly Families in Sussex, 1280–1400.* Oxford: Clarendon Press; New York: Oxford University Press, 1986.

Searle, Eleanor. *Lordship and Community: Battle Abbey and Its Banlieu, 1066–1538.* Toronto: Pontifical Institute of Mediaeval Studies, 1974.

———. *Predatory Kinship and the Creation of Norman Power, 840–1066.* Berkeley: University of California Press, 1988.

Sellar, W. C. and R. J. Yeatman. *1066 and All That.* London: Methuan, 1930.

Sheppard, June A. *The Draining of the Hull Valley.* East Yorkshire Local History Series, no. 8. York, 1958. Reprint, 1976.

———. *The Draining of the Marshlands of South Holderness and the Vale of York.* East Yorkshire Local History Series, no. 20. York, 1966.

———. "Field Systems of Yorkshire." In Baker and Butlin, eds., *Studies of Field Systems in the British Isles,* 145–87.

———. "Metrological Analysis of Regular Village Plans in Yorkshire." *Agricultural History Review* 22 (1974): 118–35.

———. "Medieval Village Planning in Northern England: Some Evidence from Yorkshire." *Journal of Historical Geography* 2 (1976): 3–20.

Siddle, D. J. "The Rural Economy of Medieval Holderness." *Agricultural History Review* 15 (1967): 40–45.

Smith, Ralph B. *Land and Politics in the England of Henry VIII: The West Riding of Yorkshire, 1530–46.* Oxford: Clarendon Press, 1970.

Stacey, Robert. *Politics, Policy, and Finance under Henry III, 1216–1245.* Oxford: Clarendon Press; New York: Oxford University Press, 1987.

Stenton, Doris M. "Roger of Howden and Benedict." *EHR* 68 (1953): 574–82.

———. *English Justice Between the Norman Conquest and the Great Charter, 1066–1215.* Philadelphia: American Philosophical Society, 1964.

Stenton, Frank M. *The First Century of English Feudalism, 1066–1166.* 1929. 2nd edition. Oxford: Clarendon Press, 1961.

Stringer, K. J. *Earl David of Huntingdon, 1152–1219: A Study in Anglo-Scottish History.* Edinburgh: Edinburgh University Press, 1985.

Sutherland, Donald W. "Peytevin vs. La Lynde: A Case in the Medieval Land Law." *Law Quarterly Review* 83 (1967): 527–46.

———. *The Assize of Novel Disseisin.* Oxford: Clarendon Press, 1973.

Taylor, John. *Medieval Historical Writing in Yorkshire.* St Anthony's Hall Publications, no. 19. York: St. Anthony's Press, 1961.

Thirsk, Joan, ed. *The Agrarian History of England and Wales,* vol. 4. Cambridge: Cambridge University Press, 1967.

Thomas, Hugh M. "A Yorkshire Thegn and His Descendants After the Conquest." *Medieval Prosopography* 8 (1987): 1–22.

———. "The Knights of the York County Court in 1212." In *Law in Mediaeval Life and Thought,* ed. Edward B. King and Susan J. Ridyard, 137–50. Sewanee, TN: University of the South, Sewanee Mediaeval Colloquium, 1990.

Thorne, Samuel E. "English Feudalism and Estates in Land." *Cambridge Law Journal* 17 (1959): 193–209.

Titow, J. Z. *English Rural Society, 1200–1350.* London: Allen and Unwin; New York: Barnes and Noble, 1969.

Treharne, R. F. "The Knights in the Period of Reform and Rebellion, 1258–1267: A Critical Phase in the Rise of a New Class." *BIHR* 21 (1946): 1–12.

Tuck, J. A. "The Emergence of a Northern Nobility, 1250–1400." *Northern History* 22 (1986): 1–17.

Turner, Ralph V. "William de Forz, Count of Aumale: An Early Thirteenth-Century English Baron." *Proceedings of the American Philosophical Society* 115 (1971): 221–49.

———. "The *Miles Literatus* in Twelfth- and Thirteenth-Century England: How Rare a Phenomenon?" *American Historical Review* 83 (1978): 928–45.

———. *The English Judiciary in the Age of Glanvill and Bracton, c. 1176–1239.* Cambridge; New York: Cambridge University Press, 1985.

———. *Men Raised from the Dust: Administrative Service and Upward Mobility in Angevin England.* Philadelphia: University of Pennsylvania Press, 1988.

Tyerman, Christopher. *England and the Crusades, 1095–1588.* Chicago: University of Chicago Press, 1988.

Vale, M. G. A. *Piety, Charity, and Literacy Among the Yorkshire Gentry, 1370–1480.* Borthwick Papers, no. 50. York: St. Anthony's Press, 1976.

van Caenegem, R. C. "Studies in the Early History of the Common Law." Introduction to *Royal Writs in England from the Conquest to Glanvill.* Selden Society, no. 77. London, 1959.

———. *The Birth of the English Common Law.* Cambridge: Cambridge University Press, 1973.

The Victoria History of the County of York, ed. William Page. Vols. 2 & 3. 1912–13. London: Published for the University of London Institute of Historical Research. Reprinted by Dawsons, 1974.

Vine, M. J. "Two Yorkshire Rebels: Peter de Brus and Richard de Percy." *YAJ* 47 (1975): 64–80.

Vinogradoff, Paul. *Villainage in England: Essays in English Mediaeval History.* Oxford, 1892. Reprint, New York: Russell and Russell, 1967.

Waites, Bryan. "The Monastic Settlement of North-East Yorkshire." *YAJ* 40 (1961): 478–95.

———. "The Monastic Grange as a Factor in the Settlement of North-East Yorkshire." *YAJ* 40 (1962): 627–56.

———. *Moorland and Vale-Land Farming in North-East Yorkshire: The Monastic Contribution in the Thirteenth and Fourteenth Centuries.* Borthwick Papers, no. 32. York: St. Anthony's Press, 1967.

———. "Aspects of Thirteenth and Fourteenth Century Arable Farming on the Yorkshire Wolds." *YAJ* 42 (1968): 136–42.

Wales, Christopher. "The Knight in Twelfth Century Lincolnshire." Ph.D. diss., Cambridge, 1983.

Walker, J. W. "The Burghs of Cambridgeshire and Lincolnshire and the Wattertons of Lincolnshire and Yorkshire." *YAJ* 30 (1932): 311–419.

Wardrop, Joan. *Fountains Abbey and Its Benefactors, 1132–1300.* Kalamazoo, MI: Cistercian Publications, 1987.

Warlop, E. *The Flemish Nobility Before 1300.* 2 vols. Kortrijk: G. Desmet-Huysman, 1975. Trans. J. B. Ross and H. Vandermoere from *De Vlaamse Adel Voor 1300.*

Warren, Wilfred L. *Henry II.* Berkeley: University of California Press, 1973. Paperback ed. 1977, reprinted 1983.

Waugh, Scott L. "The Profits of Violence: The Minor Gentry in the Rebellion of 1321–1322 in Gloucestershire and Herefordshire." *Speculum* 52 (1977): 843–69.

———. "Reluctant Knights and Jurors: Respites, Exemptions and Public Obligations in the Reign of Henry III." *Speculum* 58 (1983): 937–86.

———. "Marriage, Class, and Royal Lordship in England under Henry III." *Viator* 16 (1985): 181–207.

———. "The Non-Alienation Clauses in Thirteenth-Century English Charters." *Albion* 17 (1985): 1–14.

———. "Tenure to Contract: Lordship and Clientage in Thirteenth-Century England." *EHR* 101 (1986): 811–39.

White, Stephen D. "*Pactum . . . Legem Vincit et Amor Judicium.* The Settlement of Disputes by Compromise in Eleventh-Century Western France." *American Journal of Legal History* 22 (1978): 281–308.

———. "Inheritances and Legal Arguments in Western Europe, 1050–1150." *Traditio* 43 (1987): 55–103.

———. *Custom, Kinship, and Gifts to Saints: The Laudatio Parentum in Western Europe, 1050–1150.* Chapel Hill: University of North Carolina Press, 1988.

Wightman, W. E. *The Lacy Family in England and Normandy, 1066–1194.* Oxford: Clarendon Press, 1966.

———. "The Significance of 'Waste' in the Yorkshire Domesday." *Northern History* 10 (1975): 55–71.

Williams, Ann. "The Knights of Shaftesbury Abbey." In *Anglo-Norman Studies* 8, ed. R. Allen Brown, 214–42. Woodbridge, Suffolk; Wolfeboro NH: Boydell Press, 1985.

Wright, Susan M. *The Derbyshire Gentry in the Fifteenth Century.* Derbyshire Record Society, no. 8. Chesterfield, 1983.

Wood-Legh, K. L. *Perpetual Chantries in Britain.* Cambridge: Cambridge University Press, 1965.

Young, Charles R. *Hubert Walter, Lord of Canterbury and Lord of England.* Durham, NC: Duke University Press, 1968.

———. *The Royal Forests of Medieval England.* Philadelphia: University of Pennsylvania Press, 1979.

Index

University of Pennsylvania Press
MIDDLE AGES SERIES
Edward Peters, General Editor

F. R. P. Akehurst, trans. *The* Coutumes de Beauvaisis *of Philippe de Beaumanoir.* 1992

Peter Allen. *The Art of Love: Amatory Fiction from Ovid to the* Romance of the Rose. 1992

David Anderson. *Before the Knight's Tale: Imitation of Classical Epic in Boccaccio's* Teseida. 1988

Benjamin Arnold. *Count and Bishop in Medieval Germany: A Study of Regional Power, 1100–1350.* 1991

Mark C. Bartusis. *The Late Byzantine Army: Arms and Society, 1204–1453.* 1992

J. M. W. Bean. *From Lord to Patron: Lordship in Late Medieval England.* 1990

Uta-Renate Blumenthal. *The Investiture Controversy: Church and Monarchy from the Ninth to the Twelfth Century.* 1988

Daniel Bornstein, trans. *Dino Compagni's* Chronicle *of Florence.* 1986

Maureen Barry McCann Boulton. *The Song in the Story: Lyric Insertions in French Narrative Fiction, 1200–1400.* 1993.

Betsy Bowden. *Chaucer Aloud: The Varieties of Textual Interpretation.* 1987

James William Brodman. *Ransoming Captives in Crusader Spain: The Order of Merced on the Christian-Islamic Frontier.* 1986

Kevin Brownlee and Sylvia Huot, eds. *Rethinking the* Romance of the Rose: *Text, Image, Reception.* 1992

Otto Brunner (Howard Kaminsky and James Van Horn Melton, eds. and trans.). *Land and Lordship: Structures of Governance in Medieval Austria.* 1992

Robert I. Burns, S.J., ed. *Emperor of Culture: Alfonso X the Learned of Castile and His Thirteenth-Century Renaissance.* 1990

David Burr. *Olivi and Franciscan Poverty: The Origins of the* Usus Pauper *Controversy.* 1989

Thomas Cable. *The English Alliterative Tradition.* 1991

Anthony K. Cassell and Victoria Kirkham, eds. and trans. *Diana's Hunt / Caccia di Diana: Boccaccio's First Fiction.* 1991

John C. Cavadini. *The Last Christology of the West: Adoptionism in Spain and Gaul, 785–820.* 1993

Brigitte Cazelles. *The Lady as Saint: A Collection of French Hagiographic Romances of the Thirteenth Century.* 1991

Karen Cherewatuk and Ulrike Wiethaus, eds. *Dear Sister: Medieval Women and the Epistolary Genre.* 1993

Anne L. Clark. *Elisabeth of Schönau: A Twelfth-Century Visionary.* 1992

Willene B. Clark and Meradith T. McMunn, eds. *Beasts and Birds of the Middle Ages: The Bestiary and Its Legacy.* 1989

Richard C. Dales. *The Scientific Achievement of the Middle Ages.* 1973

Charles T. Davis. *Dante's Italy and Other Essays.* 1984

Katherine Fischer Drew, trans. *The Burgundian Code.* 1972

Katherine Fischer Drew, trans. *The Laws of the Salien Franks.* 1991

Katherine Fischer Drew, trans. *The Lombard Laws.* 1973

Nancy Edwards. *The Archaeology of Early Medieval Ireland.* 1990

Margaret J. Ehrhart. *The Judgment of the Trojan Prince Paris in Medieval Literature.* 1987

Richard K. Emmerson and Ronald B. Herzman. *The Apocalyptic Imagination in Medieval Literature.* 1992

Felipe Fernández-Armesto. *Before Columbus: Exploration and Colonization from the Mediterranean to the Atlantic, 1229–1492.* 1987

Robert D. Fulk. *A History of Old English Meter.* 1992

Patrick J. Geary. *Aristocracy in Provence: The Rhône Basin at the Dawn of the Carolingian Age.* 1985

Peter Heath. *Allegory and Philosophy in Avicenna (Ibn Sînâ), with a Translation of the Book of the Prophet Muḥammad's Ascent to Heaven.* 1992

J. N. Hillgarth, ed. *Christianity and Paganism, 350–750: The Conversion of Western Europe.* 1986

Richard C. Hoffmann. *Land, Liberties, and Lordship in a Late Medieval Countryside: Agrarian Structures and Change in the Duchy of Wrocław.* 1990

Robert Hollander. *Boccaccio's Last Fiction: Il Corbaccio.* 1988

Edward B. Irving, Jr. *Rereading* Beowulf. 1989

C. Stephen Jaeger. *The Origins of Courtliness: Civilizing Trends and the Formation of Courtly Ideals, 939–1210.* 1985

William Chester Jordan. *The French Monarchy and the Jews: From Philip Augustus to the Last Capetians.* 1989

William Chester Jordan. *From Servitude to Freedom: Manumission in the Sénonais in the Thirteenth Century.* 1986

Ellen E. Kittell. *From* Ad Hoc *to Routine: A Case Study in Medieval Bureaucracy.* 1991

Alan C. Kors and Edward Peters, eds. *Witchcraft in Europe, 1100–1700: A Documentary History.* 1972

Barbara M. Kreutz. *Before the Normans: Southern Italy in the Ninth and Tenth Centuries.* 1992

E. Ann Matter. *The Voice of My Beloved: The Song of Songs in Western Medieval Christianity.* 1990

María Rosa Menocal. *The Arabic Role in Medieval Literary History.* 1987

A. J. Minnis. *Medieval Theory of Authorship.* 1988

Lawrence Nees. *A Tainted Mantle: Hercules and the Classical Tradition at the Carolingian Court.* 1991

Lynn H. Nelson, trans. *The Chronicle of San Juan de la Peña: A Fourteenth-Century Official History of the Crown of Aragon.* 1991

Charlotte A. Newman. *The Anglo-Norman Nobility in the Reign of Henry I: The Second Generation.* 1988

Joseph F. O'Callaghan. *The Cortes of Castile-León, 1188–1350.* 1989

———. *The Learned King: The Reign of Alfonso X of Castile.* 1993

William D. Paden, ed. *The Voice of the Trobairitz: Perspectives on the Women Trou-badours.* 1989

Edward Peters. *The Magician, the Witch, and the Law.* 1982

Edward Peters, ed. *Christian Society and the Crusades, 1198–1229: Sources in Transla-tion, including* The Capture of Damietta *by Oliver of Paderborn.* 1971

Edward Peters, ed. *The First Crusade: The* Chronicle of Fulcher of Chartres *and Other Source Materials.* 1971

Edward Peters, ed. *Heresy and Authority in Medieval Europe.* 1980

James M. Powell. *Albertanus of Brescia: The Pursuit of Happiness in the Early Thir-teenth Century.* 1992

James M. Powell. *Anatomy of a Crusade, 1213–1221.* 1986

Jean Renart (Patricia Terry and Nancy Vine Durling, trans.). *The Romance of the Rose or Guillaume de Dole.* 1993

Michael Resler, trans. Erec *by Hartmann von Aue.* 1987

Pierre Riché (Michael Idomir Allen, trans.). *The Carolingians: A Family Who Forged Europe.* 1993

Pierre Riché (Jo Ann McNamara, trans.). *Daily Life in the World of Charlemagne.* 1978

Jonathan Riley-Smith. *The First Crusade and the Idea of Crusading.* 1986

Joel T. Rosenthal. *Patriarchy and Families of Privilege in Fifteenth-Century England.* 1991

Steven D. Sargent, ed. and trans. *On the Threshold of Exact Science: Selected Writings of Anneliese Maier on Late Medieval Natural Philosophy.* 1982

Sarah Stanbury. *Seeing the* Gawain-Poet: *Description and the Act of Perception.* 1992

Thomas C. Stillinger. *The Song of Troilus: Lyric Authority in the Medieval Book.* 1992

Susan Mosher Stuard. *A State of Deference: Ragusa/Dubrovnik in the Medieval Centuries.* 1992

Susan Mosher Stuard, ed. *Women in Medieval History and Historiography.* 1987

Susan Mosher Stuard, ed. *Women in Medieval Society.* 1976

Jonathan Sumption. *The Hundred Years War: Trial by Battle.* 1992

Ronald E. Surtz. *The Guitar of God: Gender, Power, and Authority in the Visionary World of Mother Juana de la Cruz (1481–1534).* 1990

Patricia Terry, trans. *Poems of the Elder Edda.* 1990

Hugh M. Thomas. *Vassals, Heiresses, Crusaders, and Thugs: The Gentry of Angevin Yorkshire, 1154–1216.* 1993

Frank Tobin. *Meister Eckhart: Thought and Language.* 1986

Ralph V. Turner. *Men Raised from the Dust: Administrative Service and Upward Mobility in Angevin England.* 1988

Harry Turtledove, trans. *The* Chronicle *of Theophanes: An English Translation of* Anni Mundi 6095–6305 (A.D. 602–813). 1982

Mary F. Wack. Lovesickness in the Middle Ages: The Viaticum *and Its Commen-taries.* 1990

Benedicta Ward. *Miracles and the Medieval Mind: Theory, Record, and Event, 1000–1215.* 1982

Suzanne Fonay Wemple. *Women in Frankish Society: Marriage and the Cloister, 500–900.* 1981

Jan M. Ziolkowski. *Talking Animals: Medieval Latin Beast Poetry, A.D. 750–1150.* 1993

This book has been set in Linotron Galliard. Galliard was designed for Mergenthaler in 1978 by Matthew Carter. Galliard retains many of the features of a sixteenth-century typeface cut by Robert Granjon but has some modifications that give it a more contemporary look.

Printed on acid-free paper.